D1378244

AGNES REPPLIER

AGNES REPPLIER

Lady of Letters

By

GEORGE STEWART STOKES

Philadelphia
UNIVERSITY OF PENNSYLVANIA PRESS
LONDON: GEOFFREY CUMBERLEGE
OXFORD UNIVERSITY PRESS
1949

02118006194011

To my

Father and Mother

Preface

It was in the fall of 1940 that I first met Miss Agnes Repplier when I was taken to call upon her by her nephew, Dr. Sidney J. Repplier. We sat and talked that afternoon in October in the Victorian parlor of Miss Repplier's Clinton Street apartment, her Grandmother Shorb's tea set spread on a little table between us, its cups serving as a series of convenient ash trays.

There were innumerable other conversations throughout the following five years, Miss Agnes invariably answering with great good humor my endless questions. Notes were taken as we talked, not only because such a procedure acted as a spur rather than as a deterrent to the essayist, but also because I was anxious to record the writer's own words as much as possible. And it was in this way that the vast majority of my information was gained. My debt to Miss Agnes is immeasurable. I can only trust that in some small way this biography will stand in evidence of my gratitude.

I am heavily indebted to Professor Arthur Hobson Quinn for the time, patience, and critical judgment he has expended on my work, as well as to Professor Sculley Bradley for his criticisms and suggestions. I am grateful to the late Miss Mary Repplier and to Dr. Sidney J.

Repplier and members of his family for their interest and help. I wish to acknowledge my indebtedness to the late Mr. Harrison Morris and to thank Mrs. Schuyler Neilson Warren and her son, Mr. Schuyler Neilson Warren, for the use of their valuable letter collections; Mrs. Spalding Jenkins, Miss Katharine Brinley, Miss Sara Newton, Mother Marie Norton-Weir, and Mr. Ellery Sedgwick for the information they very kindly offered me. My thanks also to Mr. Edward H. O'Neill for his help in matters bibliographical, and to Miss Madeleine Skelly and Miss Bertie Pearson for their work in the preparation of the manuscript. Finally I wish to thank Houghton Mifflin Company and the Librarian of the University of Pennsylvania for the facilities put at my disposal.

Philadelphia, 1948.

G.S.S.

Acknowledgments

ᵜ ᵜ

For permission to reprint copyright material in this volume, the author makes the following grateful acknowledgments:

To Agnes Repplier for selections from her collections of essays and from her biographies of Junípero Serra, Mère Marie, Père Marquette, and J. William White.

To Horace H. F. Jayne for selections from *The Letters of Horace Howard Furness.*

To Whit Burnett for a selection from *This Is My Best.*

To Appleton-Century-Crofts, Inc., for a selection from *American Fiction* by Arthur Hobson Quinn.

To the *Atlantic Monthly* for selections from various essays by Agnes Repplier and for selections from several reviews of her books.

To the *Catholic World* for "The Sphinx," "St. Mona's Lambs," and for selections from various essays by Agnes Repplier as well as for selections from several reviews of her books.

To the *Commonweal* for selections from several reviews of Miss Repplier's books.

To Doubleday and Company, Inc., for selections from *Agnes Irwin* by Agnes Repplier.

To Little, Brown and Company and the Atlantic Monthly Press for a selection from *This Book-Collecting Game* by A. Edward Newton.

To the *Nation* for selections from "The Virtuous Victorian" by Agnes Repplier and for a selection from a review by Eda Lou Walton of *Junípero Serra.*

To the *New York Herald Tribune* for selections from a review of Père Marquette and from a review of *Times and Tendencies.*

To the *Saturday Review of Literature* for selections from a review of *Times and Tendencies* and from a review by Herbert Ingram Priestley of *Junípero Serra.*

To the *Yale Review*, copyright Yale University Press, for selections from various essays by Agnes Repplier and for selections from several reviews of her books.

Contents

ꙮ ꙮ

Illustrations

CHAPTER I

Minnie

1850–1866

Ↄ Ↄ

"No family could have been more unknown to fame than mine," Agnes Repplier was pleased now and again to comment in mock complaint. And sometimes she would add with pride free from conceit, "My niche may be very small, but I made it by myself." Then, invariably, with mounting satisfaction, "And what is even more remarkable, I got it out of Philadelphia!"

As far as Agnes Repplier was concerned, at the time of her early literary struggles the heart of American letters lay in and around Boston. She was happy to point out that some years before Philadelphia had been the center, just as she would admit reluctantly that a few years later New York had taken first place. "But when I was coming along"—and of this she was very sure—"it was Boston."

For all the stir it made then, Miss Repplier felt, Philadelphia could have been quite of another world. New York was undoubtedly more commercial, and Baltimore perhaps even more foreign. But Philadelphia remained plainly inconsequential, neither one thing nor another, a legend only of what had been. And more than that, the

1

city appeared to be almost totally indifferent to those who could have lifted it into some little prominence. "A brief obituary notice in the papers was about all they ever got," Agnes Repplier would remark with finality.

It is true that the essayist never offered any detailed picture to substantiate her claim. There was no need for her to do so. Her own experience, she believed, stood as sufficient general proof. Certainly it was Boston that had first really recognized her. It was Boston that had given her her first big opportunity. And just as certainly, in those days, the city of her birth had never once opened its arms to her. "A droll city, Philadelphia," she would smile. "And tepid. Oh, so tepid."

ɔ ɔ ɔ

Before her marriage, Mrs. Repplier had been convinced that she could not do better than to marry a handsome man. But, in her daughter's opinion, although Mr. Repplier fulfilled all his wife's exacting requirements in the matter of appearance, she would have been more content had she remained single. Household cares choked her off. She discovered too late that it is difficult to be both domestic and intellectual. As a consequence, she was far from enthusiastic about married life.

Years later when Agnes Repplier's closest friend, Elizabeth Robins, was married, the essayist confessed to suffering a feeling of having been irretrievably "passed beyond," as she put it. But it may very well have been that her mother's experience stood constantly in the way of her ever surrendering her prized independence even for the security that marriage could have meant. She was, as she has said on many occasions, "like the cat that walked by itself."

Agnes Mathias was eighteen in the summer of 1850 when she met Mr. Repplier. Only a short time before she had left the Convent School at Emmetsburg, near her home in Westminster, Maryland. Tall, dark, betraying her German ancestry in her magnificent carriage as well as in the determination of her manner, the future Mrs. Repplier impressed one as striking if not exactly pretty. But more than that, she was an intelligent, even brilliant young woman.

With natural candor, the essayist once remarked that her mother had been well pleased with Mr. Repplier. Of the opinion that "a child receives his brains from his mother and his looks from his father," and perfectly aware of her own capabilities, she was more than a little satisfied with the handsome gentleman from Philadelphia. Agnes Repplier remembered her father as not very tall perhaps, but uncommonly good-looking, with features as clear as those on a Roman coin. She felt that his being twenty years her mother's senior and a widower with two half-grown sons served in the beginning at least only to add to his attractiveness.

ᴐ ᴐ ᴐ

John George Repplier, originally from Reading, Pennsylvania, had been living in Philadelphia for some years. It was there that he managed the retailing of coal for a mining business in which, with his three brothers, he was a partner. At one time, many years later, the Repplier brothers' coal lands near Pottsville were valued at more than a half million dollars. Charles, John George, George, and Joseph rightly looked upon themselves as men of some substance.

Although there were several daughters in the Repplier family, the only one to be remembered for any special reason was the eldest. She had been educated in France as a Sister of Charity, and according to family tradition, she was the first to introduce into this country the cornette, or huge winged bonnet, that distinguishes her order today.

On one occasion—so tradition also maintains, though how she came to be alone no one can explain—while traveling on a train, this Sister was engaged in conversation by a somewhat tipsy man who insisted upon occupying the seat next to hers. His unwilling partner was quite evidently dedicated to a far higher quest than the receipt of mortal man's favors, but the tippler was not to be put off by mere dress. Finally, with some sign of approaching tears, he whispered coyly that only recently he had lost his wife.

The Sister of Charity, clever and animated in spite of her inhibiting garb, retorted, "So I supposed." She paused a moment, then added, "I have noticed that when the Lord wants to make a fool of a man, He takes away his wife!"

Not all the essayist's ready wit—so ably displayed in later years—came from her mother. If, as it turned out, Agnes Repplier was not to inherit her father's "looks," by way of compensation she was at least to gain some "brains" from his branch of the family, not solely from the distaff side.

On one occasion when she was giving information to

a friend whom she had asked to write a biographical sketch of her, Agnes Repplier stated flatly that she was of French descent. But this was not quite accurate. The Repplier family, though it had originated in Strasbourg, was German in many respects. The senior Mr. Repplier had settled in the heart of the German section of Pennsylvania. There he had married a German. Even Agnes Repplier frequently referred to her paternal grandmother as "a strong German woman who rode horseback at eighty."* And several times she said of her mother, "Mathias— there's nothing more German than that." But Miss Repplier enjoyed the Gallic fiction. Although in all her reading and in all her traveling she came upon the Repplier name only once—and that, ironically enough, over a barber shop—happily it had been somewhere in France.

ಶ ಶ ಶ

Little is known of Mr. Repplier's first wife, Mary McGauley, save that in the year 1846 she died and was buried in the family vault at the Church of St. John the Evangelist, then the Cathedral of Philadelphia. It was of this church that she and her husband had been communicants almost from its founding in 1830. And it was to this church that nearly all subsequent members of the Repplier clan were to repair at times of baptism and burial.

Not long after the second Mrs. Repplier was settled in the home provided for her on North Eleventh Street, her stepsons, John George and Jacob Lancaster, both in their early teens, left Philadelphia and went to live in Reading.

* "The atmosphere must have been bad for grandfathers," the essayist once said, "for I knew neither of them."

Agnes Repplier met them only occasionally in the early days. She remembered them principally as having been the owners of a number of volumes that were to become the delight of her girlhood.

The first important books in Agnes Repplier's life, however, came through her mother. The essayist was frank to remark that Mrs. Repplier never became deeply attached to her children. But what loss this daughter may have felt in her youth as a result of her mother's seeming indifference was, as she came to realize, more than compensated for by the fact that Mrs. Repplier had turned to books for relief and escape from the trials of married life. It was a constant source of pride to Agnes Repplier that her mother had been a careful reader. And she was grateful always that English poetry had composed one of Mrs. Repplier's favorite fields.

Agnes Repplier considered her mother to have been in many ways a remarkable woman: discriminating, independent, ambitious, something of a *maîtresse femme*. "And," she would sum the matter up, "my mother was the first woman I knew who used her own mind."

ᴐ ᴐ ᴐ

On November 4, 1851, Mrs. Repplier gave birth to her first child, Mary. But Christian names apparently mattered little; nicknames were the order of the day. Because Mary was so small a baby, she was promptly called "Teedie," derived, her mother insisted, from "tiny." And "Teedie" she remained throughout girlhood.

Much to Mrs. Repplier's chagrin, as time passed, Teedie did not favor her handsome father in appearance at all.

If Mr. Repplier's features were as clear as those on a Roman coin, Teedie's were nondescript, after the fashion of a Roman coin well-rubbed.

Four years later, on April 1, 1855, a second daughter was born, duly christened "Agnes" after her mother. But Mrs. Repplier refused absolutely to have any such possible discrimination made—to her own disadvantage—between her and the child as would result from referring to them either as "Big Agnes" and "Little Agnes" or as "Old Agnes" and "Young Agnes." And because the cold, classic name would yield to no acceptably refined corruption, though for no more observable reason, she was called "Minnie."

For years the little girl suffered under what she felt was the indignity of this name. To any who dared inquire, she would declare in no uncertain terms that "Minnie" had been wished on her by the devil himself.

"April Fool," Mrs. Repplier frequently sighed, mocking herself more than her second child. Minnie too was a homely baby. As this daughter would put it, her mother was discovering that to trust to Providence in the matter of "looks" was turning out to be a chancy business.

Four more years went by, and Mrs. Repplier bore another child. This time it was a boy. Although there was an ample supply of relatives after whom she might have named him, Mrs. Repplier was tired of the almost endless list of Johns and Georges and John Georges with which both sides of the family were cluttered. Quite independently she hit upon the name "Louis."

It had a pleasing sound—Louis Repplier. It may even have been that Mrs. Repplier hoped the foreign name might work a charm on the child. But no. Though "Louis" he was christened (for some reason or other he escaped being nicknamed), the boy followed the disheartening example set by his sisters.

Whatever her mother's disappointment, Agnes Repplier has said, her father was well pleased. He was rather indifferent to the training of his children, she would admit. They never constituted any problem to him. He preferred to leave them largely to their own devices or to the instruction of their mother. But he loved them dearly, and the boy most of all, for here at last was a son to fill the gap made when George and Lancaster had left home.

"With an unconcern that can be achieved only by those sufficiently handsome not to need to care about appearance," the essayist remarked on one occasion, "my father lost no sleep over my mother's shattered illusions."

ↄ ↄ ↄ

Teedie and Minnie were as unlike each other as two little girls could be. Although neither of them cared for dolls and in this small respect were as one, in all other ways they were strikingly different. Teedie was dark, clever, precocious. Minnie was light, dull, slow to learn anything. Teedie was obedient, careful, precise. Minnie frequently had to be spanked for doing something naughty, though likely as not the very next day she would repeat whatever it was that had brought on the punishment. Teedie absorbed a great deal of her mother's attention, insisting on getting all that was to be had. Minnie, on the other hand, was shy, almost indifferent.

The older girl performed all the expected female skills

beautifully: sewing, knitting, crocheting. Minnie could
do nothing. She could not even thread a needle with any
ease. In the domestic crafts, it appeared, she was destined
for dismal failure.

Music too, her mother discovered, touched no chord
whatsoever in Minnie's being. She was unable to hum even
so familiar an air as "Yankee Doodle." Years later, when
she had become a somewhat unwilling patron of the Philadelphia Orchestra, she found it a painful business indeed
to attend a performance. For her, music was to fit properly
only into a Munich beer hall where "Wagner is thundered
at you through an atmosphere so dense with tobacco smoke
that you can't see your neighbors."

All this, Agnes Repplier would gravely confess, was
sufficiently shocking to her mother, but there remained an
even greater concern—reading. Teedie had learned at six
and quite by herself. Not so with Minnie. It seemed she
never would gain the ability.

But for all Mrs. Repplier's disturbing disappointments,
life in the Repplier home was much as one would expect.
The house itself, rising directly out of the sidewalk, was
unpretentious, one of a block on North Eleventh Street
known collectively as "City Row." The essayist remembered most vividly the second-story veranda that ran across
the rear, a favorite spot in summer above the tiny garden
below.

There were not many boys and girls in the neighborhood with whom Mrs. Repplier allowed Teedie and Minnie to play, and none who lasted as friends into later life.
"But," Agnes Repplier remarked once, "like all children,
we were entirely capable of making our own entertainment.

And we were not all blocked up with playthings as they are now."

Louis was the unfortunate one in these early days. One summer he contracted a severe case of measles that left him weak and exhausted. When he had recovered sufficiently, he was taken by his father on a boat trip up the Delaware River. This was considered a very special treat indeed, and certainly at the time it seemed an innocent expedition. But as an unfortunate result of the outing, Louis caught a heavy cold that led eventually to a stroke of paralysis. Ever after that, though for years he was subjected to all manner of treatment, he had to wear a built-up shoe on his right foot, and he never regained much use of his right arm. To his elder sister in later years it seemed almost a pity that he had pulled through. His was to be "such a scrap of a life."

ও ও ও

About the year 1863 the Repplier family moved to a large home at Twentieth and Chestnut Streets. There were many reasons for the change of residence, but apparently the one of most appeal was that Mrs. Repplier felt a "crying need for closet space" in the "City Row" house, and this new home, built for her by her husband, was equipped with "closets galore."

Not long after she had her family settled on Chestnut Street, Mrs. Repplier turned with redoubled efforts to Minnie and her education. "I was nearly nine," the essayist confessed, "and should have been showing some signs of progress." Teedie, she would add ruefully, was at the time in the happy course of covering herself with honors at the Convent of the Sacred Heart, the school, then on the outskirts of Philadelphia, to which she had been sent a short time before.

The only remarkable thing Mrs. Repplier had been able to discover in Minnie was her strong memory. And in consequence she had stocked her daughter with poetry, stanza upon stanza, page after page, endlessly. Minnie may have been slow, but she was tenacious. And what she once learned, she learned for good.

But Mrs. Repplier must have been aware of the fact that a long memory is not necessarily a sign of intelligence. She felt that Minnie would have to demonstrate more than just merely the ability to remember poems she learned vive voce in order to become worthy of her.

The next step had been to try reading. For some time Mrs. Repplier had struggled with Minnie over a little text designed, so it claimed, to teach the art of reading in as painless a fashion as possible. But Minnie and the volume were in distinct disagreement. Years later she classed it with a select group that, out of all the countless number of books she read in her youth, had caused her the most hindrance:

I learned my letters at the cost of infinite tribulation, out of a horrible little book called "Reading Without Tears," which I trust has long since been banished from all Christian nurseries. It was a brown book, and had on its cover a deceptive picture of two stout and unclothed Cupids holding the volume between them, and making an ostentatious pretense of enjoyment. Young as I was, I grew cynical over that title and that picture, for the torrents of tears that I shed blotted them both daily from my sight. It might have been possible for Cupids, who needed no wardrobes and sat comfortably on clouds, to like such lessons, but for an ordinary little girl in frock and pinafore they were simply heartbreaking. Had it only been my good fortune to be born twenty years later, spelling would have been left out of my early discipline, and I should have found congenial occupation in sticking pins or punching mysterious bits of clay at a kindergarten. But when I was young, the world was still sadly unenlightened in these matters; the plain duty of every child was to learn how to read; and the more hopelessly dull I showed myself to be, the more imperative became the need of forcing some information into me—information which I received as responsively as does a Strasbourg goose its daily share of provender. For two bitter years I had for my constant companion that hated reader, which began with such isolated statements as "Ann has a cat," and ended with a dismal story about a little African boy named Sam. . . .

But there was more to the situation than met the eye. (As for *Reading Without Tears*, one is inclined to believe it was the utter stupidity of the book rather than the difficulty of any lessons in it that offered the major stumbling block.) And as soon as Mrs. Repplier marked what lay behind the greater part of Minnie's seeming inability, she saw to it that matters underwent a drastic alteration. The result was that shortly thereafter Minnie became almost too omnivorous a reader.

Agnes Repplier freely confessed that at the time she had decided that learning to read was entirely unnecessary if there was always someone around to read to her. She had found that her mother or the nurse, Abbie, had been more than willing. And so she had preferred to let the annoying business of learning drift quite casually. She had listened rather than read.

But one day Minnie was shocked into the realization that a change in the situation was imminent. Mrs. Repplier was talking with one of her friends about the little girl's dullness in reading. "I wouldn't worry about the child," the friend said in calm conclusion. "She's just plainly deficient." As if that were any comfort to a mother who in this daughter had been cheated by a fickle Providence not only as to "looks" but apparently as to "brains" as well!

Minnie never forgot the grimness of her mother's reply: "She'll learn or die in the attempt!"

Thereafter the reading to her stopped. Mrs. Repplier and Abbie turned deaf ears to her pleadings. The books were hers for the asking; but if she wanted to discover what was in them, she must explore them alone, unaided. And after a bit that was exactly what Minnie did, the only difficulty then being that she rarely ceased.

ᴐ ᴐ ᴐ

The first book that Minnie read by herself was Hayward's translation of *Faust*, not quite the usual fare for little girls of nine or so even in the 1860's. But naught else being provided, she was forced to read grown-up books for the most part in her childhood, though of this she was never known to complain.

To her infinite delight—one advantage of having a cultivated mother—she discovered that a large supply of English letters awaited her at home. She unearthed, among other volumes, Bishop Percy's *Reliques* and a host of the popular Romantic poets of the day. She found a complete set of Maria Edgeworth, of which she grew very fond, as well as a great quantity of the inevitable pious works about which she cared not a whit.

Minnie came upon such a number of treasures and took so constant a delight in reading as to threaten on occasion her awareness of the social graces:

When I was young, all well-brought-up little girls . . . who were permitted to visit their playmates, were cautioned by careful mothers that they must on no account open a book. To sit in a corner and read, instead of joining decorously in games, was held to be unpardonably rude.

As for any sense of duty, Minnie never allowed it to stand in the way of her reading:

Once more I see the big, bare old-fashioned parlor, to dust which was my daily task, my dear mother having striven long and vainly to teach my idle little hands some useful housewifely accomplishment. In one corner stood a console table, with chilly Parian ornaments on top, and underneath a pile of heavy books, Wordsworth, Moore, the poems of Frances Sargent Osgood—no lack of variety here; The Lady of the Lake, and Byron in an embossed brown binding, with closely printed double columns, well calculated to dim the keenest sight in Christendom. Not that mysterious and malignant mountain which rose frowning from the sea, and drew all ships shattered to its feet, was more irresistible in its attractions than this brown, bulky Byron. I could not pass it by! My dusting never got beyond the table where it lay; but, sitting crumpled on the floor, with the enchanted volume on my lap, I speedily forgot everything in the world save only the wandering Childe . . . or the "Corsair," or "Mazeppa," or "Manfred," best loved of that dark group.

Mrs. Repplier, wise woman that she was in many respects, let Minnie alone to follow her own bent. In matters of what to read at least, she neither admonished nor dictated. Byron may not be generally considered the most wholesome of reading for little girls. But of this Minnie was quite unaware. "Having never been told that there was such a thing as forbidden fruit in literature," she "was spared at least that alert curiosity concerning it which is one of the most unpleasant results of our present guarded system."

ꙅ ꙅ ꙅ

Although the Civil War worked no serious direct effect upon her family, it did not pass without certain repercussions. The Maryland-born Mrs. Repplier, like many transplanted Southern women, was hotly Confederate. But Mr. Repplier remained staunchly Unionist. He was proud indeed of Lancaster who had left his Aunt Lucy's home in Reading to join the Northern forces. And he was a little grieved at his wife who had taken it upon herself, along with several other Southern women in the city, to supply the Confederate prisoners at Fort Delaware, not far from Philadelphia, with boxes of food, jelly, wine, and books. He could scarcely object to her humanitarian interest, but he was not altogether pleased that thus she would openly flaunt her sympathies.

Little of this reached Minnie or disturbed her at her reading. Even the wild rejoicings that greeted the news of Lee's surrender when it was announced in Philadelphia on April 15, 1865, remained vague and blurred in her mind. There were bonfires and parades and speeches, all blended together in the pealing of countless bells and the shouts and laughter of thousands. Everyone seemed to be very happy. But the reason for the jubilation was none too clear. The scene was largely one of confusion and made no strong impression.

The shocking news of Lincoln's assassination a few days

later was a different matter. Minnie never forgot the sight of house after house, building upon building, theaters, hotels, stores, all draped in mournful black. Even their own home bore its funereal crepe.

On April 22, at four-thirty in the afternoon, cannon sounded, one booming each minute. That, Minnie's father told her, meant the approach of the funeral train to the station on South Broad Street. And several hours later, the great procession passed the corner, crossing Chestnut at Twenty-first Street, on its way through the city to Independence Hall where the President's body was to lie in state for a day and a half.

Bands playing slow, melancholy music, the City Troop in cacophonously brilliant uniform, the mayor and officials of the city, civic leaders, hundreds of soldiers marched by. Then came the catafalque drawn by eight black horses, its canopy towering high above the people so that all might see the bier.

The entire household had gone to the corner to witness the cortege as it filed by. There they stood in respectful, awed silence with dozens of other families from the neighborhood. Everyone was most excited, but no one dared breathe a word lest, as the essayist commented years later, he be misunderstood and find himself accused of having killed Lincoln.

Suddenly a voice rose in frantic shouting, piercing the doleful music. The onlookers turned in horror to see a young girl, enchanted by the spectacle, jumping up and down, clapping her hands in ecstatic glee. Mr. Repplier was furious. It was one of the maids from his household making the disgraceful demonstration.

"Quick!" he whispered to his wife. "Get her home and lock her up, or we'll have the house burned down about our ears!" And in a flurry of apologies, subdued admonitions, and threats, they bustled the girl down the street.

Once indoors, Minnie for one felt safe. Surely, she thought, the people would understand that the maid's foolishness was none of their doing. Surely they would not burn the house down!

ତ ତ ତ

Late in the month following the Lincoln funeral procession, Mrs. Repplier gave birth to a second son. He was christened John after his grandfather, the parents said, though, as Agnes Repplier would remark, which one was anybody's guess, both grandfathers being of the same name.

"At last God has given me a handsome child," the happy mother was pleased to declare to the friends and relatives who came to admire and congratulate, for even from the very first John was a handsome boy. And as he grew older, he became more and more like his father in feature, though his hair was light.

Little Minnie adored her new brother. He was so pretty and so clever he quite occupied her time away from her precious reading. She loved just to look at him, his fair curls, his blue eyes. And there was no denying that he was clever. It seemed no time at all before he could talk or even pick out letters in the newspaper his father held for him as he dandled the baby on his lap.

One day after an afternoon's outing Abbie happened to bring John home on the horsecar. He talked with her so like a wise little gnome that an elderly gentleman on the car, amazed at the child's ability, asked the nurse how old he was. Before Abbie could answer, John spoke up. "I'm twenty-two months old," he volunteered, "and the smartest boy in town!" The story became almost legend with Minnie.

About two years later, to the infinite horror of the family, John was choked to death one night with croup. To Minnie his death seemed at the time one of the abiding tragedies of the world. Even in later years, although she fully realized that precocious children rarely fulfill their early promise, she felt that John could have lifted them all into "real fame." It had been his road in life that she had followed, she insisted. And she would add, "John was the only child both brilliant *and* handsome in which my mother ever indulged."

ꙮ ꙮ ꙮ

John's death was tempered for Minnie by new and disturbing prospects. Ever since she had learned to read, she had been studying with her mother. And though, by her own confession, she had revealed herself only an indifferent scholar, she must go to school. On this Mrs. Repplier was most emphatic.

For almost four years now Teedie had been bringing home pleasant accounts of Eden Hall, tales to which Minnie had lent only an occasional ear. She was not particularly interested in school, Eden Hall or any other. Life generally was satisfactory to her as she found it at the time.

But in the matter of education, Minnie was not consulted either as to her wishes or preferences. In her day little girls were not taken into the confidence of their parents. A decision was arrived at for her, and she was made ready to meet her prearranged future. That was all there was to it.

Eden Hall—not overly stirring to Minnie at the time, but how she was to relish her days there! How, once she had gone, she was to regret the vacations that would bring her back to the dullness of what just now she was about to quit most casually! Her life at home had been a rather solitary affair. But at Eden Hall it was to emerge into a world of inspiring friendships. At home she had been plain "Minnie," never the equal of her sister. At Eden Hall she was to become "Agnes," quite a person in her own right, no longer a lesser, comparative apology.

CHAPTER II

"Sweet Absurdities"

1867–1871

ᗡ ᗡ

The Convent of the Sacred Heart—Eden Hall—located on the northernmost reaches of Philadelphia, boasted a single main building in Minnie's day. Originally a private home of the early Victorian period, it was a plain, brownstone structure, topped by a mansard roof. A porch ran across the front, reached by wide, shallow steps. To the east had been added a wing, at the far end of which stood the Chapel, bearing a cornerstone dated 1849. On the west side extended a matching wing built during the Civil War. Possibly because of the recent anti-Catholic riots, it had been constructed mainly after sundown by candlelight, and the pointing wavered in perpetual sympathy with what had been the workmen's unsteady illumination.

The day for the girls at Eden Hall began with Mass in the Chapel. During the bleak winter months, it was cold comfort indeed they received at their devotions, for the building was unheated. But in the spring and fall, when the sun was up as early as the students, the Chapel was a pleasant place.

Mass was followed by breakfast, a meal rendered almost

silent by the rule that all conversations were to be carried on in French. A further rule stated that those students who did not indulge in such linguistic exercise were required to stand before the entire group at the end of the period alloted for eating and be marked down for their refusal. But many of the girls preferred to receive the demerit rather than submit to the stupid inanities they could manage in the foreign tongue.

Years after it had been her experience, Agnes Repplier wrote:

At that Spartan meal . . . even had we been able or willing to employ the hated medium, there was practically no one to talk to. By a triumph of monastic discipline, we were placed at table, at our desks, and at church, next to girls to whom we had nothing to say;—good girls, with medals around their necks, and blue or green ribbons over their shoulders, who served as insulating mediums, as non-conductors, separating us from cheerful currents of speech, and securing, on the whole, a reasonable degree of decorum.

Classes began at the conclusion of breakfast. As for the studies, they were quite according to the usual pattern. Minnie thought them simple if bothersome. History she enjoyed, and she was more than willing to write all the compositions the patient nun in charge could possibly read. But mathematics—"those little imps called numerals, as difficult to master as letters, and leading up to nothing but sums, which are an inadequate compensation"—was anathema to her. And French annoyed her, possibly because at the time she found it fashionable to be annoyed by the one subject the convent really endeavored to teach fully and well.

There was little time at Eden Hall for recreation. "No

one had yet discovered that play is more instructive than work, no one was piling up statistics to prove the educational value of idleness." But the girls were free certain times each day. Then they might roam the grounds in good weather or seek vicarious adventure, of a mild sort to be sure, in the library.

"Primes," the reckoning that came each Sunday afternoon, was the most exciting time of the week for Minnie. For this event the girls gathered in the Chapel under the nearsighted eyes of the Reverend Mother while one of the nuns read aloud the week's record. Here each student's deportmental as well as academic triumphs were disclosed for the whole school to wonder over.

Minnie found the ceremony entirely to her liking except on those hapless days when she was called forth to receive her reward. Fortunately, as she regarded the matter, such times were rare. But when luck was against her and the friends who felt as she—the "Hail Marys" they had said earlier in the day with an eye to warding off the misery proving to have been of no avail:

Then, over an endless expanse of polished floor, slippery as glass, we moved like stricken creatures; conscious that our friends were watching us in mocking security from their chairs; conscious that we were swinging our arms and turning in our toes; and painfully aware that our curtsies would never come up to the required standard of elegance and grace.

Although the girls at the convent were governed with what passed for an iron hand, Minnie found the discipline at Eden Hall far less stringent than at 2005 Chestnut Street. Because the rules at the convent were common to all, which was not entirely the case at home, they seemed fair. And as the essayist would blithely point out, even though you followed them—which, she added, she did not always do—you had a good time.

Minnie liked the nuns well enough, but for the most part she infinitely preferred the children. Some little girls are natural parts of a community, and she took to life at the convent with scarcely a backward glance. She was never homesick for a moment. She had a better time at school than at home; hers, she felt, was not the kind to be homesick for. Vacations were to be as desert stretches to her, and she was always glad when it came time to return to Eden Hall.

ೞ ೞ ೞ

It was on September 8, 1867, that Mrs. Repplier took Minnie to the Convent of the Sacred Heart. And on the very day of her arrival she made one of the strongest and most important friendships of her life. As she sat in the hall alone, she watched a group of girls file past her on their way to the dining room. Her mother had gone, and she had not yet been absorbed into the life around her. She was on her own now, understandably apprehensive, yet curious and excited as well.

The line of girls paused a moment opposite her, and there, directly across the way, stood one to whom her heart went out, as she would say, never to come back. The girl was not good-looking by any means, sallow somewhat, with dark, clipped hair and very light blue eyes. But Minnie felt as David must have felt when first he saw Jonathan.

"Oh, I hope she will be my friend!" she whispered to herself. And that night the two met at recreation.

It was inevitable that the two should meet sooner or later, for as Minnie shortly discovered, Elizabeth Robins—"Lizzie" at the convent—led quite a group at Eden Hall much as lambs are led to the sacrifice. And willing, devoted lambs they were. Although Minnie gathered about her a party of her own almost from the start, to them all, Lizzie's word was law. Once the older girl had accepted someone as a friend, she stood by that friend, and Minnie early swore complete allegiance to this incomparable person.

That Lizzie had condescended to take notice of her at all made Minnie very proud. Lizzie was a power at Eden Hall, though Minnie was unable to fathom just why unless, indeed, it was her seeming indifference to power. She was the ideal, the perfect friend in the eyes of the younger girl. Minnie never quite caught up with Lizzie. She never won a single prize for which her friend competed on the somewhat rare occasions when either bothered to do her best. But she loved her so she did not care. They were friends, and nothing else mattered.

ↄ ↄ ↄ

Minnie was determined from the start that, if she failed in all things else, she would cast off the distinctly hateful nickname with which her mother had blessed her and take once and for all her true, Christian name. "Minnie" she now had been for more years than she could remember. "Agnes" she would become.

And in this noble cause she enlisted the services of her friend Lizzie. To Agnes, as she was henceforth to insist upon being called, "Lizzie" was a downright insult, quite the equal of her own unbearable nickname. "Elizabeth"

Agnes   Elizabeth

she should become, and Lizzie, understandably enough, was not unwilling.

Jointly the two notified their little band. Did the other members of it realize the reason why? No matter. "Agnes" and "Elizabeth" each was called thereafter—except by the older diehards, the upper-class students, who could not, or would not, see the importance of the change.

ↄ ↄ ↄ

Agnes, Tony, Marie, Annie, Lilly, Viola, and Elizabeth formed a unique, clever group that held together tenaciously throughout their school days. It was these girls who were involved one time in the stealing of some straws from under the Bambino as he slept quite innocently beneath the glass case in the hall outside the Chapel, a measure decided upon so that each of them might have something properly sinful to confess before undertaking the retreat periodically required of all students at Eden Hall. It was these girls who gathered for themselves so unholy a conglomeration of indigestibles, including wine and cigarettes, for one particularly momentous *congé sans cloche*.

These were the daring seven who stole from their beds one night to watch the beautiful Marianus beneath the trees in the moonlight, and indeed collectively gave their hearts up to him. These were the seven who cut the numbers of their own true loves deep in their arms (each girl at the convent being expeditiously designated on occasion by a number) to prove their undying affection. These were the seven who pretended to be married and to take in marriage, at which time Agnes unwilling relinquished

Spain, the land of her heart's desire, and became, not the blessedly romantic "Princess of Castile," as she very much wished, but a quite mundane "Duchess of Tuscany" instead.

It was Agnes, Tony, Marie, Annie, Lilly, Viola, and Elizabeth who provided the "sweet absurdities" for *In Our Convent Days*. It was they who made life miserable for the mesdames of Eden Hall while making it memorable for themselves.

ᛜ ᛜ ᛜ

In later, half-serious moments, Agnes Repplier considered learning to smoke among her major accomplishments at the convent. Needless to say, at the time smoking scarcely developed into a habit. Such was to be reserved for more mature years. But beginning with the two cigarettes allotted to each girl in her little band the day they celebrated one *congé sans cloche*, Agnes and her friends would on occasion indulge in this most exciting of pastimes.

Just where the cigarettes came from is now something of a mystery, though the first had been smuggled to them by Viola's brother. The girls were allowed precious little money to spend by themselves even if they had been able to get beyond the grounds of the school to make so unconventional a purchase. But whatever their source, apparently they were available now and again.

At these delightful times, Agnes and her friends resorted to one of the attic storerooms or to a basement music studio. Sometimes they even became so daring as to go to Elizabeth's room. Being an older girl, she had a room to herself, the younger students claiming no more than a screened-in cubicle in the general dormitory.

One day the girls' irregular luxury was all but brought to a nerve-shattering disclosure. Agnes and several of her friends had gone to Elizabeth's room to smoke. After a short time of undiluted pleasure, they were interrupted by a madame attracted to the room by the odor of smoke drifting so innocently from it.

"What's this I smell?" the agitated nun called anxiously through the bolted door.

At first a terror-stricken silence answered her query. Then in a faltering voice one of the little criminals ventured, "The girls are just having their hair curled." It was a lame reply. But as they were well aware, some of the nuns would believe them no matter what—though some, on the other hand, would not. To their infinite relief, this nun believed, going her way satisfied.

The girls' consciences bothered them not a bit over the falsehood they had all been party to. For them there was a strict and undeniable difference between lying and invention. And this, in view of the harrowing circumstances, they felt was no more than legitimate invention.

ꙩ ꙩ ꙩ

If smoking proved Agnes' greatest achievement at Eden Hall, acting provided her most ignominious failure. Poor Agnes was consumed by an ardent desire to act. She could act; she *knew* she could. On the nights before an impending performance by the school dramatic group, as she lay in her reassuringly screened-in bed dreaming of what she might do, Agnes went over all the parts in the coming production. It was then that her strong memory stood her in good stead. With all the zeal and passion she was capable of mustering, she would storm through the various roles that almost always had been assigned to other girls.

Once or twice it happened that she was given a chance to display her art. But each time she was either overcome by self-consciousness that left her glued to the spot, speechless before the expectant audience, or she became so wrapped up in what was going on about her that she would never even realize when her cue to perform had arrived.

On one occasion Agnes had missed her cue as a result of living a certain play, in which she had a minor role, far beyond its actual worth. When her time to speak a few lines had come, she was unable to utter a word. After the play was over, Madame Rayburn, the dramatic coach, had tried to console the miserable Agnes:

"The scene was not spoiled," she said judiciously; "it went off remarkably well. But I did think, Agnes, that, although you cannot act, you had too much interest in the play, and too much feeling for the situation, to forget entirely where you were, or what you were about. There, don't cry! It didn't matter much!"

But Agnes was inconsolable:

Don't cry! As well say to the pent-up dam, "Don't overflow!" or to the heaving lava-bed, "Don't leave your comfortable crater!" Already my tears were raining over my blue tunic and yellow trousers. How could I—poor, inarticulate child—explain that it was because of my absorbing interest in the play, my passionate feeling for the situation, that I was now humbled to the dust . . . ?

ᕽ ᕽ ᕽ

The library at Eden Hall was small and none too inspiring in Agnes' day. There were scores of children's books.

novels of an innocuous nature to be sure, all staunchly moral, all determinedly elevating. But Agnes had gained her love of reading on stronger stuff. Chambers' *Miscellany*, of all the books in the school collection, appealed most to her. She found little use for the insipid pap designed to improve as it endeavored to entertain.

From the time of her twelfth birthday when Mrs. Repplier had given her a copy of *Childe Harold*, Agnes' favorite poet had been Byron. The library at Eden Hall was woefully lacking in the works of the romantic rebel, but Agnes knew the stories of Manfred, Don Juan, and the Childe by heart. She could spend hours merely in dreaming about them or in relating the various adventures to her friends.

The spirit of revolt in *Manfred* made it perhaps the most enthralling to her, although *Don Juan* was a very special delight. Curiously, the amorous Don never impressed Agnes particularly as far as his conquests in love were concerned. She had never been told, and it had never entered her head, that there might be something questionable about Don Juan's conduct. Most young girls learn about such matters far more rapidly from a few words offered on the sly by some initiated friend than they do from any amount or kind of reading. And so far she had escaped enlightenment.

Once as she was deep in the relating of the story of *Don Juan* to one of her schoolmates, Agnes was cut short by the sudden, horrified interruption of an upper-class student. She had just reached the incident of the Don's hiding in the bed of his inamorata when the older girl came along.

"Minnie Repplier!" the proper prude exclaimed. "Whatever are you talking about! Do you *know* what you are saying?" And she turned away with quite an evident shudder.

Agnes was angry and puzzled. In the first place, the girl had called her "Minnie Repplier"—fighting words. In the second place, she had broken in at one of the best episodes of the tale, thereby utterly destroying the spell. And in the third place, she had really seemed shocked. Over what? That Agnes could not say. If Don Juan wanted to climb into the young lady's bed, that was his business. It certainly provided an adequate place in which to hide. She pondered the matter for some time, arriving at no sensible answer other than that the older girl just did not enjoy poetry.

ↄ ↄ ↄ

Agnes had now been attending the convent school for two years. Here she had made one of the significant friendships of her life, that with Elizabeth Robins. Here her already awakened love of literature had been quickened and stimulated not only by the books at hand, slight though for the most part they may have been, but also by her contact with the older girl who was quite as avid a reader as she. At Eden Hall also she had come to assert herself, to put Minnie, the shy, awkward little girl, behind her forever. Agnes she now had become, a power, a leader herself even in competition with Elizabeth, an undeniable influence on the other children around her. Most of all, at the convent she had first tried her hand at writing, and had won the praise and encouragement of her teachers for her efforts.

Somewhat on the other side of the ledger, Agnes had revealed herself in school as one not easily coerced into doing that for which she had no particular liking. Not infrequent were her rebellions against the nuns. Although a loyal friend to those she had chosen for her own, Agnes was not one to hestitate over dismissing the objects of her scorn with devastating frankness. "Frances was first blue ribbon, first medallion, and head of the Children of Mary. There was nothing left for her but beatification . . . " Agnes preferred the less angelic. Distinctly human herself, she disliked youthful piety. "There is nothing so souring to the temper as abstinence," she felt. And she included abstaining from mischief along with such orthodox items as candy and desserts.

Two lifelong traits were brought to light during Agnes' stay at Eden Hall: courage and open intolerance of that which she considered stupid. It took courage for her to assert her independence. It took courage for her to rebel when not to have rebelled would have cost her far less trouble. It took courage for her to stamp stupidity as intolerable and then, not satisfied with mere lip service to her creed, to act accordingly.

ತ ತ ತ

But the role of rebel was a dangerous one in a convent school in the 1860's, especially when one was only fourteen. And so it happened that in July 1869, after she had finished her second year at Eden Hall, Agnes was dismissed. The note sent to her parents was diplomatic but none the less adamant: for the good of the school as well, of course, as of Agnes herself (on that point it insisted), the Reverend Mother felt . . .

Just why Agnes should have been singled out of all the little rebels there at the Sacred Heart is not altogether clear. She had not been the only troublemaker, perhaps not even the greatest. Her parents were not a little confounded by the distinction their daughter had achieved. And even she was at a loss to explain the dubious honor. But whatever the certain reason behind her dismissal, the convent days for Agnes were at an end. For her a very real world had collapsed.

She was back at home again, permanently this time, and a dull place in comparison it appeared to be. Elizabeth, Marie, Tony: all were of the irretrievable past now, or so at least they seemed. There were no young people at home but Mary and Louis. The one, having left the convent in perfect form a year since, was righteously indignant over her fall from grace; and the other was more or less an invalid. They would be slight comfort.

No more exciting, stolen adventures with her friends. No more secret confidences. Just stupid, monotonous, everlasting home duties. The prospect was far from pleasing. Even the memories of the past two years could hardly compensate for the arid waste the future promised to be.

꜒ ꜒ ꜒

If Agnes was in any degree crushed by the turn in her fortunes, Mrs. Repplier, who undoubtedly had suffered more than any other member of the family over the disgrace, was by no means defeated. The girl had proved too much for the nuns? Perhaps she could be brought to see the proper light by someone not so easy to get around. And Mrs. Repplier felt she knew just the right person.

In the fall of 1869, Agnes Irwin, who later was to be called as the first Dean of Radcliffe College, took over on Penn Square, Philadelphia, a school for girls. Mrs. Repplier had been acquainted with the Irwin family for some years. She knew that Miss Irwin, though still quite a young woman, was not only a capable teacher, but a strict disciplinarian as well. There would certainly be no indulgence of student whimsey at her school.

Having made up her mind, Mrs. Repplier arranged for the enrolling of Agnes at the Irwin School. As the essayist once commented, fathers had practically nothing to say in such matters, and children might as well have been born deaf-mutes for all they were allowed to make suggestions. But Agnes, scarcely recovered from the shock of having to leave Eden Hall, was in the main easily pleased. The truth of the situation was that she was eager for new friends such as she had made at the convent. Another school should mean another opportunity.

ᴐ ᴏᴙᴄ

Miss Irwin's School was on the whole quite different from the Convent of the Sacred Heart. To begin with, Miss Irwin herself was far removed from any of the nuns at Eden Hall, and therein lay the real heart of the difference. Miss Irwin had a profound belief in education and, startlingly enough for her day, was most emphatically not of the opinion that women could learn too much.

In view of her convictions, it is only natural that the institution Miss Irwin managed should have been in no sense of the term a "finishing school." It was a place devoted to work, to study. Nonsense in any form was not to

be tolerated there. Professionally Miss Irwin was determined, almost grim in her intransigence. Personally—to
use Agnes Repplier's own words—she was "about as de-
monstrative as an iceberg." Yet for all her austerity, she was
loved dearly by her pupils. And no one of them was to
become more fond of her than the little girl who so recently had been expelled from the convent.

Agnes found her studies under Miss Irwin much as they
had been at Eden Hall, save for one all-important difference. At this new school there was not the faintest hint of
dilettantism. Miss Irwin was a scholar with a scholar's
point of view. She always sent her pupils to "headquarters"
for their work, and by this she meant that they should
go to the original sources. Consequently her charges were
imbued from the start with a deep and sincere respect
for proper authority, particularly in matters literary.

Beyond these things, Miss Irwin's School was unlike the
convent in several other more obvious ways. It was small,
numbering only about thirty pupils or so when Agnes began her work there. And it was a day school for the most
part, except for one or two special boarding students. All
this meant that classwork was under constant close scru-
tiny and that homework became a matter of direct, personal responsibility on the part of both parent and pupil.
Though she was not pleased by any means over the necessity, each day Agnes came dutifully home with her
share of studying to do under the supervision of her
watchful mother.

ಲ ಲ ಲ

As Agnes was to realize later on, she had the type of
mind Miss Irwin heartily disliked. She was entirely com-

placent, certain she was going to do a very great deal. And from Miss Irwin she received absolutely no encouragement on this score.

Agnes soon found out, too, that Miss Irwin could not be put off with a thin excuse such as many times had worked wonders at the convent. Once when Miss Irwin asked her a question, she replied, "I'm sorry. I forget." The answer, with just the correct modulation, would on occasion at least have served in her earlier school days. But not so with Miss Irwin. "You have a tenacious memory," she told Agnes sharply, "and you have no business forgetting anything."

If on occasion a student at Miss Irwin's School tried to get out of any work assigned to her by one of the few subordinate teachers, she soon found herself face to face with the headmistress who took charge until a change in the pupil's work was effected. And here only, in the case of Agnes, did Miss Irwin have to acknowledge defeat. Agnes had been having trouble with mathematics. Everyone comes upon opened and closed doors in life, and mathematics, she was sure, was a completely closed door to her. So she had informed her teacher, and the teacher in desperation had gone to Miss Irwin. As a consequence, the headmistress supervised Agnes' work throughout one whole, painful, seemingly never-ending week.

At the end of the time, having managed no appreciable improvement in her pupil's accomplishments in this particular field of study, Miss Irwin announced coldly, "Agnes, you did yourself a grave injustice when you labeled yourself 'stupid' in mathematics. You are simply *impervious* to mathematics." And she emphasized the word uncomfortably.

For all she might have been afraid of her on occasion, Agnes came eventually to admire Miss Irwin completely. Even at the time of her schooling, she recognized the fact that, as she would say, Miss Irwin "saw things thoroughly and she saw them whole." For her part Miss Irwin apparently realized that Agnes was an unusual child. But the teacher discovered also that she was easily turned aside, and she was determined from the beginning that the girl should not allow herself to be turned aside.

At first Miss Irwin was impatient with Agnes. Now and again she was cuttingly caustic.

On one occasion she asked a pupil if she knew how the crowns of England and Scotland came to be united. The answer was correctly given. James the Sixth of Scotland and First of England was the monarch who united them. Delighted to observe any scrap of knowledge that had not been part and parcel of the day's lesson, Miss Irwin asked: "And whose son was he?" The child pondered for a moment, and then said: "I know that Queen Elizabeth was his mother, and I did know who was his father, but I have forgotten." "I wish you would try and recollect," observed Miss Irwin persuasively. "It would throw an interesting light on history."

And again:

A clever little girl, who thought as well of herself as clever little girls are wont to do, informed her class that "Lycidas" was an elegy on John Keats. When the discrepancy of dates was somewhat sharply pointed out to her, she said with the air of one making a generous admission, and rather expecting to be contradicted: "It was stupid of me I know." To which Miss Irwin made weary rejoinder: "Don't dwell on the obvious. Go on with your reading."

Agnes was the unfortunate pupil involved on both counts, the object of Miss Irwin's scorn on these and many other occasions.

In the main, Miss Irwin's School was almost equally
both a disappointment and a source of real pleasure to
Agnes. It was not another Eden Hall, as she had fondly
hoped it would be. Now school was a dull matter of daily
trips back and forth, of stupid evenings under the lamp-
light at 2005 Chestnut Street, of endless tasks about the
house in free time. What she would not have given to
have been back at the convent! How she dreamed, calling
on her staunch memory and most ardent imaginative
powers! But it was no use. The convent days were over.

The present, real and uncomfortably changed from the
blissfulness of what had been, was the insolvable problem
now. Not that Agnes really disliked the work at Miss
Irwin's. Not that she had made no new friends. But the
school could not hold a candle to the convent as far as she
was concerned. At Miss Irwin's there was no Marie, no
Tony, and most lamentable of all, no Elizabeth.

That there were certain compensations for her at the
Irwin School Agnes Repplier could not deny. And far
from the least of these was the headmistress herself. Daily
she became of more and more importance to the young
girl. Even in her most rebellious moments, moments when
she was exasperated out of all patience because she could
not do as she pleased when she pleased, Agnes was conscious of Miss Irwin. And there were times when Miss
Irwin took on almost godlike proportions in Agnes' eyes.
She was everlastingly grateful to her mentor for the months
she spent with her over *Childe Harold*. And the day Miss
Irwin gave Agnes a copy of Keats's poems to read by herself wiped out with a single sweep many of the faults she
had found to carp about.

Of even more immediate appeal to Agnes than the

headmistress were the books she uncovered at Miss Irwin's School. Here she discovered that one was never at a loss for something to read, something important, something satisfying. No longer the almost constant recourse of necessity to Chambers and his dozen-times exhausted *Miscellany*. Here there were books aplenty, books to be read and reread.

But without doubt the greatest benefit Agnes derived from her attendance at the Irwin School was in her writing. Upon the merest suggestion at the convent she had written verse—dearest of all to young hearts—stories, sketches, even plays. But it was at Miss Irwin's that she received her first important criticism. The headmistress knew that Agnes' book interest could indicate a corresponding interest in writing. Before long she found that it did, and so she provided the girl with every opportunity to exercise her youthful talent.

Not always was the teacher pleased with her pupil's work. And never did Miss Irwin unbend sufficiently to the bandying of idle pleasantries merely for the sake of being agreeable. She was not one to hestitate over speaking her mind even when to do so might offend. But she never allowed her sharp wit or incisive satire to come between Agnes and what even then seemed might possibly be her work in life.

If writing was to be Agnes' career, then there was only one road to success and that lay clearly marked. This road and none other would Miss Irwin allow her charge to follow, and she sought with every power at her command to block any alluring bypaths. It was in the field of writing she was most determined that Agnes should not go astray.

ง ง ง

But all was not sweetness and light for Agnes at Miss Irwin's School by any manner of means. The fact that Miss Irwin was a friend of her mother's or that the headmistress seemed to take a special interest in her literary endeavors was no reason for Agnes to suppose that she was immune to the discipline of routine studies at the School. Now and again Agnes wished that Miss Irwin, by virtue of her interest in her, was not so constantly aware of her presence. Because Miss Irwin was, Agnes sometimes felt that she was not a little imposed upon. It was difficult, even impossible, for her to slip by whatever the matter at hand.

There were in consequence not a few clashes along the way, minor forays, to be sure, from which Miss Irwin invariably came off the victor. It was not fair, the girl thought. I cannot *always* be wrong, she would tell herself. And on occasion, to test the strength of her wings, Agnes would set out deliberately to express her independence. Sometimes she frankly defied the headmistress, quite openly baiting her in the process. Perhaps at these times Miss Irwin saw through the ruse. Possibly she was entirely conscious of the act going on around her. But for the most part she endured the girl's outbursts with a calmness that could have been born only of the knowledge that, after all, she did have the upper hand.

ɔ ɔ ɔ

For a year and a half Agnes met the problems and delighted in the joys of Miss Irwin's School before the inevitable happened. The patience of the nuns at Eden Hall had been exhausted after two years of near rebellion on the part of the little girl. It was small wonder that the not nearly so patient Miss Irwin gave out after only three terms. The marvel may be that she had been able to keep control of herself so long. But the end came again for Agnes, and this time it really was the end.

One day in class Miss Irwin gave Agnes a certain book to study. And quite suddenly Agnes decided that she was not interested in studying that particular book. Indeed, she was not interested one iota in that particular book. With characteristic independence she tossed it on the floor. She would not read, she would not study, and that was that.

A stricken silence followed, marked at length by a sharp intake of breath on the part of all the other assembled students. Miss Irwin's dignity as she retrieved the volume so mutinously discarded was awesome beyond belief. But nothing was said at the time, nothing was done, no punishment was meted out—just then.

That afternoon, after she had returned from school, Agnes saw Miss Irwin come along Chestnut Street and turn up the steps before her home. She thought little of it; Miss Irwin was a friend and frequent visitor. She thought little, too, of the fact that Miss Irwin and her mother were closeted for quite a time in the front parlor. She thought even less about the whole affair when dinner passed without mention of the afternoon's performance. The intermittent qualms of the afternoon and early evening grew less and less disturbing. That night Agnes slept without a twinge of regret or tremor or insecurity.

The next morning when it came time for her to get ready for school, Agnes put on her hat and coat and gathered up her pencils and books. She descended the stairs from her room as she had done on countless previous mornings, prepared to offer a hasty farewell to her mother waiting in the lower hall. Suspecting nothing, she missed entirely the drawn look about her mother's mouth, the thinness of her lips.

"Where are you going?" Mrs. Repplier asked the girl who was about to slip past her.

What was wrong, Agnes wondered. Could she possibly have forgotten? "To school," she whispered with becoming if unnatural meekness.

"You can take your hat and coat off," Mrs. Repplier continued in a disturbingly quiet way, "because you are not going back to school."

"Not going to school?" It sounded incredible!

"No, you are not going to school—now or ever again. Miss Irwin came yesterday to say she had borne quite enough."

Agnes was shocked into defiance. "I don't think Miss Irwin had anything to bear," she said.

"I can judge only by what I have had to bear myself." And Mrs. Repplier turned majestically away.

Agnes was dumfounded. But she knew even in that horrible moment that dismissal from Miss Irwin's School was not the blow leaving Eden Hall had been. Although she realized fully that she would miss the school, although in a sense she hated to leave, still she felt a stirring sense of exhilaration over Miss Irwin's having turned her out, as she would say, "neck and crop." After all, there was something in that, she decided, something quite satisfactory.

CHAPTER III

Career

1872–1884

For the most part Agnes Repplier was not unduly wor-
ried over her dismissal from Miss Irwin's School. Like
many moderately clever girls, she thought she could educate herself, and she turned at once to a self-devised course
in reading. She decided then and there that she would become a scholar. But before very long, she discovered that
she really could not educate herself in any formal sense
of the word at all. Little more was possible for her than
to make herself well read.

Agnes Repplier did not quite agree with Elizabeth Robins who once remarked, "I never learned anything after
I was sixteen, but by way of compensation I knew it all
then." But she was confident of her ability. She would never
have thought of admitting that leaving Miss Irwin's had
been anything even remotely approaching a misfortune.

In time Agnes Repplier realized that, although she had
high ambitions, she lacked the necessary means to their
realization. She wanted an education, but she had no one
to help her to it. Alone, she merely floundered. What she
was to attain, she felt in later years, was no more than a

tolerable framework on a weak foundation. If she did have to admit to herself now and then that it is no easy job to keep up study by oneself and that one good mind to lead her would have been everything, still she kept bravely going, reading the more, the more alone she felt herself to be.

Miss Irwin or her mother could have meant a great deal to her, but the young girl had willfully cast them both off. And Mrs. Repplier was determined that no longer should she waste time and money on this rebel daughter's education. Two schools had been enough; there would be no more. Miss Irwin, though she could see Mrs. Repplier's point of view readily enough, was horrified at the thought of leaving Agnes to nothing more certain than her own devices and a somewhat defiant determination to show her elders that they had been mistaken in what had appeared to be her undependability at school. Frequently she would urge Mrs. Repplier to reconsider—though she herself never offered to reinstate the girl in her school. But no, Mrs. Repplier had made up her mind, and that was the end to it.

ↄ ↄ˙ↄ

A few months more than sixteen, Agnes Repplier set out on her own. French, thanks to her mother's early training and the convent's efforts, she had well in hand. Latin she read with ease. Horace was for her a constant joy, the delight, she felt, of every right-thinking mind. But English letters remained then and always her main source of stimulation. In them she read unceasingly and with an amazing ability to find the distinctly uncommonplace.

Memoirs and biographies gave her more pleasure than fiction, and poetry offered her its wealth of beautiful exactness.

From whatever she read, even in those early days, she extracted what she felt to be the best, storing up ideas, phrases, whole sentences that were to feed her mind and pen throughout her entire career. Although she had not then begun to keep the notebooks she found so valuable in after years, her memory was strong and fresh, and she filled it with her random, useful gleanings. Later in life, she read mainly what may have been necessary to her trade. But at the beginning it was a happy feasting in every direction, with the young girl seemingly never sated.

ꙮ ꙮ ꙮ

While she was filling her mind and heart with the wonders of literature, Agnes Repplier was also trying her hand at writing. Quite understandably, at that time she scarcely thought of herself, she would say, as one day becoming a famous anything, let alone a famous author. But she could no more keep from pen and paper than she could successfully steel herself against opening a new book.

Words were the only things she understood, Agnes Repplier declared; she had a "passion for words." She experienced the keenest pleasure of all when she was putting them down on paper, one after another, in orderly, precise fashion. Words, she felt, are like jewels, and she handled them as carefully as a jeweler his precious stones. She believed in the *mot juste*, and with solitary diligence she would search for it, depending on nothing but her books and her inner sense of rightness.

The youthful writer did all her work quite by herself, and few persons indeed ever saw her early attempts. Like most beginning authors, she was timid about revealing her efforts. But to her chagrin, she found that she could not keep her work entirely to herself as she devoutly wished she could. Now and again her mother would insist upon being shown what she was doing.

Fortunately, as Agnes Repplier saw the matter, Mrs. Repplier was in general much too busy with her household cares to bother to any great extent with her. Mary's days for some time now had been given over largely to teaching Louis the fundamentals of the three R's, in the course of which, incidentally, she was exhibiting no striking display of patience. Her father, as always, was far more concerned with providing for the family than he was in the individual members of it. And so Agnes Repplier read and wrote undisturbed, largely unmindful of the course of things around her.

ง ง ง

One day Mr. Repplier announced simply and undramatically that he had lost his money. The essayist remembered that he was very calm, quiet, and rather pathetically ashamed. But not so her mother. She was anything but calm. How did it happen, she wanted to know. And so Mr. Repplier related the short, sorry business: he had sold his coal holdings. Mrs. Repplier was shocked and hurt that he had done such a thing without even mentioning it to her and said as much. What had he done with the money? He had invested it in iron. And who had advised him to do that? Mr. Repplier told her: an Irishman, a redheaded Irishman,

and worse luck, a Protestant to boot. Now Mrs. Repplier
had the answer. You *know* you can't trust an Irishman, she
told her husband. As for a Protestant—well, that made the
chicanery doubly certain. And there was nothing left then?
Mr. Repplier was afraid not—nothing but the house. He
had invested his money in a foundry down on the Delaware River, and the venture had proved unsuccessful.

Immediately Mrs. Repplier assumed full charge of the
situation. Something had to be done, and Mrs. Repplier
took it for granted that she herself was the only one capable of doing it. At least the house was saved. Eventually
no doubt they would have to give it up. It would be far
too expensive for them to maintain under the circumstances.
But for the time being they would stay where they were.

Mr. Repplier said that he had thought he could perhaps
go back into the coal business as representative for one of
the larger New York firms. It would be only on a commission basis, but it would be something. Yes, Mrs. Repplier
agreed, it would be something.

Next she turned to the girls. Louis was after all still only
a child. "Mary," she announced firmly, "you can teach.
But," she added in warning, "you'll have to show more
patience than you have with Louis." Mary, it seemed, where
business was concerned, understood that patience would
most certainly be a more than necessary virtue. She promised to play her role with Griselda-like endurance.

There had been a day when Mrs. Repplier liked to suggest that her younger daughter take the veil. One conse-
crated to the church in the immediate family would be a
mark of distinction. But Agnes Repplier knew she could
not become a nun merely because her mother wanted her

to be one. "Why, I'd lose my immortal soul," was her comment. And for all concerned, it had been wise of Mrs.
Repplier not to have pressed the point.

"As for you, Agnes," her mother went on, brushing
aside any earlier thoughts of an unproductive life for the
girl in a nunnery, "you, of course, can write." Mrs. Repplier was very sure of that. There was no question in her
voice, and indeed the younger Agnes was perfectly willing
to offer her little art in the interest of family fortune. She
was delighted that at last she would be able to show her
worth, not that she had ever been particularly bothered
over what others thought of her, but because now she knew
she could write inasmuch as she would have to write. From
that very moment she was fired with both desire and need,
the best of all possible goads for the artist.

ᴐ ᴐ ᴐ

Agnes Repplier, more than ever the determined writer,
worked hard, giving over her whole mornings without fail,
then resting in the afternoons and evenings. She was slow—
more remarkable for that than for anything else, she would
say—composing the first rough draft straight through,
"working like mad" for a few days while her idea was still
fresh in mind. Then she would go back for revisions, a
system that stayed with her throughout her entire career.
She always had plenty of words; she liked them, considered them marvelous things. But although she thought then
and ever that English is the best of all known languages,
she declared it "a hell of a nuisance to get it right."

Agnes Repplier knew—it seemed she had never not
known—that somehow, somewhere inside her there was

something. But she brought it out only with a great deal of trouble. She understood how to write even if she did not have anything to say, and half-seriously she would admit many years after to never knowing which is the better attribute for an author to possess. She had no particular message certainly in the early days, but she could phrase what she did have to offer surely and well.

Though it all may have been a struggle, the essayist was equal to the task. She had ambition and she had books. And in addition, there was the ever-present pressure to earn money, though in this regard she was always careful not to write down merely for the sake of income. Money was a real need, but she knew from the start that reputation was even dearer. "God forbid that I should ever degrade writing for the sake of money!" she would say over and over again.

In the beginning, Agnes Repplier earned five or ten dollars, on rare occasions fifteen, for the little sketches, stories, and poems that found their way into the Philadelphia newspapers. Not much perhaps, but at least it was encouraging. Though she tried each one, offering material to any editor who would take it, the *Sunday Times*, she discovered, was most receptive of all the city journals of her time. And fortunately her parents evidenced no qualms over her publishing in a paper designed to be hawked on the Lord's Day. Their only concern, she has said, was over the amount of money her work would bring. If something she wrote was rejected by one paper, she would send it to another, going from big to little, till finally it was accepted. Remarkable as it may seem, there was never to be anything all the way from those very first serious attempts down through the full and productive years that was not eventually published somewhere.

In after years, Agnes Repplier came to realize that she had had nothing like the competition in her apprentice days that she would have had fifty years later, and she felt herself to have been undeniably lucky. She believed that luck plays a large part in anyone's success as a writer, and freely admitted that it certainly had in her own. Her great good fortune, she felt, was that she had come at a time when New England had plenty to offer and when yet there was still room elsewhere. It is true that she had experienced few of the troubles authors are supposed to have at the start. But then, she never expected to jump to the top in one mighty leap. She was quite satisfied to work her way up, and she had both the courage and determination to persist in her slow if steady climb.

Agnes Repplier may have been very young and overconfident in the beginning, but she was as certain then that she could write as she was after she had won her place. She experimented carefully in her early writing, following no model, feeling her way cautiously. And in it all, she tried to do her best. Hers was an unbounded admiration for English. She endeavored with all the artistry at her command to develop what from her extensive and well-chosen reading she had come to consider to be a good style. This uncompromising excellence she strove to inject into all that she wrote: into the early essays, short, simple pieces concerned mainly with the little of life she knew; into the stories that somehow just would not turn out to her expectations; into the poems which were few in number, for, she has said, she never flourished in poetry and was as a result inclined rather to keep these productions for the most part to herself.

Whatever the matter in hand, Agnes Repplier worked hard always and with a depth of sincerity far beyond her years to achieve a precision, a nicety, a clearness of expression that would be effectively literary as well as pleasingly entertaining. If form was to count more than content, the form at least would be excellent.

ↄ ↄ ↄ

Some six years after Mr. Repplier made his momentous announcement concerning his money affairs, he and his wife decided that it would be far more practical for them all to move to a smaller house and try to rent their home on Chestnut Street. Mr. Repplier was failing in health, and his commission business in coal was not overly prosperous. Then, too, though they tried valiantly enough, neither daughter was earning a great deal as yet. It was, Agnes Repplier would say, a rather gasping existence they led at this time.

And so the problem of finding a new home arose. The family looked here and there throughout the city. They would not even consider moving from Philadelphia; in this they thought much as the essayist was to think in her more mature years. After all, Philadelphia was home, and they were above everything else Philadelphians. Finally, after persistent seeking, they came upon a place in West Philadelphia on Locust Street a few doors beyond Fortieth. A three-story, tight-row house—a far cry from 2005 Chestnut Street—with a front piazza on which, they pointed out in an effort to console themselves, Mr. Repplier might sit in the summer months, and a tiny patch of garden in the rear: not the best by any means, but they had to agree it would serve their purpose.

They prepared forthwith to move: eliminating, combining, packing, unpacking. All the servants of more affluent days except the cook had long since been reluctantly dismissed. But even though it was something of a pinch to keep her on, Julia—famed for her kidney stews—journeyed out with the family.

ↄ ↄ ↄ

Established shortly on the very last fringes of civilization, as she most emphatically considered anything west of the Schuylkill to be, Agnes Repplier took up her work in the second-floor front room at 4015 Locust Street. No matter where she might find herself, the writing must continue. If ever a fortune was to be made, small as it might be, she saw that she apparently was the one destined to make it. She had the promise and the will. She must be the means.

West Philadelphia was not without its real drawbacks. Mary Repplier's pupils all lived in town, and consequently each day she had to pack off to the "City" to keep up her work. Her mother would joke about it, saying that Mary traveled like a milkman from door to door. But it was no joke, especially in the winter months, with waiting on a windy, snowy corner for a horsecar an uncomfortable necessity.

Agnes Repplier found it a great inconvenience to live such a distance from the libraries in the center of town, and she had a well-grounded mistrust of the circulating variety, a mistrust aided and abetted by her mother and fostered

as well by her training under Miss Irwin. The Library of
the University of Pennsylvania was quite near at hand, but
it was not one with which she was familiar—not like the
Library Company, with its gloomy but amazingly full
Ridgway Branch on South Broad Street.* Miss Repplier
disliked jaunting to and fro—frequently she was not equal
to it physically—and she longed for the easy days when a
trip to the library had been a matter of only a few minutes.

ভ ভ ভ

Elizabeth Robins, following her graduation from Eden
Hall, had taken up her friendship with Agnes Repplier
again. Miss Robins had turned to writing seriously some
time before her friend, and she had made enviable strides.
But then, Charles Godfrey Leland (no blood relative,
though she called him "uncle") helped her whenever he
could. Agnes Repplier remembered that a few years later
it was he who sent one of Elizabeth Robins' papers off to
the *Atlantic Monthly*, and thereby brought about her first
appearance in that magazine.

Perhaps on occasion Miss Repplier regretted that she had
no one "to give her a boost now and then," but in the main,
she rather enjoyed walking alone. Whatever she would accomplish, she would tell herself, would be on her very
own, with no one else dividing the credit. Still, Elizabeth
Robins was getting somewhere—there was no denying that
—whereas even now she was little better than an amateur
with only a few minor feathers in her cap.

* The essayist once wrote to a friend: "Of all the misbegotten build-
ings in the world the Ridgway Library is the worst. Dark, dismal,
depressing, inconvenient, it is a haunting horror . . . "

Mrs. Repplier had told her younger daughter all along that she would have a hard time of it establishing herself as a writer. But she encouraged her in her work because she knew it was all she could do. She was perfectly sure that the girl could write, and more than that, she was perfectly sure that she must.

And Agnes Repplier herself realized as much as her mother that she could not afford to be discouraged. She found that there is nothing like the spur of necessity to drive one on. She was coming to see as well that what you are interests the world very little—unless, as she would say in the Philadelphia phrase, you come down from a "Signer." The world, she discovered, is moved only by what you do. And so she worked with all the energy she could muster, taking her pleasures where she found them: in the fact that she was trying diligently; in the small amounts of money that came in recompense for her efforts; even in the excitement of seeing her name in print.

ꙮ ꙮ ꙮ

One day, almost ten years after Mrs. Repplier had laid down the law to her daughter in the matter of her writing, a short story of Agnes Repplier's was accepted by the *Catholic World*, the magazine established some twenty years before by Father Hecker. Isaac Thomas Hecker early in his life had been interested in both the transcendentalist experiment at Brook Farm and in Bronson Alcott's colony at Fruitlands. He had been an intimate friend of Thoreau, whom, after his own conversion in 1844, he had tried to bring into the Catholic Church. In 1865 he had founded the Missionary Priests of St. Paul the Apostle—known generally as the Paulist Order—and some seven years later had begun publishing the *Catholic World* of which he acted as editor.

January 1881—a date to remember! And the amount received, fifty dollars, was perhaps the most gratifying reward Agnes Repplier was ever to earn. Mrs. Repplier's single comment in the face of such success was a somewhat resentful "You never showed that to me" to which her daughter made no reply. A smile of mingled pride and superiority seemed best at the time.

"In Arcady" tells of a young man, a Mr. Bevan, who, having gone to the country one fall to recuperate from an illness, finds himself caught in a pretty party of children watched over by the angelic Natalie. After five weeks of the most genteel and indirect of courtships imaginable, Mr. Bevan proposes to the nursemaid, commenting somewhat loftily on the result:

She was ready indeed to trust her precious future in my hands, but the surrender was made without one single word to ratify it.

Before long, quite without the slightest provocation, Natalie dies, and the following autumn Mr. Bevan, musing on what might have been, murmurs:

It is October now. The fruit hangs ripening on the trees; the red leaves deck the brown and wearied earth; the setting sun flared crimson in the west; but the golden gates of Arcady have closed upon me, and in this world I shall enter them no more.

Sixty years after its publication, when the story was recalled to its author, she quoted this final paragraph without hesitation, smiled, and remarked: "You might have thought I was a hundred!"

$$\mathfrak{O} \ \mathfrak{O} \ \mathfrak{O}$$

Not many months after the publication of "In Arcady," Mrs. Repplier was taken suddenly ill. For years apparently, though no one had suspected it, not even she herself, she had been the victim of cancer, a disease which later was to attack her writer-daughter. But whereas Agnes Repplier, when she first noticed the symptoms, was to submit to immediate and completely curative medical attention, with Mrs. Repplier the disease had made such inroads upon her that no help was possible.

Her family was distraught. Barely fifty, she was not old. They were not prepared to meet this tragedy. But their regrets and wondering protestations could effect no change. In August 1882, Mrs. Repplier died and was buried in the family vault at St. John's.

Though each one of them felt Mrs. Repplier's passing as he had felt no other grief, it was her daughter Agnes who missed her more than any. When, four years later, she won her way into the *Atlantic Monthly*, she found her success like ashes in her mouth because her mother was not there to share it with her.

And the loss remained. She once wrote to a friend in sympathy upon the death of his mother: "I am glad she saw your hardwon and well-merited success before she had to die. My mother, who pushed me steadily on, died before anything was gained; and nothing has been the same to me since, because no one cared as she cared."

But the writing had to continue. Now more than ever

Agnes Repplier realized her responsibilities. She must take care of her brother, her father, even her sister to some extent. This was the charge her mother bequeathed to her.

ᕴ ᕴ ᕴ

. The month following her mother's death, Agnes Repplier appeared again in the *Catholic World*, this time with a highly romantic story under the alluring title: "Last Pages in the Journal of Eve de la Tour D'Arraine." From the vantage of eight decades, its author was to dismiss it lightly as "clever if a little dull," though she thought even then that the name she had concocted for its leading character was very beautiful.

The "Last Pages" tells of a group of aristocrats awaiting execution in the melancholy days of the French Revolution. Eve is betrothed to Maurice, but apparently she does not love him, nor, as it turns out, is she even willing to pretend to any affection in order to make his last moments on earth happier. When an abbé, who has come to administer the last rites to the couple, offers out of the goodness of his heart to marry them so that they may meet death in the approved fashion as man and wife, Eve is quite indifferent to the suggestion. Maurice inquires as to the depths of his lady's love, and she replies with amazing neutrality:

". . . It is true, Maurice . . . I cannot love you as you deserve, and I never could; but perhaps in heaven God will give me a larger heart, and you can enter into it . . . "

The "Last Pages of the Journal of Eve de la Tour D'Arraine" is, in brief, fiction at its most romantic and romance at its most traditional. Its author was trying earnestly, but she had far to go before she would truly find herself.

The month following the appearance of the "Last Pages," Agnes Repplier published an essay in the same magazine that, about a year before, had opened its friendly doors to her. "The Good Humor of the Saints," though not among her best by any means, is quite in what was to become her most effective vein. Here for the first time she made extensive use of her reading in the fashion that was to be characteristic of her later writing. She quotes from a number of writers: Thomas a Kempis, Abbé Retord, Cardinal Newman, Bishop Tabert, and of all other possibilities, Samuel Johnson, who must have felt himself something out of place in the company of such distinctly sanctified men.

The purpose of this essay was to offer the point of view that a sense of humor is not incompatible with other-worldliness. And the conclusion drawn is that "enough has been said to show that a keen sense of humor may keep pace with our spiritual advancement, each helping on the other." The importance of this paper lies not in any small wisdom it may present, not in the choice of authorities gathered in proof thereof, but in the fact that it is an essay, recognizably the progenitor of an almost countless number that were to follow.

In the January 1883 issue of the *Catholic World*, Agnes Repplier published one of the very few poems of which she ever felt sufficiently sure to offer to the reading public. "The Sphinx," inspired by the French painting "Le Repos en Egypte," picturing the Holy Family resting at night in the arms of the desert leviathan, reveals not only its author's sense of the dramatic—here well restrained—but also her careful play with words, the ability to choose her "jewels" with a delicate feeling for the nuances of poetry.

All day I watch the stretch of burning sand,
   All night I brood beneath the golden stars;
Amid the silence of a desolate land
   No touch of bitterness my reverie mars.

Built by the proudest of a kingly line,
   Over my head the centuries fly fast:
The secrets of the mightly dead are mine,
   I hold the key of a forgotten past.

Yet ever hushed into a rapturous dream
   I see again that night—a halo mild
Shone from the liquid moon; beneath her beam
   Travelled a tired young Mother and her Child.

Within my arms she slumbered, and alone
   I watched the Infant. At my feet her guide
Lay stretched o'er-wearied; on my breast of stone
   Rested the Crucified.

ↄ ↄ ↄ

The year following the publication of "The Sphinx,"
1884, marked a turning point in Agnes Repplier's career.
It was this year that she met Father Hecker, who set her
once and for all on the road she was to follow with only
occasional deviation throughout her mature literary life.
Miss Irwin may occupy the initial place and Mrs. Repplier a seat in the judges' stand, but Father Hecker holds
rank as the first professional critic to concern himself with
Agnes Repplier, essayist.

Early in the year Agnes Repplier had published, again
in Father Hecker's *Catholic World*, a quasi-tragic tale
called "A Story of Nuremberg." About July 1884, she
traveled to New York and by some happy chance met,
face to face, the editor who had given her the opportu-

nity she had sought so long. Although she could not later recall all the details of their meeting, evidently he had had his fill of Repplierean romance. Quite as evidently too, he saw in this young writer—she had turned twenty-nine the April before—a talent wasted because so largely misdirected. Hence he gave her the advice that within a few years was to change Agnes Repplier, story writer of sorts, into Agnes Repplier, essayist par excellence.

In a paper of a quarter century later, Miss Repplier tells of this meeting and its consequences:

The first criticism I ever wrote was an essay on Mr. Ruskin (how many years has it been since essays on Ruskin had a market?) which was undertaken by the advice of Father Hecker, and was . . . published in *The Catholic World*. Father Hecker told me that my stories were mechanical, and gave no indication of being transcripts from life. "I fancy," he said, "that you know more about books than you do about life, that you are more a reader than an observer. What author do you read the most?"

I told him "Ruskin"; an answer which nine out of ten studious girls would have given at that date.

"Then," said he, "write me something about Ruskin, and make it brief."

That essay turned my feet into the path which I have trodden laboriously ever since.

Agnes Repplier thus learned that you have to write what is in you. And it is to her great credit that she received the editor's criticism in the spirit in which it had been offered. Thereafter, she was to be primarily an essayist, and fiction she was to consider almost as much a closed door to her as some years previously she had found mathematics to be.

"Ruskin as a Teacher," the essay produced upon the

suggestion of Father Hecker, is brief if nothing else. That much of the editor's advice had been taken quite to heart. But far more important than mere length is its form and content wherein its author proved that she had caught the full significance of Father Hecker's injunction.

In this critical essay, Agnes Repplier tries first of all to show that, in spite of Ruskin's anti-Catholic attitude in his earlier writings, he needs must turn sooner or later to the "holiness of Catholic art," and that "in all his books we trace the change as it comes slowly and surely." Then, having justified her choice of subject, so to speak, she goes on to point out the lesson he teaches: that work done for base gain inevitably ends in failure.

In conclusion, finding in the English critic's later books "a sense of failure which saddens without angering him," she asks: "What has been the secret of his failure?" But the question, no doubt quite wisely, she leaves largely unanswered save to suggest that "out of his own mouth is he condemned when, in all humility, he acknowledges that sin unfits for labor."

In the manner of presentation, "Ruskin as a Teacher" is familiar essay more than a little tinged with criticism. It reveals in its form, if not a mature artist, at least one who is entirely aware of the possibilities of her chosen type. Here is personal comment that transcends mere idiosyncrasy; here is individual viewpoint that is sufficiently broad to allow of further interpretation. There is not a great deal in it that is particularly arresting. But the essay is keen in its way, succinct in its expression, and original in its appraisal.

This paper on Ruskin is, obviously, of books rather than of life. And in that, no matter what its shortcomings, it is important because, to paraphrase Agnes Repplier's own words later, it represents the first real step of its author along the path which she trod laboriously ever after.

"The Good Humor of the Saints," now nearly two years in the past, did little more than point one way out of a great many. "Ruskin as a Teacher" made fulfillment of the earlier promise almost if not quite a reality.

ꙅ ꙅ ꙅ

The December after "Ruskin as a Teacher" appeared, Agnes Repplier published in the *Catholic World* a second poem, "St. Mona's Lambs," and accompanied it in the same issue with an essay, "An Apostle of Doubt," written as obviously as the Ruskin paper in the pattern Father Hecker had set for her.

The poem shows even more than "The Sphinx" Miss Repplier's ability to handle the simplest words for their fullest meaning:

Deep in the Irish forest's leafy shade
The holy Monacella knelt and prayed:
"Have mercy, Lord, on what Thy hands have made!"

And as she knelt a little, wounded hare,
Sore spent and hotly press'd, came limping there
While rang the hounds' fierce baying through the air.

One bitter glance the hunted creature threw,
Then, as the pack came straining into view,
Quick to the virgin's pitying bosom flew.

There nestled panting, while the royal maid,
Uplifting her soft finger-tip, forbade
The dogs' approach, and trembling they obeyed.

And I have heard that ever since that day
"St. Mona's lambs" the little children say,
As from their path the wild hare scuds away.

But if pursued, oh! then say pityingly,
"God and St. Monacella succor thee!"
And the dear Saint its advocate will be.

"An Apostle of Doubt," far more important than the
verse in view of the essayist's later work, is concerned
with an account of the Reverend Hugh Reginald Haweis,
an Englishman of considerable versatility, being, as he
was, writer, artist, musician, and preacher of St. James's,
Marylebone. His faith was Anglican, but Agnes Repplier sees in him for all his seeming anti-Roman Catholicism an attitude toward the church both worthy and winning, even though possibly inadvertent as far as the clergy-
man was concerned.

ʊ ʊ ʊ

One aspect of all these early writings—stories, poems,
essays—that even the most casual reader of them could
not fail to notice is that they are directed toward a Roman
Catholic audience. Many years later, in a paper called
"The Young Catholic Writer: What Shall He Do?" the
Reverend Talbot Smith presented the case of a young
writer friend of his who had failed apparently because of
his faith. And he had come to the somewhat startling conclusion that the beginning Catholic writer should "conceal
his faith . . . lest it blight his literary reputation."
In answer Agnes Repplier wrote:

At the risk of being profoundly egotistical, I venture to
offer my own experience as a refutation of this casuistry;

and I do because I am a plain example of a "lesser light," whose publisher and public are assured—a small public, be it said, small as befits the modest nature of the illumination. In the first place, far from being repulsed at the outset by Catholic magazines, as was Father Smith's unfortunate correspondent, I met with encouragement and a helping hand . . . I have *never* in all these years found it necessary to ignore, much less conceal, my faith. I could not if I would. When faith is the most vital thing in life, when it is the source of our widest sympathies and of our deepest feelings, when we owe to it whatever distinction of mind and harmony of soul we possess, we cannot push it *intentionally* out of sight without growing flat and dry through insincerity. Nor have I ever been able to trace my failure on my part to an editor's distaste for my creed. When I have failed, it was because my work was bad—a common cause of collapse, which the author for the most part discredits. Nor have I ever been asked by editor or publisher to omit, to alter, or to modify a single sentence, because that sentence proclaimed my religious beliefs. It is not too much to say that I have found my creed to be a matter of supreme indifference to the rest of the world as it is a matter of supreme importance to me. Moreover, the one book [*In Our Convent Days*] which I have written which has a Catholic background—a book designed for my own people, and which I thought would be acceptable only to those who, having shared my experiences, would also share my pleasure in recalling them—has been read with perfect good humor by a secular public. It is impossible for me to believe that anybody cares what catechism I studied when I was a child, or what Church I go to now.

This is the considered opinion growing out of the experience of a mature writer. It was Agnes Repplier's conviction twenty-five years after her first appearance in the *Catholic World*. But, although it belongs to a relatively distant period, it is of interest here because it reveals an attitude patently hers at the start even if unexpressed in so many words until years later.

In the beginning, it is clear that Miss Repplier was naturally not a little conscious of what would appeal. She was trying to sell, and as a consequence was tailoring her productions to her potential audience. Her church had not only not impeded, it had actually helped.

Natalie of "In Arcady" is a Catholic. All the characters in "Last Pages in the Journal of Eve de la Tour D'Arraine" profess the same faith. With the exception of Johnson, every saint and near saint, every writer referred to in "The Good Humor of the Saints" is a Roman Catholic. "The Sphinx" tells of the Virgin and her Child. And so on throughout the list. In each effort the author was winning her way, so to speak, by means of her church. Although her subjects were neither doctrinal nor controversial, it is not unfair to assert that she began her real career with and by the aid of her faith.

As a consequence of Agnes Repplier's finding in her belief not only a stimulating font of inspiration, but a satisfactory source of profit as well—though perhaps it would be not quite accurate to insist that such had been more than happy chance—her field had remained narrow and her appeal limited. The *Catholic World* had proved a staunch friend, and never was she to desert its pages even when other magazines were to give her a wider field. But hers was a more inclusive talent. She needed a greater outlet.

Her debt of gratitude to this particular journal and its editor was deep. She had come far even in the three years since she had first reached its pages and had gone on to follow Father Hecker's sound advice. But although she may "never . . . have found it necessary to ignore, much less conceal" her creed, Agnes Repplier was to learn that not always could it be her constant focal point—not always, that is, if she expected to test the full limits of her power. The *Catholic World* had in the main readers of one faith only. Father Hecker had given her the chance, and she had made the most of her excellent opportunity. But (to recast Boethius) "when the world is overcome, the stars are yours," and Agnes Repplier had mastered the *Catholic World*. Now another world—perhaps even the star of the ancient philosopher—lay waiting for her.

The Atlantic Monthly

1885–1886

೧ ೧

There was no doubt that Agnes Repplier had firmly established herself as a regular contributor to the *Catholic
World*. Stories and essays of hers appeared in the January, March, June, August, and October issues for 1885,
followed by a poem in November of the same year. The
essays showed a steady growth toward the final perfection their author was to achieve, but the stories revealed
little improvement over her first melodramatic attempt.
"The Tragedy of Beningbrough Hall," for one, is replete
with every properly appalling Gothic trapping: low,
eerie cries; mysterious death; screams in the night; suicide
—all culminating in a sudden, retributory hanging. And
the poem, "St. Winifred's Well," beginning:

> Caradoc, son of Alen, the king,
>   Hath loved, and loved in vain.
> He planned a day of reckoning:
>   "Give heed, O maid! till thy death-knell ring!
>   Short shrift, ere thou be slain."

although somewhat after the manner of an early English
ballad, catches only a passing shadow of the innocent
charm of "St. Mona's Lambs."

But slight though the intrinsic worth of these papers may be—particularly when viewed in the light of full fifty years of notable accomplishment—this much is certain: work was being done, constant conscientious effort was being put forth, and, most important, the essay was coming to play an ever-increasing role. Daily Agnes Repplier was realizing with crescive force the fundamental truth of Father Hecker's advice to her.

ɔ ɔ ɔ

Every morning, promptly at nine, Miss Repplier would proceed to her study and take her place at a tidy desk watched over by a portrait of Keats after Severn's sketch. Though she had heard and read that some authors wrote their best at night because of the thought-conducive quiet, Agnes Repplier found that for herself the morning was the most propitious time of all. Generally at night she was too worn out to do much else than play a game or two of whist with her sister, her brother, and her father. And even this was managed more out of a sense of duty than of desire or from any great interest in the game.

Although some forty years later she went so far as to take lessons in contract bridge with several of her closest friends, in the early days the essayist's attitude toward the modest progenitor of that complicated combination of numerology, augury, and polite calumny may be summed up in the words of a note of hers to a friend in which she admits to cordially detesting the game and adds: "Mary and I have been asked to a card party. Come and we'll refuse to play."

But on more occasions than she liked, because of her

father's failing health, Agnes Repplier felt it her obligation to amuse him as best she could, and whist was his single pleasure. She and her sister were not young in regard to cards. Euchre they had been taught before they had sense for any more elaborate game, though whist had followed shortly thereafter. From their pre-convent days, Mr. Repplier had coached them in various such games. It was the only use to which he could put girl children; it was all he thought women needed to know. In their father's eyes, card-playing constituted education.

And perhaps in the early days the girls had found cards a better way of spending an evening than in doing nothing or in reading books they already knew by heart. But although as a result cards were to resolve themselves into the routine procedure night after night, Miss Repplier was inclined to confess that such was not her favorite way of spending time. In later generous moments she would admit that perhaps whist offered a little in the way of education—how to get along with men, for example, "and that is something to learn"—or that it had provided a worth-while discipline. But during these years the game was scarcely entertainment for her. She considered whist a consummate bore, and only with considerable difficulty did she conceal the fact.

ᘓ ᘓ ᘓ

Writing was Agnes Repplier's real interest, with reading and people—clever, ingenious people—crowding close. Family, for all the love and devotion she bore them, never constituted "people" to her. No one of them had provided her with even a remotely adequate foil, not even her mother.

Her closest friend, Elizabeth Robins, seemed the perfect combination of all things worthy. For years the two
had gone hand in hand, discussing their work and ambitions without either jealousy or doubts. A good-natured
rivalry, carried over from their convent days, existed between them, the source of stimulation to them both.

Though Elizabeth Robins worked with considerable
ease and she only with great effort, though because of an
earlier success Elizabeth Robins was discouragement if
also encouragement to her, though Elizabeth Robins had
the help of her "Uncle" Charles Leland and she had no
one but herself on whom to depend, Agnes Repplier felt
she deserved a wider public than she had yet found, for
she honestly believed her own work better executed than
that of her friend. If perhaps it was more limited in its
appeal—before she really found herself, that is—still it *was*
better writing, or at least so she would console herself in
the face of what to her were Elizabeth Robins' disheartening triumphs.

Some four years before this time, in July 1881, Elizabeth Robins had appeared in the *Atlantic Monthly* by
way of an essay called "Mischief in the Middle Ages." The
two friends had been overjoyed at the almost undreamed-
of honor. Little more than a beginner then, Agnes Repplier had only in her fondest fancies allowed herself to
think of such success. The *Atlantic Monthly!* That was
the greatest, the most inspiring end of all! And Elizabeth
Robins—working quietly, unpretentiously, effortlessly, as
it seemed to her friend—had made it. Agnes Repplier confessed to having thought she would die if she did not get
in also.

In dark moments, she would despair of ever achieving

this goal. Then she would endeavor calmly to consider the whole situation. Her friend was only a tolerable scholar, really no better than she herself. Although Miss Robins had no pronounced religious preferences, neither had she any stupid prejudices against religion. Was she narrow, damagingly bigoted, Agnes Repplier would ask herself. Most emphatically no, though perhaps she had allowed creed to limit her field. She had directed her work to a large extent toward the *Catholic World*, it was true, and no doubt it would be wise to try consciously to widen her scope, to let distinctly Catholic subjects lie fallow for a while.

Was it then that Elizabeth Robins was a better workman than she? This Agnes Repplier could not see, for she was convinced that she was far more capable of putting her whole heart and soul into her work than was her friend. The answer? There was no answer save work, she would sigh. More and more work.

For all her rationalization, Agnes Repplier had found it hard to watch Elizabeth Robins climb: one paper—the first—in 1881, five in 1882, more in 1883, and all in the *Atlantic Monthly*. But if Miss Repplier felt discouragement over Elizabeth Robins' success in writing, she experienced an even greater sense of having fallen irretrievably behind when one day early in 1884 she received a note from her friend stating simply and succinctly: "Greatly to my surprise, I find myself engaged to Joseph Pennell."

Joseph Pennell, the artist! Perhaps he was homely—"as ugly as sin," Agnes Repplier described him. Perhaps he was somewhat careless about his appearance; a friend told her that he knew "Joe Pennell is engaged because he is a scrubbed-up Pennell." Perhaps he liked a bit too much to quarrel; a plain speaker, he wasn't a Quaker for nothing, she would say. Perhaps throughout the coming years she was to feel that Elizabeth Pennell was to waste a great amount of time and effort patching up the difficulties her husband provoked. But at least she had someone to offer her real help, someone upon whom she might lean, someone to add his strength to hers. And more than just that, he was decidedly well on the way to becoming a world-famous artist.

If he was, in Agnes Repplier's opinion, a dull man; if in later life she was to feel that Elizabeth Pennell had done her best work when she was not collaborating with her husband; if she saw little about their association that could be labeled ecstatic; still she was forced to admit even in those days when independence seemed almost unreasonably precious that Elizabeth Robins was very fortunate indeed. The why of Mrs. Pennell's love always remained something of a mystery to Agnes Repplier, but anyone could have seen that Pennell loved his wife dearly. And perhaps Miss Repplier envied her friend this even more than she envied her success in writing. Yes, it was a shock, Elizabeth Robins' marriage and subsequent going to England with her husband. But Agnes Repplier's near future was to bring some compensation. At least the *Atlantic* was to break upon the shore for her too.

ᔕ ᔕ ᔕ

Although it had been years now since the disgraceful if momentarily thrilling episode in her school, Miss Irwin, busy woman that she was, never lost contact with her rebel pupil. No doubt she may have been under the very real impression that young Agnes had thought too much of herself in those days, that, in fact, she had been almost insufferably smug, as she herself would later confess. And certainly she was at no time interested in her in a merely personal way. But she was always ambitious for the girl.

Never going quite so far as to offer to criticize Agnes Repplier's writing—nor was the coming author overly anxious to allow her former mentor to see any before it appeared in print—she did have faith in the young woman, and she was vitally concerned in her work. Throughout the ten or so years that Miss Repplier had been earnestly striving not only to satisfy her artistic sense but to line the family pocketbook as well, Miss Irwin had remained a driving force behind all the effort she put forth. The more progress she made, the greater the need of further progress, or so the essayist felt if ever she were to justify Miss Irwin's evident belief in her.

Even though the older woman may only indirectly have aided the young author in the question of style or subject or field, she proved a decided factor in Agnes Repplier's career inasmuch as almost without seeming design she provided the writer with a goal quite as dominant as and perhaps even more pressing than any she had set up for herself—that of winning a nod of approval. Once she had put her mind to a thing, Miss Irwin drove with relentless energy toward its attainment. Long before, she had come to the decision that the girl had ability worthy of her attention, and Agnes Repplier, be it said, was never unaware of the fact that this someone who mattered was watching her.

ꙮ ꙮ ꙮ

Elizabeth Robins Pennell and Agnes Irwin had been Agnes Repplier's friends from her childhood. They had both known her long before she had ever published, or indeed, had even thought of publishing a single word. Harrison Morris, poet, and later editor of *Lippincott's Magazine,* was her first "literary" friend. He won a place for himself at a time—the middle 1880's—when Agnes Repplier was extremely flattered to find that she had something of a following, though by no means did this lessen her appreciation of him. And he was to continue through the years as confidant and trusted adviser in all matters pertaining to her career to a degree more intimate than even Miss Irwin achieved.

Although when Morris first met Agnes Repplier he was engaged in business, still he always made time somehow for arts and letters. It was through Louis, then employed by Mr. Repplier as general clerk in his retail coal trade, that the two became acquainted, and Harrison Morris with his taste for the excellent in writing was as delighted with the society of another author as Agnes Repplier was to find a literary admirer.

Before very long, Harrison Morris became almost one of the Repplier family. He would travel west from his home on North Twentieth Street of a Sunday afternoon, and first off, together with Louis, would be sent to "rush the growler," as they were pleased to call it, before sitting down to a long session of good talk topped by one of Julia's famous suppers. Kidney stew was her most meritorious dish, and it was quite a standing joke that Morris would send word he was coming out on such and such a Sunday "to eat Julia's kidneys."

It was Harrison Morris who introduced Agnes Repplier to Dr. Morris Jastrow, long a professor of oriental languages at the University of Pennsylvania; to Dr. Felix E. Schelling, the great Shakespearean scholar of the same university; and, most exciting of all, to Walt Whitman. It was Morris later on who was influential in Agnes Repplier's being honored by membership in the National Institute of Arts and Letters. But it was the man himself who counted, not what he was able to bring with him. First as "Dear Mr. Morris" and then after twenty years (no hasty familiarity here) even to almost twice twenty more as "Dear Harrison," he proved his friendship for Agnes Repplier time and time again: in little ways, with Christmas baskets of fruit and wine, with birthday congratulations, with keen critical taste, with all the thoughtful, blended kindnesses of years of understanding companionship.

No doubt there were others greater than he, particularly as a pseudo-omniscient world views position. There may have been others closer than he, degree in such matters being for the most part of vain hazard. But no one proved more enduring.

ಌ ಌ ಌ

Agnes Repplier's life was to be singularly free of all considerations involving the heart rather than the head. It is true that in her younger days she was interested in one of her Uncle George's sons, Frank Repplier, to a more than cousinly degree. But any possible thoughts of marriage were completely prohibited by both church and family.

Some sixty years after, with octogenarian detachment, Agnes Repplier would point to Cousin Frank's having married a New York woman of means as proof that he had not been exactly heartbroken over the affair. Even a later friend, a young Englishman who had come to this country bent on making his fortune but very sensibly had returned to his native heath to marry one instead, was perhaps little more than a passing fancy as far as the essayist was concerned.

If the truth be admitted, Miss Repplier was not the kind to offer men encouragement. Her wit and cleverness were generally far too brilliant for all but the hardiest. She may very well have frightened more than she attracted—and this in spite of the fact that by her own frequent, free admission she much preferred the company of men to that of women and was to number not a few of the most important of her day among her friends.

ꙅ ꙅ ꙅ

The year 1886 began with enough evident progress over the past to hint of even more satisfying achievement. In January, the *Catholic World* published "A Still Christmas," a short story that for lack of melodrama, for simple, unaffected characterization easily surpassed all the stories Agnes Repplier had offered the public since she had first started. It tells of an English family during the winter of 1653 when, by Puritan order, a ban had been put on all "papist," festive (the terms being more or less synonymous) recognition of the Christmas season. "No Christmas! No Christmas! No Christmas!" the herald proclaimed as he walked through the deserted city streets. But in a certain Catholic Cavalier household there was to be a Christmas celebration even if behind drawn curtains, modest and subdued perhaps, for the father and son had fallen in a lost cause, but a fitting celebration nonetheless.

The effect of this simple little story is that of truth itself, truth becomingly decked in fiction-finery. No need for whole-cloth cutting in "A Still Christmas." And because the essentials had been drawn from solid fact and warmed by sympathetic insight the effect is as real and appealing as that of history.

February brought in the same periodical a biographical sketch of Joost van den Vondel, the "greatest of Holland's poets," who, coming as he did at the end of the sixteenth century, "had assisted at the birth of Dutch literature and nourished its vigorous growth." Apparently this essay was inspired by a reading of *Studies in Northern Literature*, for it begins—as, indeed, were so many that followed to begin—with a quotation, here from Gosse's work.

This was Agnes Repplier's true field, one of her most congenial points of departure: a comparatively obscure figure out of literary history—obscure, at least, for the English reading world—to be treated with all the certainty and care that scholarly research and a literary-loving mind could summon. No path did the essayist tread with more assurance than the byway in literature, and in "Joost van den Vondel" her step is sure.

ɔ ɔ ɔ

The following month, March, was undistinguished by any publication. But as it turned out, that was only the quiet before the great event, for—the most gratifying of all possible gifts to mark her thirty-first birthday—in April, the *Atlantic Monthly* printed "Children, Past and Present." With this essay, Agnes Repplier considered her future to be firmly set.

For almost fifteen years she had been writing and publishing before she gained a hearing in a "real" magazine, as she called the *Atlantic*. To those who would suggest that such effort showed considerable perseverance, she would insist smilingly that it had revealed instead merely a considerable need of money. No matter. This at last was realization. The fruit of determination, necessity, whichever it may have been—or a combination of the two, as no doubt it was—this at long last was success sufficient for the most exacting and, moreover, vindication of belief even to herself.

For as long as she could remember, *Harper's Magazine* had been an accepted adjunct to the Repplier household. Month after month, year in and year out, it could be found on a table in the front parlor. Its lengthy serials and elaborate illustrations were favorites with them all, and to Mr. Repplier in particular *Harper's* was almost a necessity.

It took Agnes Repplier to effect a change. The *Atlantic*, she would say proudly, came in with her. Just why she should have picked this magazine instead of the other may be explained in part by the fact that even after her publishing days had begun, it represented the taste of the brightest corner of the American literary world—even though perhaps the effulgence was on the wane.

The *Atlantic Monthly* had, since its founding, offered a host of worthy old and new writers. Its editors—always a fascinating, impressive breed to Miss Repplier because, as she would say, they decide things—had been brilliant men; and Thomas Bailey Aldrich, its present head, was well within the established tradition. Perhaps at times she was to find it a little dull, but she could find excuse as well. It is human nature, she would point out, to be dull. And for her the *Atlantic* exhibited a sound sort of dullness; it was never trivial nor common. If dull, it was not stupid— a difference; and it was always worth while, always readable.

For almost a generation, the *Atlantic Monthly* had been the gospel of Bostonians, and Agnes Repplier felt it quite good and wise of the city to hold on to it so securely. Boston, she was certain, would stand by the *Atlantic* so long as there was an *Atlantic*. Not only this, but Miss Irwin knew and loved the magazine. She was perhaps as familiar with Boston as she was with Philadelphia—later even more so—and her word was not to be doubted by Agnes Repplier. If Miss Irwin held the *Atlantic* in the highest esteem, there must be good reason indeed; it behooved her not to question but to seek.

Most important of all perhaps, the essayist had observed that this Boston by-product (she liked to remark that it was so distinguished the reverse seemed quite possible) was kind to new writers. It was on the constant lookout for fresh talent. And Agnes Repplier herself had long since set her cap for the prize.

ꙮ ꙮ ꙮ

As a result of the modern tendency to desert the broad beaten roads of history for the bridle-paths of biography and memoir, we find a great many side lights thrown upon matters that the historian was wont to treat as altogether beneath his consideration. It is by their help that we study the minute changes of social life that little by little alter the whole

aspect of a people, and it is by their help that we look straight
into the ordinary every-day workings of the past, and measure the space between its existence and our own. When we
read, for instance, of Lady Cathcart being kept a close
prisoner by her husband for over twenty years, we look
with some complacency on the roving wives of the nineteenth century. When we reflect on the dismal fate of Uriel
Freudenberger, condemned by the Canton of Uri to be burnt
alive in 1760, for rashly proclaiming his disbelief in the legend of William Tell's apple, we realize the inconveniences
attendant on a too early development of the critical faculty.
We listen entranced while the learned pastor Dr. Johann
Geiler von Keyersperg gravely enlightens his congregation
as to the nature and properties of were-wolves; and we turn
aside to see the half-starved boys at Westminster boiling their
own batterpudding in a stocking foot, or to hear the little
John Wesley crying softly when he is whipped, not being
permitted even the luxury of a hearty bellow.

Thus does "Children, Past and Present" begin. The keynote of the essay follows in the next paragraph:

Women, workmen, and skeptics all have reason enough to
be grateful they were not born a few generations earlier;
but the children of to-day are favored beyond their knowledge, and certainly far beyond their deserts.

From this, Agnes Repplier weaves a fascinating "bridle-
path" through all the dour austerity of youthful discipline
in days happily long past. Mrs. Wesley, Mrs. Sherwood,
Lady Balcarras, Harriet Martineau, Madame Quinet, the
Marquise de Montmirail, Lady Mary Wortley Montague;
St. Anselm, Bertrand du Guesclin, Guibert de Nogent,
Chateaubriand, John Stuart Mill; the monastic schools of
the Middle Ages, Eton, Westminster; Mr. and Miss Edgeworth's *Practical Education*, Mrs. Barbauld's "highly correct and righteous little volumes," Miss Sewell and her

Principles of Education: each yields a singular oddment of information, each feeds the author in her thesis.

And the great wonder of it is, not that the information is there for the using, nor indeed even that the thesis is admirably demonstrated, but that Agnes Repplier was able to come upon such a remarkable array as she musters here to prove her contention. Where, how, when, by whom led? The answer lies in the intellectual curiosity, in the painstaking research, in the eternal quest for the out-of-the-way that motivates so much of the essayist's work. That which is surface and readily recognized, with few exceptions, is not for her. No one loved more "to desert the broad beaten roads of history for the bridle-paths of biography and memoir" than Agnes Repplier. And few were better able to handle with deftness, or color with fascination that which "the historian was wont to treat as altogether beneath his consideration" than she.

"Children, Past and Present," though not by any means sprung full-blown out of a profitless past, represents nonetheless a startling advance over what she had done previously. There had been the unusual before; there had been the felicity of execution. But nowhere in all her earlier work were these two qualities so happily blended.

Agnes Repplier has smilingly confessed to a sense of mystery surrounding the very real fact that the *Atlantic Monthly* accepted "Children, Past and Present." Perhaps one can be blinded by proximity, or very likely one may on occasion choose whimsically to be mystified. But the reader, who must remain forever on the outside, can see, and he who puts whimsey away for the moment can understand.

CHAPTER V

Books and Men

1886–1888

Once the first step had been taken, the going grew much easier: one essay followed "Children, Past and Present" in 1886, four in 1887, and another in 1888. The *Atlantic Monthly* had become a regular outlet for Agnes Repplier's writings. "On the Benefits of Superstition" gathers a sheaf of strange, bewildered beliefs of our credulous forebears. Throughout its pages there runs only the faintest suggestion of pungency, too playful to be called malice, and not even the most sensitive shade could conjure resentment against the author's delicate mocking.

"Curiosities of Criticism" ranges all the way from the whining of Lord Beaconsfield, who, sorely needing "emollient for his bruises," held to the contention that "all critics are necessarily wrong in all cases," through "the pure absurdities of criticism" to the just conclusion that "it is folly to rail at the critic until we have learned his value; it is folly to ignore a help which we are not too wise to need." Though critic herself and in theory at least not one to take up cudgels for the author, Agnes

Repplier puts both sides of the issue with such perfect balance that neither critic on the one hand nor writer on the other can claim to have come off completely unscathed, or for that matter, more than just a little damaged.

"The Decay of Sentiment," a lament that "the old springs of simple sentiment are drying fast within us," and "Some Aspects of Pessimism," a gentle reminder that "self-satisfaction, if as buoyant as gas, has an ugly trick of collapsing when full-blown, and facts are stony things that refuse to melt away in the sunshine of a smile," evidence a sufficient tongue-in-cheek attitude to forestall the reader who might be tempted to whisper "false." "What Children Read" offers a plea for the rich, ripe books of a bygone day, the books that children used to read, and a hearty denunciation of the "Dotty Dimple and Little Prudy" nonsense of a less enlightened even if modern age. "The Cavalier" suggests that if the Puritan "has been wafted into universal esteem by the breath of Carlyle his great eulogist," then it is equally true that "the Cavalier still waits for his historian." These papers make up the remainder of the *Atlantic* essays of this initial period.

Over the same months that she had been offering these essays in the *Atlantic Monthly*, Agnes Repplier was publishing as well in her friend of long standing, the *Catholic World*, and had found entry also into another magazine, *Lippincott's*. Of the half-dozen papers in all that appeared elsewhere than in the Boston journal, the most important is "Marius the Epicurean" of the former for May 1886, and the most typical, "Modern Word-Parsimony" in the latter for February 1888.

The first is really an extended analysis, "the harsh out-

line of a book which Mr. Pater has enriched with all the
rare charm of scholarship, with luminous descriptions of
a dead past, and with touches of a subtle philosophy inter-
woven deftly and gracefully among its pages." The lesson
it teaches, the essayist concludes, is "to help us to be as
happy as we can, by increasing and refining our sensations,
by identifying ourselves with every form of beauty, and
by opening our hearts freely to all higher emotions." In
Pater, Agnes Repplier found a kindred spirit, one whom
she might and did long cherish, for some years after she
had written this careful examination of the book she was
to hold a little group of listeners spellbound in an out-of-
the-way English inn by her keen appreciation and delineation of it.

"Modern Word-Parsimony" is more typical perhaps in
that it reveals the incisive wit of its author, for which
characteristic in general she was to be so justly remembered, whereas "Marius the Epicurean" had been too
earnest a paper to allow of even the slightest persiflage.
In this paper, Agnes Repplier regrets the loss in present
literature of the "languid grace" of that in the past, although here, as so frequently in her writing, the reader
is never certain to what extent she means to be taken
seriously. Be that as it may now, she writes, literature
"stands stripped like an athlete for the course, carrying
nothing that may interfere with its primary object of
getting rapidly over the ground." And of this the implica-
tion stands clear: the author is distinctly of the opinion
that, like the athlete of popular fancy, such unfettered
literature may well be far more fleet of body than nimble
of mind. With an unmistakable shaking of the head, she

looks sorrowfully to the day when it may be "possible for us to grow more parsimonious still."

ɔ ɔ ɔ

Although, in years past, Miss Irwin had many times told Agnes Repplier that Boston had spoiled her early authors with too much praise and had even insisted whenever her former pupil had complained of being overlooked that a little neglect is good for a young writer, not many months after the essayist had gained entrance into the *Atlantic Monthly* the older woman informed her that it now was time for her to go to Boston. To Agnes Repplier's asking why, out of her knowledge Miss Irwin gave irrefutable reason: "Boston is prepared to be hospitable to you. And your readers are ready to welcome you. You have a great chance, and you take it by the Boston end."

Miss Repplier protested that she did not want to go to Boston—the prospect of such a trip unnerved her beyond measure—that she did not want to go anywhere. She was perfectly content to remain quietly at home. But Miss Irwin was not to be put off; she brushed all objections aside. "Nonsense! Boston is keener than Philadelphia—as well you may have suspected. Boston will be good to you." And as things turned out, that it was indeed.

Nonetheless, with considerable misgivings, Agnes Repplier set out alone for Boston. Even though she was as sure of Miss Irwin as she was of the seasons, she was desperately afraid: afraid of Boston itself, afraid of its people, afraid of the reception she might receive—or, worse, of being perhaps totally ignored. There could be no doubt that Miss Irwin knew best—the safest source of small comfort—and she had given her a sheaf of letters of introduc-

tion. Perhaps all would go well. Aldrich knew of her coming: his reply to her note so informing him had been most
cordial. But *Boston!* Boston does not care for the opinion
of anyone outside of Boston, she kept repeating. Who or
what am I to go to Boston?

But the essayist might well have saved herself all the
worry: this first trip (there were to be many in the years
to come) proved to be ten days of "riotous gaiety." Her
immediate impression of the town was that it seemed quite
small for all the important people in it. Although Boston
may have been full of distinguished persons dying out at
a great rate—Thoreau, Emerson, Hawthorne, Longfellow
—still there was no denying the fact that it as hub had carried on the intellectual life of the country for a hundred
years. In her opinion it had an unbeatable tradition. She
felt that it had largely passed out of the creative into the
critical stage by the time she arrived, that to all intents and
purposes New England had ceased to flower on any large
scale when she came on the scene. Still, once she had visited the city, she knew that it had far more to offer than
Philadelphia, and that she really did have to go there to
meet people who counted. Bostonians, she discovered,
"tossed their minds." They did not just talk about anything, but always about something; and they had an infinity of conversation. In Boston, she was happy to see, people met intellectually.

On that first exciting trip, Agnes Repplier settled down
in a small hotel, not quite certain what would happen, nor
just how to go about things. But before long, she was
caught up in a dazzling whirl of dinners, receptions, and
teas, meeting as she went everybody big and little.

Boston may have been very pleased with itself, but it

was friendly, and far more charming than she was to find New York later on. The city truly seemed curious about her, and her coming caused "a little flutter," as the newspapers put it. But that was to be expected: after all, she was of the *Atlantic*, and the *Atlantic* was even more of Boston than she had imagined it to be. She found herself as a result famous if, as she felt, in a queer sort of way.

Aldrich was kindness itself, he and his charming, handsome, rather superior wife. Bostonians called Mrs. Aldrich the "Amber Witch," after the fairy-tale character, because of her collection of amber and the amber jewels that she never seemed to be without. But it was the editor himself who charmed Agnes Repplier beyond measure, the most brilliant talker she was ever to know. Prone to laugh at what he held dear, rather a scoffer at things, sardonic, gay, amusing: this was Mr. Aldrich. He really was not like Boston at all, she thought, being far too light-tempered, far too light-minded, irreverent even toward the city itself. Miss Repplier found him fond of the trivialities of life, but, she decided, even Boston must like to be amused on occasion.

Although he never stressed the literary side of his life, she was quick to learn of his reputation as editor of the *Atlantic*, which, always somewhat on the heavy side, had been brought around, she felt, to gayer things through his efforts. Yes, Mr. Aldrich was all that she could have dreamed of, all and more; for not only was he a delight with his witty talk, but he was completely generous to her as well with the attention he showed her. Through him and Miss Irwin's friends who came out in gallant force to entertain her, she met all the important persons left.

There was old Dr. Holmes, kindly, chatty, tottery, a little in his dotage; and Whittier, friendly, assured, if not exactly interesting. There was Sarah Orne Jewett, whose short stories Agnes Repplier sincerely admired. Charming, handsome, pleasing, she was the shyest, most reticent woman with whom the outlander from Philadelphia was to become acquainted.

Agnes Repplier met Mary E. Wilkins Freeman on several occasions, but she found her dull in conversation, sealed up as it were, seemingly uninterested in anyone. And there was something mysterious about her as well. Agnes Repplier wrote years later:

It was said of her that she absolutely refused to so much as open other people's books lest the pictures etched so clearly in her mind should grow blurred and confused. I rather think she knew how thin as well as fine was the vein of ore she worked, and that she had resolved none of it should be lost.

She was a small, thin, fair-haired woman. Seen across the room she looked like a girl. Seen close at hand she looked older than her age. She dressed sedately; but, sitting near her one day after luncheon, I noticed three brilliant and beautiful rings on her left hand. They blazed so proudly that my eyes constantly strayed towards them, a circumstance she was quick to observe. "I can't help it," I murmured apologetically. "They will be looked at. They are so lovely."

Miss Wilkins moved them round and round her thin little fingers. "They are beautiful," she said. "Week before last I was so low in my mind, so dull and dispirited, that I came up to Boston and bought these rings to cheer me up."

Never in my life had I been so staggered by a simple piece of information. In the first place, the thought that a book (Miss Wilkins had published but one) might, like Ali Baba's cave, be overflowing with jewels, gave me a new and exalted view of authorship. In the second place, I had never imagined rings as things one bought for oneself like hats and stockings.

They were things given, or bequeathed by great-aunts. Low spirits are common to us all; but who save Mary Wilkins, straight-forward, circumscribed, sure of herself, and as unimaginative as a hatrack, would have thought of curing them with rings?

Julia Ward Howe, Miss Irwin had warned, was an alarming person, reminding one of nothing more than a parrot about to pounce. And Agnes Repplier found that Mrs. Howe rather made this pose her role. No doubt she was a wonderful woman. She cared for causes in a way that aroused envy in the essayist, who claimed she herself always found it difficult to be moved deeply by a cause. But Mrs. Howe was almost overbearingly masterful. And she did not take the trouble to converse with you; she just let out a few words now and then. Although the essayist was to know her well, she never quite conquered her fear of "The Battle Hymn of the Republic," as she flippantly labeled Mrs. Howe.

Undoubtedly the most important figure Miss Repplier met on that first trip to Boston was Lowell, a lordly man, imposing in manner and speech. Somewhat self-conscious, not a little self-centered, he appeared to the Philadelphian to be rather condescending in his attitude, though, as she would say charitably, perhaps he could not help it. Cold, standoffish, kind but frozen, he was, after all, she had to admit, a great man, and very impressive. But then, Agnes Repplier would tell herself in later years, at the time she had been rather easily impressed.

Amusingly enough considering the position he occupied, it was Lowell who, unconsciously to be sure, provided Agnes Repplier with the most delightful tale of all to relate to her friends back in Philadelphia. She was being entertained at the home of one of the most prominent society women in Boston. Everybody of importance was there—everybody including Lowell. Having left her wraps on the second floor, the essayist had come down to the reception room to discover that unfortunately she had neglected to bring her glasses. They remained tucked away with her things in the cloakroom. Standing idly by outside the ring of social and literary giants gathered for the occasion, she lamented her having been so careless. She was much too shy to go upstairs to get them herself; and yet, without the glasses, she felt awkward and ill at ease. And to add to her general discomfort, she saw that, of all persons, Lowell was descending upon her, inquiring as he came up why she had not joined the others.

"I'm quite unhappy," she confessed in a small voice, "because, you see, I've left my glasses upstairs, and I can't see a thing."

To her pleased surprise, Lowell immediately offered to get them for her. Having been reared in the idea that men do things for women—though later experience, she would say, was to cure her of the notion—Miss Repplier expressed her appreciation of his kindness, and told him just where the glasses might be found.

But during Lowell's brief absence on the mission of mercy, the full significance of her naïveté was made clear to her. A woman present at the reception—totally strange to the newcomer—having noticed that he had been speaking to her, asked where Lowell had gone. Agnes Repplier innocently informed her, "To get my glasses."

The stranger was obviously shaken. "You mean *Mr.*

Lowell has gone to get your glasses?" she asked in frank unbelief.

Taken aback, the outlander gasped assent, and the woman stalked away in shocked amazement. Agnes Repplier was embarrassed and confounded. Whatever else Lowell might be, she felt, he was a man, and more than that, he was at home. She, on the other hand, was a woman and a stranger. Surely he was not too great a person for common politeness. Boston *must* find him boring, she sighed in guilty confusion over her *faux pas*, yet apparently it continues to adore him.

Taking all things into account—even her unfortunate misuse of the lordly Mr. Lowell—Agnes Repplier had been perfectly enchanted by her trip to Boston. She felt that the debt she owed the city could never be repaid, that she had found another true friend, perhaps the greatest. One really has to go to Boston for inspiration, she decided. She herself—though only on the urging of Miss Irwin, be it admitted—had turned to Boston as a flower to the sun, and there she had come upon a light and brilliance equal to none to be gained elsewhere. Truth to tell, she confessed, her head rocked at the very thought of the reception she had received. No other words could possibly express her reaction to it.

But if her head had been understandably turned by Boston, it was swiftly unturned again by Philadelphia. Back home, she was merely Agnes Repplier, a relatively insignificant writer living quietly west of the Schuylkill. Here she found no inspiration other than that coming from pride and necessity. Here she found no open-arms reception, and this in spite of her "triumph" at Boston.

Here she found only obscurity, the obscurity, she felt, that is Philadelphia itself.

And yet, it was but in passing moments that the essayist aspired to Boston. She would remain faithful to this droll town with its obscurity, its neglect, its indifference. Philadelphia suited her somehow, all of it, even the indifference. "Once a Philadelphian, always a Philadelphian" might be stupid, Agnes Repplier realized, but even she could not be different. Then too, she had discovered, Bostonians so openly felt her coming from Philadelphia a pity that she declined absolutely to regard it thus. "Philadelphia?" they would ask, pausing invariably to digest the horrid fact. Yes, Philadelphia. That is my home. Besides—and she would smile—winter in Boston is very cold.

ව ව ව

Early the following summer, in 1888, Mr. Repplier, ailing for some time, was taken seriously ill. The piazza that July was deserted. The blinds were drawn in his room to keep out the hot Philadelphia sun, hotter and more uncomfortable, Agnes Repplier declared, than that of equatorial Africa. Slowly, day by day, he gave up. He had so little to fight for now it seemed; seventy-six was long enough to live. The first week of July brought the end, and he was buried in the vault at St. John's where six years before his wife, Agnes, had been placed.

The death of her father was not the shock to Agnes Repplier her mother's passing had been. He was always in his way more fatherly perhaps than Mrs. Repplier had been motherly, and yet he had never come very close to her. For all her faults—no one was more aware of them than this daughter—Mrs. Repplier had become almost a necessary force, and the essayist had felt because of her an urgent need to prove her worth. By her very begrudging them their interference with her life, Mrs. Repplier had tied her children to her with a bond more real because more obvious than that of the casual if sincere love their father bore them. There was sadness but little sorrow in his passing, and for Agnes Repplier the future had not lost the desire-to-justify it once had lost.

છ છ છ

In the spring of the same year in which her father died, Miss Repplier came to the conclusion that she wanted to publish a collection of her better essays, and she chose her first seven *Atlantic* papers for the volume. There were several reasons why she made the decision, but the most important was she had become convinced that a book is a necessary form of advertisement for a periodical writer. "It is a great help to a writer to publish a book," she would offer in somewhat oblique explanation to those of her friends who inquired. Then, too, although this was merely secondary, Elizabeth Pennell had long since published several books, and Agnes Repplier was not one to allow her former convent mate to get ahead of her.

Fearful lest no company would want to risk the publishing of her essays, and none having up to this time volunteered to do so, the essayist wrote to a well-known Boston house offering them her work on a subsidized basis. Morris, who had had experience in the business of publishing, advised her in the matter. Although her Boston trip had almost exhausted her small reserve of funds, both he and she thought it a venture not a little worth-while.

And as Miss Repplier would say in later years, "I had no hesitation—which was a help."

Although the Boston firm of her choice agreed to publish a slim volume, they made it painfully clear that she was very probably throwing her money away. There was no market for essays, they informed her. But Agnes Repplier had made up her mind; she was not to be deterred by any considerations of money. This was far too important for debilitating caution. Having considered the question seriously, she was certain of what she wanted. Very well, the Boston firm replied to her letter brushing aside their objections. But remember that we warned you. And the edition was, upon their strong suggestion, reduced from a thousand copies to eight hundred, to protect her, they said, from too great a loss.

Some years later, after the book had gone through several printings, the publishers generously wrote her in congratulation. Aren't you glad you didn't take our advice, they asked in effect.

"*Books and Men,*" Agnes Repplier wrote to Morris, "is to come out on September 29th," and she asked him if he could possibly manage some newspaper publicity for her without too much trouble. Then on October 2, 1888, another letter to her good friend:

My copies of the essays have just arrived; neat quakerish little books with an air of deprecating modesty about them that forcibly suggests the most remote corner of the bookseller's shelf. I can see them already shrinking bashfully into their appointed nooks and powdering their little gray heads with the dust of the undisturbed.

But in February of the following year she was able to write Morris again in great excitement that only fifty-seven copies of the first edition were left. "Do you think

it possible I will have a second?" she added in some wonder. No fear—the book went into twenty all told. The advertisement Agnes Repplier had sought, it seemed, was a
success.

In November and December following its publication,
reviews of *Books and Men* appeared, and gratifying for
the most part they were. In the Boston *Post* it was stated
pleasantly if in somewhat reverse-compliment fashion that
the seven essays comprising the volume had "already made
some reputation for their author among those who have
literary tastes and enjoy a book which finds in them its
only excuse for being." This reviewer called particular
attention to the two essays on children, and concluded
with a dubious flourish: "A better companion in reading
which shall entertain and rest the mind and yet have some
value, the season has not brought."

As was to be expected there were reviews also in the
Atlantic Monthly and the *Catholic World*. In the latter
magazine the critic wrote: "As for men, the men in these
pages are, after all, the men of books, who sometimes dif-
fer from the men one meets in broadcloth or in tweed,
awaiting their apotheosis into calf-skin and gilt lettering"
—proof positive that Father Hecker's ghost was still at
large.

This then was the making of a book; this the coming of
age of a writer. Perhaps not all was soft words and pretty
compliments; perhaps not all was ease and sure success.
But there was satisfaction in the business even along with
the carping of a few voices, and the doubts involved. And
there was the keen sense that a reputation was being forged
in lasting fashion. Now, Agnes Repplier felt, she had become an author in very deed.

CHAPTER VI

Wider Worlds

1889–1892

ⴹ ⴹ

In October 1889 Agnes Repplier wrote to Harrison Morris:

Miss Irwin wants me to give five or six public lectures on literary subjects in Lent, when she thinks people will have nothing better to do with their time than to come to hear me. The idea is appalling, and I may say frankly that what partly discourages me is that dismal warning of Dr. Jastrow's that my opinions were unpalatable to women, on whom, of course, I should have to rely for an audience. There would be no use of lecturing, if I cannot please, and yet, when a woman like Agnes Irwin urges any measure, it seems unwise to resist. What do *you* think?

Morris thought well of Miss Irwin's suggestion, and, doubly fortified if still none too sure of herself, Miss Repplier began to make ready for the Lenten series. These, it turned out, were but by way of preparation for the ultimate test.

As with the essay writing which, upon Miss Irwin's advice, Agnes Repplier had taken "by the Boston end," so also with her lecturing. The real start came, not at Philadelphia, but in the "Hub" before an awe-inspiring

group of select ladies of the very highest order. After
all was over on the afternoon she spoke, a friend reported
to the essayist that she had overheard two members of
the audience commenting upon her talk.

"It was a brilliant lecture," one said with a note of in-
contradictability in her voice.

The other conceded that it had been and added: "She
speaks very well. Where is she from?"

"Philadelphia," said the first.

"Philadelphia? Phila*delphia?*" with a rising inflection
that went up to the ceiling. "Well, she must be a Bryn
Mawr woman."

The story delighted Miss Repplier, who found it most
amusing that in Boston at least, whenever the proud city
of Philadelphia was concerned, the tail should wag the
dog. But let them have their quirks, she told herself. The
test had been a success.

Agnes Repplier soon discovered that lecturing had
every advantage to it save being a pleasant thing to do.
Topics were easy to find, for in general she drew from
her essays. "The Mission of Humor" was to be her most
popular, and even she liked it the best inasmuch as it
allowed her to tell one story after another. Although
she did grow inordinately bored with repeating herself,
still she was not required to spend more than a minimum
of time in preparation. All this made for little trouble.

But the drawbacks were annoyingly unavoidable.
Never very strong, the essayist found it quite an effort
to make herself heard in a large hall. And it was not until
years later that Augustus Thomas gave her his sound
advice: "Look after your consonants, and your vowels

will look after themselves." Of even greater discomfort
to Agnes Repplier was the necessity of remaining after
a talk to be entertained. She would far rather hurry
away. She did not like the unnerving business of coming
face to face with the members of her audience. But for
all the trials, Miss Repplier could rarely resist the temptation to speak whenever she received a call. Lecturing made money for her. That was the fundamental
advantage.

Although her lecturing was to take her traveling in
the United States for more than thirty years, never was
Agnes Repplier to feel it had repaid her quite so generously as one night in Richmond. After her talk, an elderly gentleman in the audience came up to her.

"Your name is Repplier," he said. "Are you by any
chance related to a Mrs. John George Repplier of
Philadelphia?"

The lecturer told him that she was indeed Mrs. John
George's daughter.

"Well, I am glad to meet you," the man went on.
"You see, I was a Confederate prisoner at Fort Delaware,
and your mother sent me cakes and jelly and books. I
have never forgotten her. I am very happy to be able to
thank the daughter for her mother's kindness to me."

ꙅ ꙅ ꙅ

It was about this same time, too, that Agnes Repplier
felt she both was ready for and could afford a trip to
Europe, an initial trip that was to be followed by numerous others through the years. Miss Irwin may have
had a hand in the matter, and anything recommended

by Miss Irwin generally became an absolute necessity to Miss Repplier; but the essayist really needed no encouragement here. Travel in Europe came naturally to her.

"I saved money, went to Europe and spent it," Miss Repplier at eighty and more was proud to confess. "To go abroad should be the rational ambition of every writer. As soon as I had a thousand dollars in hand, I went off to Europe—thank heavens!' This was after her parents were dead and she was free to come and go more or less as she pleased. As she would say, "For years London and Paris had been calling as hard as they could call." Now she could answer.

It is true there was the rather terrifying business of the sea voyage about which she had heard so many uncomfortable things. Mrs. S. Weir Mitchell kindly offered her cure for *mal de mer:* go to bed as soon as you set foot on the boat and stay there until land is reached on the other side. But Agnes Repplier would willingly have risked seasickness a dozen times for one trip abroad.

She never went to Europe for the scenery. She could not abide Switzerland, with looking at mountains and streams apparently the only occupation at hand. Travel abroad to her meant meeting people and seeing cities. "There is no thrill quite like that of arriving in a strange city for the first time," she would explain. Through the years she was to come to know certain parts of France and of England with almost native familiarity.

Rome became an understandably particular favorite. Her initial visit was on the suggestion of Archbishop Ryan who insisted that no Roman Catholic goes to Europe for the first time without seeing Italy. Though she remembered that the weather had been blazing the June she was there, she found the city all she could have asked. In addition to its undeniably romantic atmosphere, Venice also had an equally undeniable smell to it, Miss Repplier discovered. But it was not disagreeable to her. The tourists were the only nuisance. They would insist upon singing on the Grand Canal.

Berlin she found a curiously disciplined place. Agnes Repplier lived there in constant fear of being arrested for doing something contrary to the law—like walking the wrong way on the street, she would complain in amusement. And she was very happy to escape before her incarceration. But Munich was a real delight, especially the beer gardens. No one stays at home at night in Munich, she decided, not even the grandmothers.

Brussels seemed to the essayist a feeble imitation of Paris, a city in its turn that appeared somehow alien to her. London remained always way above Paris in her affections. Had she gone abroad permanently, she most certainly would have chosen it to live in as had the Pennells. There was not a brick about it that did not appeal to her. In a measure it seemed her rightful home; her literary home it had been for nearly thirty years.

The first trip abroad came in the summer of 1890. Agnes Repplier and her sister, Mary, went together on the *Normania* and traveled four months, mostly on the Continent with a few weeks in England at the very end of their stay. Perhaps it was not to equal some of her later trips, for it was a hurried affair. But it was the first, and that alone made it memorable.

When in Rome Agnes Repplier sent Harrison Morris some violets from the graves of Shelley and Keats. "We

visited the Catacombs," she wrote him, "our guide being a
Trappist monk who had been released from his vows of silence for the occasion. And he certainly made up for lost
time! I kept trailing behind, looking back, wondering what
it would be like to be lost there, until the guide must have
thought I was either a Protestant or a lunatic."

The essayist and her sister reached England the day of
Cardinal Newman's death, and "London was all agog.
Madame Tussaud's—where we went last night—has two
figures of him," she wrote to Morris, "one of them brand
new, with his hand resting on a table of black velvet, to indicate the general mourning."

In London she met Elizabeth Pennell whom she had not
seen for several years. "Every promise of her youth has
bloomed into a delicious fulfillment, and of all the charming things in London, she seemed to me the best," she wrote.

Her praise of England was rapturous, especially of the
way in which people spoke. "After French, Dutch, German, Flemish, to say nothing of American, the mother
tongue was made doubly blessed by being so sweetly
spoken . . . The charming intonations of the English fill
me with wonder and regret. Why can't I speak in that
way?" Some years later, more in earnest than in jest, Miss
Repplier was to suggest that we in this country give over
the study of foreign languages and learn how to speak English instead.

That first trip made of Agnes Repplier a confirmed trav-
eler. If in a way it was not entirely to her liking, the mis-
takes had been largely her own fault and she would know
better the next time. Italy, France, and England most of all
had more than lived up to their promise.

ಬ ಬ ಬ

In the 1880's one's literary life was not complete without membership in a Browning Society, and Philadelphia had its little band of worshipers that gathered monthly to do honor to the Victorian poet. According to the essayist, the group to which she belonged had no social standing whatsoever and very little real merit. It was made up for the most part, she came to feel, of thwarted souls who could not get their composings published and so read them instead.

"We encouraged each other in mediocrity," was her comment in later years. And yet the society reached out in the right direction. "It endeavored to keep letters alive," she said, adding, "which was certainly a noble enterprise, even if in Philadelphia it was much like keeping a selection of corpses moving about."

Of far more consequence was the Contemporary Club, begun in 1886 and continuing to the present day. Over the years, Agnes Repplier was to be actively engaged in its organization, acting as president for several terms as well as contributing frequently in other capacities. Dedicated to the business of promoting discussion of matters of the day, the Contemporary Club engaged speakers ranging all the way from Walt Whitman to Margaret Sanger and surveyed topics from evolution to the American Indian.

On many occasions Miss Repplier was the speaker of the evening, though there were times when she refused if she felt herself unequal to the situation. Once when Harrison Morris asked her to take part in a debate on Shakespeare, she wrote to him declining his invitation: "I do not assign to myself the task of imparting what I don't know to the world."

Most frequently she was merely looked to for "words" when the meeting was turned over to the audience. It was

then that she shone forth, her ready wit pointing her remarks. Indeed Talcott Williams, then of the Philadelphia
Press, and she became so well known for their comments
and countercomments that they were dubbed "Tall-talk
Williams" and "Agnes Reply-er" by the members of the
club who squirmed with delight as the fur flew.

In 1886, Agnes Repplier was instrumental in getting
Walt Whitman to address the club. Somewhat fearful of
what he might have to say and rather disarmed by his back-
country farmer getup when he appeared on the scene, she
was infinitely relieved to hear him speak "beautifully, well
within bounds, and with a charming grace and manner."

Years after the Whitman meeting she presented Henry
James to the club members. A surprise of another sort resulted on this occasion, for the immaculate author turned
out to be a dismal disappointment. Horace Howard Furness
wrote of it to his sister:

After dinner [Agnes] told me much of her introduction of
Henry James at the Contemporary Club. As she memorized it
at the time, she repeated it to me, almost word for word, and,
my faith! it was charming, sparkling with most felicitous
phrases. Indeed, from what I have heard of the evening, her
speech eclipsed Henry James's, whereof the delivery was almost irredeemably bad. . . .

Forthright always, Miss Repplier wrote once to Harrison
Morris: "I am told that you declined to ask Mr. L. D. to
speak at the Contemporary meeting. If this be so, I congratulate you. I heard him last Sunday. He is a worm."

It would scarcely be exaggeration to say that those meetings of the Contemporary Club at which Agnes Repplier
spoke, either extemporaneously or from the platform, were

always the high lights of the season. Though she never forgot her genteel origin, she never hesitated to speak her mind. And she spoke with pungency and éclat always.

೨ ೨ ೨

In 1891, the essayist published her second volume, *Points of View*, made up of eight papers first printed in the *Atlantic Monthly* and one from the *Catholic World*. Of the entire collection, well received by critics and public alike, two essays have particular significance.

At the Contemporary Club meeting for March 1888, a group of men, including Agnes Repplier's friendly adversary Talcott Williams, had considered the subject "Books Which Have Helped Me." The discussion set Miss Repplier to thinking, and in July 1889 she published in the *Atlantic* a paper entitled "Books That Have Hindered Me." It began:

So many grateful and impetuous spirits have recently come forward to tell to an approving world how they have been benefited by their early reading, and by their wise-chosen favorites in literature, that the trustful listener begins to think, against his own rueful experience, that all books must be pleasant and profitable companions.

Agnes Repplier's own experience had indeed been "rueful." There was that "horrible little book called 'Reading Without Tears'" which had plagued her early life. There was *Sanford and Merton* which had had the unfortunate effect, not of filling her with regard for the righteously industrious, but of giving her a "sneaking preference for the drones and butterflies of earth." And there were many others. She concluded her blithe paper:

Those who read these simple statements may not, I fear, find them as edifying or as stimulating as the happier recollections of more favored souls; but it is barely possible that they may see in them the unvarnished reflection of some of their own youthful experiences.

Agnes Repplier thought the essay one of the most amusing she had written. Of course, it should be included in her latest volume; it was too good to be ignored. Even the censure of her cousin Frank Repplier, who considered the essay a disgracefully flippant and shameful effort and had begged her not to put it in, could not change her mind.

In the October 1889 issue of the *Atlantic*, Miss Repplier had offered an essay called "Fiction in the Pulpit." In it she took to task the novelist with a "call," the public that wants to be edified as it is entertained, and, in general, the "intrusion of ethics upon art," especially literary art. George Eliot, Charles Reade, Dickens, George Moore, Howells: all come in for their share of criticism.

But what made this paper particularly memorable was that Lowell read it and approved of it. He wrote to Horace Howard Furness: "I have just been reading with great enjoyment an essay on 'The Novelist in the Pulpit' of Miss Repplier, who, I believe, is a friend of yours—truly delightful!" The letter was passed on to its author who was understandably elated by the praise. This was recommendation indeed. And what was perhaps even more gratifying, evidently the great man had forgiven her the trouble she had put him to over the business of her glasses on that first trip to Boston.

"A Plea for Humor," a third essay in the volume, is a cry for less drabness in literature. It ends with a characteristic display of wit: "This age of Apollinaris and of lectures is at fault, and . . . it has produced nothing which can vie as literature with the products of the ages of wine and song." "Literary Shibboleths," one of the best in the collection, offers in addition to a strong attack on pretense in reading, fine discriminating criticism of Russian and French fiction. But it is perhaps in "English Love-Songs" that the essayist is most effective. The paper presents a winning plea for the youthful beauties of Elizabethan and Caroline poetry as opposed to the analysis of the Brownings. And the evidence in behalf of the older love songs is unmatchable: "They are the models for all love-songs and for all time, and, in their delicate beauty, they endure like fragile pieces of porcelain, to prove how light a thing can bear the weight of immortality."

Points of View had gone beyond *Books and Men* as surely as "Children, Past and Present" had surpassed "Ruskin as a Teacher."

ʊ ʊ ʊ

It was through Harrison Morris that Agnes Repplier met Walt Whitman. She found him a most astounding old man, though very simple, kind, and hospitable. He was boarding at the time in Camden, which to her mind was just about the most melancholy of all possible ways of living. She was inclined to feel that part of Whitman's difficulty in getting along was due to his representing that city across the Delaware. What, she would ask, is Camden?

On their first meeting Whitman served Miss Repplier whiskey in a china toothbrush mug. She drank it heroically. His little room was littered with old newspapers, and she was certain that one lighted match carelessly discarded would send him into another world.

As for his poetry, the essayist admired it though she felt he had written only lines here and there that were truly worth remembering. She recognized that he always had the courage to be just what he wanted to be, that he never allowed anything to interfere with his life, and this she found an admirable quality. But she felt him to be an incurable poseur. He loved his indecency, she insisted, clinging to it with almost embarrassing ardor.

Then there was Thomas Eakins, the artist, who was very eager to paint Agnes Repplier's portrait. But she rather feared his uncompromising realism. She was tall and thin —"I would have had a much harder time of it had I been dumpy," she would remark—and she was perfectly willing to admit that she was "no beauty." She really was apprehensive of what Eakins would do to her, for, of course, he would have said it was her "character."

George W. Childs Agnes Repplier met socially. She thought him greatly overpraised, even though he was a considerable philanthropist. "You have a brilliant future," he said to her on their first acquaintance. "Come to my office soon." As if *that* constituted the entrance to a brilliant future, Miss Repplier would laugh. But she did call on Childs several times, and on each visit he presented her with a cup and saucer. They were as much his mark as ten-cent pieces later on in New York were Rockefeller's. Miss Repplier gathered quite a collection. But she thought he must reserve better ones for more important personages.

Dr. S. Weir Mitchell and Horace Howard Furness were undoubtedly Agnes Repplier's two most important literary friends in Philadelphia. Mitchell had a charm all his own. He was kindness itself to her, professing to admire her books more than he really did, she felt, out of a spirit of pure friendliness. A stately sort of person, he liked the formalities of life, and he entertained extensively.

Miss Repplier considered Mitchell's novels dull if able. He wrote with real ability, but she thought his people never came to life. She thought, too, that he composed very charming verse although not true poetry. She was of the opinion that his medical reputation contributed greatly to his literary reputation, and that he was very proud indeed of the latter if somewhat indifferent to the former.

Once a friend of Agnes Repplier's asked Mitchell to autograph one of his books for her. "I'd be delighted, my dear," said the doctor. "Which would you prefer?" Quite seriously the young woman mentioned a medical treatise. Mitchell was furious. "You impudent hussy," he stormed. "Just for that, you'll get none."

According to the essayist years later, Horace Howard Furness "inherited" her from his father, the Reverend William Furness, a well-known Unitarian minister of the city. "He was a saint," Miss Repplier would say of him, adding, "and I am loath to acknowledge Unitarian saints!" A kindly, alert old gentleman, he had first become interested in the writer through her papers in the *Atlantic*. "Do you happen to know a Boston woman who is contributing to the *Atlantic* over the signature 'Agnes Repplier'?" he wrote to his friend Agnes Irwin, who, he knew, was well acquainted in Boston. "Bless you," Miss Irwin wrote in reply, "she lives at your very door. Once she was a student in my school in Philadelphia, and she lives there today."

After the death of William Furness, Agnes Repplier continued her friendship with his son Horace Howard. The Shakespearean scholar and she had many interests in common, books and cats being the dearest to their hearts. Again and again Miss Repplier visited Horace Furness at his home in Wallingford, frequently staying for several days at a time. Although the scholar was totally deaf, and somewhat sensitive about his disability, with the aid of an ear trumpet the two spent hours in good talk about books and people and their feline pets.

Their friendship was far closer than that between the essayist and Mitchell, and there was nothing formal about their association. On one occasion following a visit by Agnes Repplier, Furness wrote to his sister: "You know how universally I am derided for my heated house. In this connection Agnes made me laugh. I felt a draught from the pantry which I feared was blowing on her back and asked if she so felt it. Her reply was instant and hearty: 'I thank God, I do!' " Nothing even remotely of the sort could have occurred at one of Mitchell's evenings.

Although he was deaf, Furness was a remarkably effective reader, particularly from his beloved Shakespeare. Everyone acknowledged his artistry, but no one was more certain of it than his sister Nannie. One evening the scholar was reading from *Hamlet* to a group of friends, Miss Irwin, Agnes Repplier, and Nannie among them, gathered in his library. Each one was charmed by his sensitive interpretation, and Nannie most of all. She sat in utter stillness, watching every movement of her brother's lips, every gentle gesture of his hand. When he had finished, Nannie remained quiet a moment. Her eyes glistened, her gaze never wavering from her brother's face. Miss Irwin stepped quietly up to her. "He didn't write it, you know, Nannie. Shakespeare did," she said.

As for Harrison Morris, that friend of long standing, the formalities were breaking down between Agnes Repplier and him. One day he made bold to ask her and Miss Mary to dinner at the Falls Restaurant on the Wissahickon, and she wrote him:

It is so very good in you to want to give me this pleasure that, for once and once only, I will lay aside my principles, abandon my sentiments, and resign myself into your hands, to enjoy all you wish to provide. My sister, having no such principles to resign, will be much pleased to accompany us.

And again, in answer to one of his notes to her, the essayist commented: "What nice paper you wrote on; the first I have ever seen from you which fitted its envelope. I admire it very much."

ᴆ ᴆ ᴆ

In the meantime, for all the lecturing, clubs, and friends, Agnes Repplier was working steadily and with as great care and precision as ever. A fourth magazine had been opened to her: *Life*. Almost weekly for thirty years she was to contribute to the humorous journal. And on occasion the larger papers for the more serious periodicals began as little sketches, scarcely a hundred words in length, that appeared in its pages.

Eighteen-ninety-two saw the publication of two more volumes, one of Agnes Repplier's own writing, *Essays in Miniature*, and the other a collection of poems for children, *A Book of Famous Verse*, of which she acted as editor. *Essays in Miniature*, made up of sixteen papers, is lacking somewhat in the same excellence of style as *Points of View*, though it is not without its quotable passages. But Agnes Repplier herself recognized the volume as not being up to the standard of her best work. Concerning it she wrote in reply to a note from Harrison Morris: "The book *is* bad. I guess I ought to know."

Essays in Miniature may have added little to the distinction of its author, but *A Book of Famous Verse* brought pleasant accompaniment, for it served as a second link in a growing friendship between Agnes Repplier and Andrew Lang, the English author and scholar, an epistolary friendship that had begun with her first essay in the *Atlantic*.

CHAPTER VII

Varia: Of Friends and Travel

1893–1900

೨ ೨

In the spring and summer of 1893, Agnes Repplier took a trip west, on which she chaperoned two of her young friends, Agnes and Sarah Boone of Baltimore. The Boone girls had been students at Eden Hall where Miss Repplier discovered them when she returned to lecture there upon one occasion. In addition to the trip west, the three were to enjoy several seasons abroad together. And although the older woman was rather of the opinion that she never constituted the model chaperone, the girls thought her the ideal companion.

Throughout almost the whole of the western trip, Agnes Repplier was concerned over the title for her latest collection of essays. En route to Denver, she wrote to Harrison Morris:

I have been thinking up some more titles which I submit to your judgment . . . Friends and Foes, Friends and Fables, An Idle Hour, Studies in Idleness, Essays in Idleness. The last I love, and will make a brave fight for, if it has your sanction. The sound at least is good. . . .

111

Evidently Morris did not sanction "Essays in Idleness" but made other suggestions instead, for from Coronado Beach, California, Miss Repplier again wrote him: "I have promptly abandoned Essays in Idleness, and thank you heartily for both your letters. But, in truth, the substitutes please me no better."

The letter concluded on a pathetic note:

My natural imbecility is enhanced by fatigue and suffering; for what *do* you think I am doing in this most beautiful and glorious place? I am having the mumps for the first time in my life . . . As for my book, it must go without a title, I fear. . . .

Morris responded shortly with another suggestion. And Miss Repplier answered from Santa Barbara:

Thanks for *Criteria*. It is fine, but a little pretentious. I have sent it at once to H M & Co. [Houghton Mifflin Company] together with all the others, and left the choice to them . . . Miss P. gave me four titles. *Appreciations*, which belongs to Mr. Pater. *Dicta*, which belongs to Mr. Birrell. *A Sheaf of Essays*, which is bad, and *Perceptions*, which is good, and which I also sent to Boston.

Two weeks later from Monterey, the essayist again posted her friend and adviser as to her progress in the matter of a book title. In her letter she enclosed a note from her publishers who had chosen her favorite, "Essays in Idleness," as they said, "in spite of your own misgivings and the positive feeling of your 'skilled friend.' " Miss Repplier explained: "I wrote them at once to use the one of *all* the titles they liked best, and I have washed my hands of the matter. But I am reinstated in my own conceit."

As for the country, she "loved Yosemite, the glades by the Merced River, and San Francisco." And she added, "I think that you would have enjoyed seeing me perched on a vicious grey mule, riding up one of the Yosemite 'trails,' in a state of mingled terror, bliss, and misery."

But Harrison Morris was not to be put off so easily. He suggested "Criteria" again as a title. And Agnes Repplier wrote him from San Francisco:

Upon my soul I think Criteria is fine. But you see my papers are none of them critical. If they were, don't you think I would jump at such a title? But how can I write about cats* and such like, when I want to call the book Criteria?

And then, to soften her firm refusal of Morris' suggestion, Miss Repplier continued:

They have beautiful cats in the Chinese Quarter of San Francisco. And they are all so tame and friendly! Down in the dreadful underground dwellings where the poorest people live, a dear little Chinese girl brought a splendid, huge Maltese cat, and placed him in my arms.

Such sights as I have seen! The Chinese opium dens, and gambling hells, and theatre, and Joss House, and tea rooms! Such pretty Chinese women! Such fascinating shops! Such splendid moonlight flooding their beautiful gilded balconies. Really this is a delightful city, and we are having a delightful time. Jim Corbett the prize fighter is at our hotel, and sits near us in the dining-room. We admire him immensely, and went last night to see him in an idiotic pugilistic play called Gentleman Jack. There were two finely realistic scenes; one where he is training for his fight with Mitchell, and one where he wins it. We all sat in a row, and applauded until the house shook. None of us had ever seen a prizefighter before . . . I have just been requested to tell the New York World "How I rest." A paper of two hundred words called "Agnes Repplier's Methods." I explained that I didn't rest, and so could not oblige them.

* "Agrippina" was to be the lead essay in the collection.

From the Hotel Del Monte in Monterey, the business of book titles now safely settled, Agnes Repplier wrote Harrison Morris:

The hotel is superb, and holds seven hundred people—mostly, as far as I can gather, millionaires. No other type of person appears to abide in California. Everybody says everybody else is worth twenty millions. It has a lovely sound . . .

On by boat to Alaska, where "the sea was so calm that we steered close up to the gleaming walls of ice, towering high over our heads, and every shade of blue from pale sky to indigo," back and through the Yellowstone, then on home. The trip had been a revelation to Agnes Repplier: the Pacific coast was very beautiful, she found, particularly in comparison with the Atlantic coast she thought "so damned unattractive."

ᵔ ᵔ ᵔ

Essays in Idleness came out in the fall of 1893. Of the eight papers contained in it, those on "Leisure" and "Wit and Humor" are perhaps the most interesting. The essayist writes in the former:

It is self-culture that warms the chilly earth wherein no good seed can mature. . . . And for the training of one's self, leisure is requisite; leisure and that rare modesty which turns a man's thoughts back to his own shortcomings and requirements, and extinguishes in him the burning desire to enlighten his fellow-beings. . . . To study Greek in order to read and enjoy it, and thereby make life better worth the living, is a possibility that seldom enters the practical modern mind. . . . It is in his pleasure that a man really lives; it is from his leisure that he constructs the true fabric of self.

The second of these two essays offers a penetrating distinction between wit and humor:

Wit is artificial; humor is natural. Wit is accidental; humor is inevitable. Wit is born of conscious effort; humor, of the allotted ironies of fate. Wit can be expressed only in language; humor can be developed sufficiently in situation. Wit is the plaything of the intellectual, or the weapon of nimble minds; humor is the possession of all sorts and conditions of men.

Essays in Idleness was well received. The reviewer for the *Atlantic* spoke of Agnes Repplier in the same breath as of Charles Lamb and Leigh Hunt, which was gratifying to say the least. And in the *Book News Monthly*, the essayist read of her work:

Miss Repplier's style is captivating, without being at all grand or elaborate, and she has a vigor that is positively masculine, combined with fine feminine sensibility. . . . She is certainly one of the most interesting figures in contemporary life.

In spite of her own misgivings and the missing sanction of Harrison Morris, *Essays in Idleness*, title and all, had come off well.

ꙮ ꙮ ꙮ

In October 1893, Agnes Repplier wrote to Morris:

Will you write a story—a very short biographical notice for me for Scribner's *Book Buyer*, to accompany my picture which I have consented to send them? You need not say civil things, and I fancy you are already in possession of the few meagre facts. Born in Philadelphia—French extraction*—(That sounds well, and excuses a great deal). Thirty-six [actually thirty-eight], last April—(This hideous detail might be softened vaguely). Wrote first for newspapers at home—Then for Atlantic Monthly—Mr. Aldrich my first good friend—Boston my most amiable critic—five books, counting the "Book of Famous Verse" . . .

* Of a rather thin distillation, as a matter of fact; but Agnes Repplier had inherited her mother's fiction, though she was not altogether taken in by it.

The *Book Buyer* asked me to send the name of some one they could ask to write the notice; and Mrs. Wister* being in Chicago—you are my only hope.

This letter was followed by another giving further information on the request of Harrison Morris:

Here are some points.

1. While it took years to teach me to read, and while I never could learn to cipher, my memory, as a little child, was considered abnormal. My mother taught me orally interminable poems, which I learned without labour, and loved without understanding, held by the beauty of the words. "A simple and sensuous delight."

2. What I know—such as it is—has always been acquired in the same unconscious spirit, and through the pleasure I took to it. All that I have ever striven to learn has been speedily forgotten.

3. I can only work in the morning and for three or four hours. Then I grow tired and stupid. The pleasure is gone, and I have to stop. So I don't accomplish a great deal, try as I may. Neither do I work with ease, but with infinite painstaking.

4. I dearly love social life, and amusing people. But I abhor (and here my French blood counts) the intrusion of serious matters into idle talk. I like conversation as an art, and in all arts, the form is more to me than the substance.

Harrison Morris willingly complied with the essayist's request, sending in a few weeks' time a sketch for her approval. As might be expected from one so careful in all her writing, Miss Repplier came upon a few statements in it to which she took polite but adamant exception. Morris referred to her family as "The Reppliers;" he stated that Mrs. Barbauld had been read to her at home; and he remarked that "The genius of cleanliness presided over [her desk]."

* Mrs. Caspar Wister, sister of Horace Howard Furness, and translator of a number of German novels.

Agnes Repplier returned his sketch to him post haste plus three changes:

Thank you very much, and please, *please* pardon the three corrections I have dared to make. "The Reppliers," like the Jameses or the Robinsons, sets my teeth on edge. I have never read or heard a word of Mrs. Barbauld's in my life, and I never want to.* And I cannot bear to have the world informed that I am clean—It is like telling it I am virtuous. One hopes so indeed!

For the rest, you are far too kind—I am neither so clever nor so nice, I fear, as you have made me out.

Harrison Morris made the alterations suggested by his subject, and the sketch was duly published in the January 1894 issue of the *Book Buyer*, becoming thus the first of a series of biographical accounts of the essayist that were to appear now and again to the delight and interest of her ever-growing public.

ᔕ ᔕ ᔕ

The spring of 1894 found Agnes Repplier again accompanying the Boone sisters on a trip, this time to Europe and the Near East. On the journey to the West, she had discovered that they were the best of traveling companions. Although some years her junior, they never seemed to realize the difference in ages, except that Miss Repplier felt them kinder to her than they would perhaps have been to a younger woman.

The trip began none too auspiciously. From Paris Agnes Repplier wrote to Harrison Morris:

* Apparently Miss Repplier had forgotten her reference to Mrs. Barbauld in "Children, Past and Present."

Mr. Talcott Williams has just given me the doleful information that Miss Irwin has been offered the head of Radcliffe, Harvard's Annex, and that he fears she will accept. If Boston steals her from us, I shall be more unhappy and more furious than words can ever express.

Boston did "steal" Miss Irwin from Philadelphia and her friends there, and Miss Repplier was for a time at least "furious." But the future actuality was to pass before the pressure of other matters, just as now even the very thought of it was to be dimmed by the excitement of the trip before her, the main high light of which was to be the meeting, so long looked forward to, with Andrew Lang in London.

ᔓ ᔓ ᔓ

Shortly after "Children, Past and Present" had appeared in the *Atlantic Monthly*, a correspondence had sprung up between Agnes Repplier and Andrew Lang. It had been entirely of his provoking, induced, it seems, by her more or less casual reference to Guibert de Nogent in that essay.

Lang's letters to her, which arrived steadily at frequent intervals, Miss Repplier found almost unpardonably difficult to decipher, taking the better part of a month for her to spell out. But they were well worth all the effort. The essayist found Lang to be a scholar who took himself lightly, an unbeatable combination as far as she was concerned. He was flippant to the last degree, but she never grew tired of his lightheartedness, for his was a flippancy grounded on solid worth.

At about the same time she had edited *A Book of Famous Verse*, Lang published a somewhat similar collection which he called the *Blue Book of Poetry*. And considerable banter had passed between the two over their work. Lang's selection had been made *con amore;* that was plainly evident. He had had a free hand. But Agnes Repplier had been requested—almost required—to include certain poems for which she held no great love.

Guibert de Nogent, *A Book of Famous Verse*, a steady correspondence, and now at long last the meeting. Miss Repplier wrote to Harrison Morris:

Mr. Lang is sulky and irresistibly charming; tall, lean, grey, and very handsome; with a single eye glass, a delightful smile, and a manner at once awkward and supercilious. He gave me a beautiful dinner when I first reached London, and was very good to me afterwards.

Lang took Agnes Repplier to a cricket match at Lord's "where, for once, he brightened into real enjoyment." But after the grand scrimmage of baseball, of which the American was very fond, she found cricket dull indeed. It seemed an overly gentlemanly game in which the players apparently did nothing but strike beautiful attitudes.

Later the two went to the British Museum, to the Grafton Gallery, and to tea. As it turned out, to her great amusement, Miss Repplier had to lend her escort the money to cover the cost of the refreshment, for Lang discovered that he had only two shillings sixpence in his pocket. His companion was equally amazed both by the Englishman's bland unconcern and by the fact that, for a wonder, she had the necessary amount with her.

During the course of her stay in London, Agnes Repplier was taken by the attentive Lang to one of Mrs. Humphry Ward's receptions—"a trifle dull"—and to supper

at Gosse's—"which was not." Then there was a "Bohemian"
dinner at Elizabeth Pennell's and a "very staid luncheon"
at Mrs. Fisher Unwin's "where we talked about anarchy
and women's rights." The round of events, which Miss
Repplier found perfectly overwhelming, came to a fitting
and imposing conclusion with an introduction to Saints-
bury of considerable and unassailable renown.

Lang had executed his duty with gentlemanly correct-
ness. But he had had enough. "He bade me a cheerful farewell when I left London," the essayist confessed years
later, "and he never wrote to me again. The inference is
tolerably plain. . . . "

ॐ ॐ ॐ

Agnes Repplier wrote to Harrison Morris from Ullswater, wishing him well on his coming marriage to Miss
Anna Wharton, daughter of Joseph Wharton of Philadelphia:

We have "rested" now at Ullswater in a most admirable hotel,
with the lakes at our feet, and a chain of mountains girdling
us round, and any number of beautiful walks—which we don't
take—stretching in every direction. We are the only Americans here, and the English people, I am sure, think that we
are mad, or have lost the use of our limbs.

Ambleside, and Grasmere, and Rydal, and Keswick, all the
exquisite country which Wordsworth and Coleridge made
holy ground, would delight your eyes and heart. At Grasmere
you can follow Wordsworth step by step, recognizing each
source of inspiration. At Hawkshead is still standing the dear
old grammar school where he went as a boy, and had so much
liberty given him to roam. His grave at Grasmere is very simple, and his little monument in the church not half so fine as
Southey's at Crosthwaite. But then, Heaven knows, Southey

1n21-rtg.u

deserves all that admiring friends could do for him. De Quincey, Hartley Coleridge, and Clough have left their records here; and in the hotel at which we stayed in Bowness there is still preserved, in the little old bar, the chair that Christopher North sat in when he ate the famous suppers of the "Noctes."*

We sail three weeks from to-day, a melancholy thought for those who hate the sea. We try not to think about it, and yet, with feminine instinct for self-torture, we remind each other continually how brief our respite is. . . .

ᔆ ᔆ ᔆ

The next half-dozen years were crowded and important ones for Agnes Repplier. In them she was to travel twice again to Europe, to see the publication of three more books, to undergo a serious operation, and growing out of this last, to make a friend who was to be her staunch admirer and companion for many a happy year.

On both the trips abroad Miss Repplier was accompanied by Sarah and Agnes Boone. An infinity of places had been missed on the earlier journey, and Baedeker's handy little volumes—"one star, look at; two stars, look hard; three stars, look very hard"—were never out of reach.

Other books traveled with them, too. One summer it was Carlyle's *Frederick the Great*, out of which they would read to each other while waiting for train connections. The Boone girls agreed after wading through the seventeen volumes Carlyle had managed to fill that they knew no one in real life half so well as they knew Frederick.

The second trip, coming in 1900, was made particularly memorable by an audience with the Pope. Not always did the "Woos," as Agnes Repplier called her charges, perform

* *Noctes Ambrosianae,* a series of imaginary conversations by John Wilson (Christopher North), *Blackwood's Magazine,* 1822–35.

as they were supposed to, but on this august occasion their behavior was beyond reproach. Miss Repplier was almost as impressed by their unwonted dignity as she was by the pontiff himself.

Wherever they went, whatever the sight to see, Agnes and Sarah were agreed that their chaperone—this incomparable person who in a moment of whimsey had written on her passport: "Face, broad; Complexion, sallow; Mouth, too large"—was not only the "best in Philadelphia," as Lady Astor once said in their presence, but, indeed, the best in the world.

ତ ତ ତ

In the Dozy Hours, published in 1894, a collection of twenty short essays, is one of Agnes Repplier's best volumes. The title essay presents a delightful account of authors for "the dozy hours" and their "bedside books." Charles Lamb and Madame de Sévigné among the letter writers, Jane Austen among novelists, Herrick, Marvell, Gray, Cowper, Keats, and Tennyson among poets: these the essayist heartily recommends.

The essay on "Lectures" is one of the most appealing in the volume.

Is it industry or a love of sport which makes us sit in long and solemn rows in an oppressively hot room, blinking at glaring lights, breathing a vitiated air, wriggling on straight and narrow chairs, and listening, as well as heat and fatigue and discomfort will permit, to a lecture which might just as well have been read peacefully by our own firesides? . . . The necessity of knowing a little about a great many things is the most grievous burden of our day. It deprives us of leisure on the one hand, and of scholarship on the other.

"Reviewers and Reviewed" offers a witty yet reasonable defense of the harried critic:

It is urged . . . against newspaper critics that they read only a small portion of the books which they pretend to criticize. This, I believe, is true, and it accounts for the good-humor and charity they display. If they read the whole, we should have a band of misanthropes who would spare neither age nor sex, and who would gain no clearer knowledge of their subjects through this fearful sacrifice of time and temper.

The essayist asks in "Sympathy," a paper deriding the business of digging up little faults of great men:

What can we say to people who talk to us anxiously about Byron's unkindness to Leigh Hunt, and Dr. Johnson's illiberal attitude towards Methodism, and Scott's incomprehensible friendship for John Ballantyne: who remind us with austere dissatisfaction that Goldsmith did not pay his debts, and that Lamb drank more than was good for him, and that Dickens dressed badly and wore flashy jewelry?

Her answer is characteristically direct:

I don't care what Dickens wore. I would not care if he had decorated himself with bangles, and anklets, and earrings, and a nosering, provided he wrote "Pickwick" and "David Copperfield." If there be any living novelist who can give us such another as Sam Weller, or Dick Swiveller, or Mr. Micawber, or Mrs. Gamp, or Mrs. Nickleby, let him festoon himself with gauds from head to foot, and wedge his fingers "knuckle-deep with rings," like the lady in the old song, and then sit down and write. The world will readily forgive him his embellishments.

In the Dozy Hours proved no real task for Agnes Repplier. And it was received with the same quiet, sincere enthusiasm that had greeted her previous books. *Philadelphia,*

too, undertaken at the request of Macmillan for their
"Travel Series," and brought out in 1898, save for the necessary research involved, went easily enough. But *Varia* was
a different matter.

As with *Essays in Idleness*, it was not the selection of the
individual papers that caused the concern, but an appropriate title. In February 1897, Agnes Repplier wrote to Harrison Morris, her confidant in all such matters: "Do you
think 'Life and Letters' would be a good title for my new
book? It will have five literary papers, two historical ditto,
and two sketches of travel. Or 'Letters and Life'?"

Morris responded with a list of suggested titles. And in
reply Agnes Repplier wrote: "Mrs. Oliphant has pre-
empted 'The Primrose Path' for one of her novels. I like
'Voyages at Anchor' immensely if it be appropriate. 'By
Land and Letters' combines the travel sketches and literary
papers."

Later she sent him a lengthy collection of titles, confess-
ing: "I am played out. And none are good. It is the hardest
thing in Christendom . . . "

But Morris was not discouraged. He made further suggestions, among them the title finally adopted.

In the fall of 1897 the volume appeared, and early the
following January Miss Repplier wrote to her friendly
adviser: "I did not send you Varia, because I was oppressed
with doubts as to whether you wanted it, though it be
your god-child. I am glad you do, and it will be a pleasure
for me to give you the book."

Harrison Morris read *Varia* with keen enjoyment and so
informed its author. "I am glad you like Varia," she wrote
him, "that is if you really did like it, and those were not

lying civilities you uttered. I am very much pleased with the title, although I have been asked if it were a novel I had published. People think it a heroine's name."

The critics were not so deceived. They recognized *Varia* for what it truly was. "Miss Repplier's function in literature," one commented, "is that of the busy bee. She hovers over and enters into books . . . and returns thence laden with stuff . . . which will pass very well for honey." And another said of this latest volume: "It has insight and humor; it is light-hearted and open-minded."

"The Eternal Feminine" offers a protest against

the monotonous repetition of a phrase which catches and holds the public fancy by virtue of its total lack of significance —"the new woman." It has been received with seriousness by those who read the present with no light from the past, and so fail to perceive that all femininity is as old as Lilith, and that the variations of the type began when Eve arrived in the Garden of Paradise to dispute the claims of her predecessor. "If the fifteenth century discovered America," says a vehement advocate of female progress, "it was reserved for the nineteenth century to discover woman;" and this remarkable statement has been gratefully applauded by people who have apparently forgotten all about Judith and Zenobia, Cleopatra and Catherine de Medici, Saint Theresa and Jeanne d'Arc, Catherine of Russia and Elizabeth of England, who played parts of some importance, for good and ill, in the fortunes of the world.

"The Deathless Diary" is of particular interest, for in it the essayist makes and justifies a confession:

Four ways there are of telling a curious world that endless story of the past which it is never tired of hearing. History, memoir, biography, and the diary run back like four smooth roads, connecting our century, our land, our life, with other centuries and lands and lives that have all served in turn to make us what we are. Of these four roads, I like the narrowest best. . . . Diaries tell their little tales with a directness, a candor, conscious or unconscious, a closeness of outlook, which gratifies our sense of security. Reading them is like gazing through a small clear pane of glass. We may not see far and wide, but we see very distinctly that which comes within our field of vision.

In "Cakes and Ale" Miss Repplier strikes a note akin to that of "English Love-Songs" several years earlier. She declares in this essay:

Why, we may drink nothing stronger than tea and Apollinaris water all our lives; yet none the less the mad music of Elizabethan song will dance merrily in our hearts, and give even to us our brief hour of illogical, unreasonable happiness.

"Old Wine and New" is a lament that modern history books have fallen far below the happy standard of centuries past. Froissart and his *Chronicles* are unfortunately no longer considered proper models, the essayist points out. She comments with telling effect:

No one of the sister Muses has lent herself so unreservedly to the demands of an exacting generation as Clio, who, shorn of her splendor, sits spectacled before a dusty table strewn with Acts of Parliament and Acts of Congress, and forgets the glories of the past in the absorbing study of constitutions. She traces painfully the successive steps by which the sovereign power has passed from the king to the nobles, from the nobles to the nation, and from the nation to the mob, and asks herself interesting but fruitless questions as to what is coming next. She has been divorced from literature . . . and wedded to science, that grim but amorous lord whose harem is tolerably full already, but who lusts perpetually for another bride.

For all the concern its title had given Agnes Repplier, *Varia* meant only delight for her readers.

ᕤ ᕤ ᕤ

In later years Miss Repplier was never quite certain just how she came to know that the same disease which had caused her mother's death was making sharp inroads upon her own none too strong constitution. Never a very robust person, she was feeling weaker, more tired than usual the winter of 1896, though no word as to the real nature of her illness crept into her correspondence with Harrison Morris, recipient of all manner of trials as far as her books were concerned.

But one day she did write calmly and quietly of it to Sarah Boone in Baltimore. "There's no disgrace about cancer," she explained. "So I don't see why I need keep it a secret. It's not as if I had contracted it through some wilful act of my own."

Dr. J. William White of the University of Pennsylvania Medical School, a surgeon of considerable fame, was recommended to her by her physician. She went to him and was told that an operation would be all that could save her. And with the same calmness that she had written to Sarah Boone, she received the news. It had all come about too suddenly for her to be frightened. If an operation was necessary, then the sooner over with, the better.

Throughout her remaining years, Agnes Repplier felt that she owed her life to White, as, in all actuality, she did. But more than that, after the operation had been successfully accomplished and a strong bond of friendship had grown up between the bluff, sports-loving doctor and his gratifyingly brave patient, she felt she could not get along very well without him. It was always a source of amazement to her after White's death some years later that she had indeed outlived the man who she was certain was keeping her alive.

In her biography of White, Miss Repplier wrote:

Above and beyond all other qualities must be reckoned his
courageous acceptance and enjoyment of life. He feared it as
little as he feared death. He never held back his hand from
its favours because they carry danger in their wake. He never
inquired too curiously if the game were worth the candle. He
took royally what was his, and paid the price in full. There is
a matchless sentence of Mr. Chesterton's which describes, as
no words of mine can ever describe, this sane and valorous
attitude: "The truest kinship with humanity lies in doing as
humanity has always done, accepting with sportsmanlike relish
the estate to which we are called, the star of our happiness,
and the fortunes of the land of our birth."

These gifts Dr. White took unshrinkingly from the hand
of fate, and of them he built the strong and splendid fabric of
his life.

No tribute could have been more simply put nor more
sincerely felt.

꘎ ꘎ ꘎

It was the year 1900. Agnes Repplier was approaching
the midway mark. Not very far in the future she was to
offer *A Happy Half-Century* to her readers.

And in the main it had been happy. She had accomplished
her duty tour of the United States with more pleasure than
pain; she had reveled in the luxurious abundance of Europe.
She had made many friends for herself, if a scattering of
enemies—crabbed souls who never knew when not to take
her seriously. But most of all, she had won a reputation that
was well on its way to being the envy of those who aspire
to write, not for the glutton masses, but for the gourmet
few.

Agrippina

1900

ᴆ ᴆ

Although Agnes Repplier owned more than one cat down through the years, the nearest and dearest to her heart always was Agrippina. In telling of a successor to this famous feline, she wrote:

There is something indescribably sweet in the quiet, self-respecting friendliness of my cat, in her marked predilection for my society. The absence of exuberance on her part, and the restraint I put upon myself, lend an element of dignity to our intercourse. Assured that I will not presume too far on her good nature, that I will not indulge in any of those gross familiarities, those boisterous gambols which delight the heart of a dog, Lux yields herself more and more passively to my persuasions. She will permit an occasional caress, and acknowledge it with a perfunctory purr. She will manifest a patronizing interest in my work, stepping sedately among my papers, and now and then putting her paw with infinite deliberation on the page I am writing, as though the smear thus contributed spelt "Lux, her mark," and was a reward of merit. But she never curls herself upon my desk, never usurps the place sacred to the memory of a far dearer cat. Some invisible influence restrains her. When her tour of inspection is ended, she returns to her chair by my side, stretching herself luxuriously on her cushions, and watching with steady, sombre stare the inhibited spot, and the little grey phantom which haunts my lonely hours by right of my inalienable love.

Even Nero (a hard name perhaps for an innocent kitten, but what else might Agrippina's first-born be called?) could not replace Agrippina. True, she was not the first in point of time. There had been cats—and dogs, though of these Agnes Repplier was never particularly fond—in the early days of her childhood. They all had vanished after a few weeks so mysteriously that even then the little girl had suspected some heartless outside force, such as her mother. But Agrippina, that first cat of the essayist's maturity, remained forever first in her affections.

She had been presented to Miss Repplier by a friend who brought her wrapped snugly in a muff. And from the moment she laid eyes on her, Agnes Repplier knew that this would be the only cat. Poor thing—she was not destined to live very long, and perhaps the shortness of her earthly career made her the more pathetically endearing. Agrippina died in kitten-birth, a worthy and noble end, no doubt, but tragic too.

Once, years after, Miss Repplier was asked with becoming circumlocution if she had ever allowed Agrippina to exercise her natural prerogative. (This was before the cause of the cat's death had been made known to her interrogator.) The essayist laughed gleefully. "My dear," she said when she had regained sufficient control of herself, "I preached virginity to Agrippina till I was blue in the face. But she'd howl, so I'd kiss her and put her out in the alley!"

In all things just, Agnes Repplier was not one to condemn her little charge to the same fate that was to be her own. She had the generosity to allow Agrippina to consort with her common friends, for, as she would confess, "I hadn't any choice in the matter."

ꙮ ꙮ ꙮ

It was while Miss Repplier was living in the Locust Street house that Agrippina was brought to her. And it was on the little desk in the second-floor front room that Agrippina was wont to play. There she and her mistress would pass the time, the author in endeavoring conscientiously to write while the cat was just as bent on keeping her from so doing.

At Sunday-night supper Agrippina was guest of honor. She took precedence even over Harrison Morris and Dr. Jastrow, most frequent partakers of the feasts. Jastrow was almost as fond of the cat as was her owner. He thought it only right that Agrippina should come first. But not so Morris. And with the unerring judgment that only cats possess, Agrippina invariably chose his lap on which to settle down comfortably.

One evening Agrippina took it into her uninhibited little head to climb first to the mantelpiece, then to jump six feet to the top of a bookcase, next to hang precariously from a dangerously swinging picture, and finally to land squarely on the protesting Harrison Morris seated on a sofa below.

"Miserable stable-born cat!" he exclaimed. "The airs she gives herself. Might think she was a royal princess!"

Miss Repplier and her other guest were doubled over with delight. And even Agrippina seemed pleased with her performance.

ᴏ ᴏᴊᴏ

Agnes Repplier always doubted persons who talked of the affection of their cats. "Their very indifference is so honest," she would protest. "What they hold back rather than what they give attracts. 'It is more blessed to give than to receive'—and you do with cats. A dog pathetically tries to break down the barriers between him and you, but a cat lives its own life. A cat withdraws. We know little about them—although they're wise little beasts."

Cats are without morals, she insisted always, and they are perfectly democratic. Dogs are snobs, preferring a mate in their own class. But as for cats, any old tom in the alley will please them. Consider Agrippina. She had a black lover, an alley lover. But he suited her. She was completely satisfied with him even if he had never seen the inside of a decent home. Agrippina was democratic. And Agrippina was the best of all.

The essayist much preferred ordinary cats to the pedigreed variety. "They're far more intelligent, anyway," she would explain. And females were more to her liking than males—even though "they *will* have kittens." As for altered toms, she had no use for them, although such had not always been the case. In her convent days, "altar cats," as she had mistakenly thought them called, were the source of considerable speculation and mystery to her. She supposed them to be some peculiar church breed that only the very pious might own.

Cats have always got on with scholars, Agnes Repplier knew, because scholars sit still for long periods of time at their work. Cats like quiet people. They heartily approve of a sedentary life—in others, that is. And, of course, her own incomparable cat approved, though she never exhibited any profound respect for her mistress' learning.

"Oh, yes, it's a great thing to be dowered with beauty," Miss Repplier would admonish Agrippina. "And it's especially great for a female. You were born beautiful, remember—no merit to you, you little beast . . . And it's very unfair, dear, I'll tell you now. Very unfair. You'll be cherished all your life long. Yes, Agrippina, Providence is as unfair to cats as to women. Because you're such a beauty, you'll have a happy time of it all the way. Many an alley cat has just as good a heart, but no beauty. Nothing but brains —as I have. And nobody wants them. But they support me. Which beauty doesn't always do."

And then as Agrippina would prepare to forestall further comment by curling up and going to sleep: "There, now! What would I be doing if I slept all the time? What walls would be about me? I can't please anybody just by lying asleep. But you . . . Well, you don't have to work for a living. And I suppose you wouldn't care if I wrote like Shakespeare. You blind little cat!"

ᴐ ᴐ ᴐ

There is a sweet and sunny corner of the Elysian fields, where drowse and play, and drowse and play forever, a little band of cats, whose names, imperishable as their masters', are household words today. We know them well, these gentle furry ghosts, lifted to immortality by the human hands that fondled them in life. We know the white Muezza whom Mohammed loved, and Bouhaki of Thebes, proudest of his proud race, and Dick Whittington's thrice famous cat that made his master's fortune. We know this sleek and shining tortoiseshell, for she is Selima, fair and ill-fated, whom the glint of gold-fish tempted to her grave. This pensive pussy with clear topaz eyes shared Petrarch's heart with Laura; this splendid beast, red as a fox and stately as a lion, is Chateaubriand's Micetto, the sovereign Pontiff's gift; and his no less arrogant companion sat, it is whispered, by the side of Wolsey, when the butcher's son was Chancellor of England.

Montaigne's great cat is here, indolently supercilious as in old earthly days; and Victor Hugo's Chanoine, the sleepiest puss in Paradise; and Baudelaire's mysterious pet, with pale fire gleaming 'neath his half-shut lids; and Moumotte Blanche and Moumotte Chinoise, rivals for M. Loti's fluctuating affections, and the superb dynasties, both white and black, that ruled for years over M. Gautier's heart and home. Here, too, is "great Atossa," sung into fame by Mr. Arnold; and that sedate and serious tabby who slept too long in Cowper's bureau drawer. And—honored of all their race—here are two happy and distinguished cats whom we cannot remember without envy, nor name without respect,—Dr. Johnson's Hodge, and Hinse of Hinsefeld, the wise companion of Sir Walter Scott.

Into this august assembly, into this sacred circle, I fain in moments of temerity would introduce a little shade who stole too soon from the warm sun, and from the simple joys of life. She was dearly loved and early lost, and the scanty honours years of toil have brought me I lay at her soft feet for entrance fee. May Hodge and Hinse champion her cause with the Immortals for the sake of the unfaltering love I have ever borne their masters, and may her grace and beauty win for her what my poor pen is powerless to attain! Dear little ghost, whose memory has never faded from my heart, accept this book, dedicated to thee, and to all thy cherished race. Sleep sweetly in the fields of asphodel, and waken, as of old, to stretch thy languid length, and purr thy soft contentment to the skies. I only beg, as one before me begged of her dead darling, that, midst the joys of Elysium, I may not be wholly forgotten.

> "Nor, though Persephone's own Puss you be,
> Let Orcus breed oblivion of me."

This the Foreword to Agnes Repplier's book about cats, *The Fireside Sphinx*, which she humbly offered to the memory of her beloved Agrippina.

She sent a copy of the volume to Horace Howard Furness at whose "Lindenshade," in Wallingford, the remains of Agrippina lay buried. He wrote in reply:

After reading your exquisite, exquisite Preface last evening, I breathed a holy vow that Agrippina's resting-place should be incontinently marked by a headstone, diminutive but proportionate. Is the simple name carved therein sufficient? or will you send me the years of her birth and death?

Had she any love of humour beyond the resources of her tail, whereby she would relish the addition of "Requies-cat"? Not for worlds would I cause that shade a shade of annoyance. . . .

Do you remember in which direction, North or South, her poor little head rests? Our house faces due South.

The thoughtful word was passed along to Harrison Morris with considerable satisfaction seeing that he had borne the cat no love: "Dr. Furness," Miss Repplier wrote, "is putting up a marble stone over Agrippina's grave. I am deeply touched, and very much pleased."

And she added: "I do hope you'll like [*The Fireside Sphinx*]. I adore it—quite impersonally—and don't dare to pick it up, lest I waste my time re-reading it. That comes of doing—once in a lifetime—something one wants to do."

ɔ ɔ ɔ

Of all Agnes Repplier's friends, Horace Howard Furness alone loved cats as much as she. Whole evenings were spent between the two in doing nothing more than relating the various exploits of their particular pets. Cats were worthy of their talk, they felt; the subject needed neither explanation nor apology.

Together they sympathized with an unfortunate if beautiful cat, belonging to a New England friend of the essayist's, that was required to consume its meal in the kitchen along with the servants and out of a common, ordinary dish, whereas Ruzzie, a superannuated setter of the same household, had a collection of fine Russian bowls from which to eat.

"And to think," Agnes Repplier exploded with mounting indignation as she told the lamentable story, "Mrs. W. said she would rather hear Ruzzie lapping his water—which he does with a horrid noise—than listen to a symphony concert! Of course, I said I would, too," she was forced to admit in view of her own well-known dislike for music, "but it was a bitter alternative."

For years Furness had owned a striped cat of uncertain origin that answered—when he wanted to—to the name of Romeo. He was, as Miss Repplier declared, quite a regular institution, the principal actor in a little comedy that took place every twenty-four hours with the regularity of clockwork. Night after night, when it came time for him to shut things up securely, the patient Shakespearean scholar would go out onto the porch of his home and call: "Romeo! Romeo!" To which plaintive cry his friend could not keep from adding, "Wherefore art thou, Romeo?" on those occasions when she was witness to the performance.

Furness' particular love was reserved for two Siamese cats he imported with the express purpose of raising a long line of thoroughbreds. But however mating may be managed in catteries Miss Repplier could never understand, for as she put it, "Banshee had a common alley lover, and Banquo sired bastards all over the country!"

It is true that as kittens they were affectionate little creatures. (Later, the essayist noted, they were too occupied with family affairs—and not of Furness' choosing, either—for so simple an expression of feeling.) He had written to her upon their arrival:

I am longing to show you the pride of my heart and the joy of my soul:—two Siamese kittens!

I did not dare to ask you to come and see them until now.

After an ocean voyage, during which they had never been taken out of their box, I couldn't diagnose the state of their health with sufficient assurance to venture to exhibit them. But now I believe them to be so far convalescent that their bewitching antics would fascinate the soul of a Danish wolf-hound. Of their effect on your tender heart I dare not think . . .

I am a little selfish in my wishes that the kittens may show off before you in their best style, because if they are sluggish I shall have to perform their antics myself, and I'm a little stiffish in the joints for playing with a cork and a string. But I'll do my best, although it is a little rough on my dress coat when I have to lie on my back and claw the cork with my legs.

Miss Repplier lost no time in paying her respects to Banquo and Banshee, as Furness shortly thereafter reported to his sister:

On Monday Agnes Repplier came hither to dinner . . . solely to see the Siamese kittens. And her enthusiasm was entirely satisfactory. The minute she entered your parlour, where I was seated, with the little creatures scurrying hither and thither, she seated herself on the floor and gathered the kittens into her bosom, exclaiming with delight over their affectionate purrings. It must be a stony heart, fit only for stratagems and spoils, that can resist them.

But before very long, Banshee—and presumably Banquo as well—was up to the questionable tricks for which fate and her democratic nature had marked her. And one day Miss Repplier received a pathetic note from her learned friend announcing his darling's first misstep:

Four little strangers were welcomed yesterday into this feline and unfeeling world, but one immediately departed this life without waiting for his allotted other eight.

Of the three survivors, one is as black as my hat,—possibly blacker seeing that this article was purchased last summer in London,—and the other two are one mottled all over. Pray God, the mother has been honest!

I knew you'd want to have the earliest news.

Fortunately for Banshee and her offspring, Furness was no narrow-minded puritan. He was as concerned over the welfare of the latest addition to his household as he would have been had the union of which they were the result been honored with his blessing.

When Miss Repplier asked if she might call upon the new arrivals, he wrote her an anxious note in reply:

Come every day to see Nannie, but don't expect to see the cherubic kittens or their ma just yet. The latter has caused me some anxiety; I feared she was feverish, and she was certainly greatly excited. So I have enjoined the strictest seclusion, which is to last until the little ones are well on their way to sturdy health, and can be brought up stairs to see company.

After providing a most luxurious bed for the future mother —the very kind of bed I should have chosen for myself—what does she do but select an old box with five straws in it, in the darkest corner of the cellar!

If you have any sympathy which is going to waste, bestow it on the woebegone pa, who is literally heart-broken over the inexplicable disappearance of his idol—or is it that he sniffs kittens in the wind and would like to have a go at the toothsome dainties? After the experience of the old box, cats' nature is somewhat of a problem.

When the kittens are presentable, their fond mother will not be as proud to show them to you as will be

Yours affectionately,
H H F

ᴆ ᴆ ᴆ

Banquo, Banshee, Nero, "the grocer's cat," even an unsung tom by the name of Carl, each had its place in Agnes

Repplier's affections. And there were other cats as well: a little sleeping kitten made of clay, a seated cat modeled after some ancient royal favorite, the pictured tabby that played for all time within its wooden frame upon the wall. But none of these could ever measure up to Agrippina. "A one-cat woman, that's what I am," the essayist would say.

And she never tired of telling the story; it was both joy and sorrow to her:

Once, long ago, a little grey cat sat on my desk while I wrote, swept her tail across my copy, or patted with friendly paw my pen as it travelled over the paper. Even now I put out my hand softly to caress the impalpable air, for her spirit still lingers in the old accustomed spot. I see her sitting erect and motionless in the superb attitude of her Egyptian forefathers, her serious eyes heavy with thought, her lids drooping a little over the golden depths below. After a time they close, and her pretty head nods drowsily; but, like a perverse child, she resists the impelling power, straightens herself, and flings a glance at me which says, "You see how wide awake I am." Then very, very slowly, sleep touches her with soft, persuasive finger. She sinks down, down; the small proud head is lowered; the gleaming eyes are shut; a half-articulate purr grows fainter and fainter until it melts imperceptibly into the soft and regular breathing which betrays her slumber . . .

But that is not quite the end. Devotion brings the story to its close:

I stop my work and look at her, or rather I look at her ghost, the inspiration of this poor book, written to do her honour. It is finished now, and Agrippina sleeps. I lay it gently down before the shadowy presence. It is her password to Elysium. It is my offering to her, and hers to the Immortals, that they may give her place. She has waited for it seven years. Little grey phantom, haunt me no longer with reproachful eyes. I have kept my word. I have done my best. And the book belongs to you.

But did the "little grey phantom" recognize what lay behind so wistful a dedication? Perhaps she did. There was a
certain lifelong friend who, in a moment of rashness, also
claimed undying affection for her pet. "But she had a husband, and you can't be mad about a husband *and* a pussy
cat, you know." Of that Agnes Repplier was well aware.

Yes, Agrippina must have understood and thanked the
gods-that-be for her good fortune.

CHAPTER IX

A Happy Half-Century

1901–1909

ɔ ɔ ɔ

Some half-dozen years or so before the publication of
The Fireside Sphinx, Agnes Repplier and her brother and
sister moved back into the "City." They had had enough of
the benighted atmosphere of West Philadelphia, and now
that their parents were long since gone and they themselves
were managing quite adequately there was nothing to prevent such a return to "civilization."

First came an apartment on Spruce Street near Twelfth,
and then a few years later, another at Nineteenth and Chestnut streets. There were to be two more removes before
the migratory essayist and her brother and sister would
come to settle finally on Clinton Street just east of Tenth.
It was in an apartment in this house, with its Victorian parlor on the first floor and the bedrooms on the second, that
Agnes Repplier found at last complete satisfaction. It suited
her, as she would say, "right down to the ground." Within
a short distance of Wanamaker's store—the center of things
for all Philadelphians—within as easy reach of St. John's,
it appeared to be ideal for her. And it was as living in the
Clinton Street house that in later years Agnes Repplier was

141

remembered by her out-of-town visitors as well as by her
Philadelphia friends.

"Agnes Repplier? Oh, yes, she lives on Clinton Street,
doesn't she? I've seen her many times," was to become a
commonplace with her both curiously indifferent yet
withal proud fellow citizens. Clinton Street, its ancient Co-
lonial homes now broken into apartments and in some instances housing students attendant at near-by Jefferson
Medical College, provided a congenial, genteel setting for
the eminent lady of letters.

And Miss Repplier's being there was not without its
occasional diversion for other residents of Clinton Street.
It was reported in a Philadelphia paper that on one occasion the essayist complained to some collegiate neighbors
of hers about their carelessly tossing rubbish into the back-
yard. She wrote them a polite but insistent letter, request-
ing them to clean up the offending trash and "kindly in the
future not to be so neglectful." The students attended to
the business with almost unheard-of promptness. Although
the removal cost them five dollars, they were indifferent
to the expense involved. They had sold the famous author's
autograph for twice the amount.

ᴆ ᴆ ᴆ

In 1899 Harrison Morris had accepted a position as editor of *Lippincott's Magazine*, a position he was to hold for
the following six years. And because Agnes Repplier had
known him so long and so well, she frequently would make
requests of him that she would never dream of asking of
other more remote editors.

Miss Repplier's friend and medical adviser, White, it

seems, was not content merely to see his name appear now and again in technical journals. Not so shy about his writing as his literary friend had been in the early days about hers, he would offer his work to her for criticism. A paper recounting his experiences at housekeeping one summer at Norfolk, England, which his friend found readable and practical but far too long she consented to revise, and wrote to Morris suggesting it for his magazine. "But," she made it plain, "if I give it my precious time, I want it to run some chance of publication."

Harrison Morris was as good a friend to Agnes Repplier as she to the doctor: the paper was accepted, to be duly offered to the public. The essayist wrote in gratitude to the kindly editor: "You know [Dr. White's] name counts for a great deal more than mine, and people vastly prefer to read things that are not written by professional authors." Though, she added, she had of late been pushed for time, "we all have our moments of weakness, and my particular desire just now is to see this paper through."

If it gave White any pleasure to think himself an author, and if she could help bolster his belief in himself along such lines, the least Agnes Repplier felt she could do was to offer him her services. After all, he had performed the utmost for her when she had needed him the most. And more than that, he was her friend.

ɔ ɔ ɔ

It was in 1902 that Agnes Repplier received her first outstanding honor, the degree of Doctor of Letters from the University of Pennsylvania. Horace Howard Furness delivered the presentation address:

We have invited to be here present, on this occasion, Agnes Repplier, because she has revived the art, well-nigh lost in these days, of the Essayist. Slightly to change the well-known words, there is no province of the Essayist that she has not touched, and there is nothing which she has touched that she has not adorned. Her wisdom is illuminated by her wit, and her wit is controlled by her wisdom. Under her clear and searching gaze all blown pretence lies shriveled. To her, the by-ways of literature are as familiar as the high-ways, and into no nook or covert have her silvery feet strayed that they have not led us into "a purer ether, a diviner air" and revealed to us quickening springs and glittering fountains. Her Fireside Sphinx, with well sheathed claws, will play immortally, in the fields of Asphodel, with Lesbia's sparrow. She has told us the story of our own dear City, and into thousands of homes her voice brings learning and elevation, purity and refinement, "fair thoughts and happy hours."

Therefore, we present her to the Provost that she may receive from the University the Academic Degree of Doctor of Letters.

There were to be many more honors added to this one. But none was to be more gratifying than this first received in the city of her birth and at the hands of her good and generous friend.

ↄ ↄ ↄ

In the summer of 1902, Agnes Repplier again traveled abroad, choosing Cornelia Frothingham as her companion for the trip. The essayist had known Miss Frothingham for some years. She was sister-in-law to Charles Brinley, a prominent figure in Philadelphia intellectual life, the head of the Society for the Extension of University Teaching. The "University Extension," as the organization was generally called, brought prominent speakers of the day to the city somewhat after the fashion of the Contemporary Club. But with the Extension, the meetings were open to the general public, whereas the Contemporary Club gatherings were for members and occasional friends only.

For years Agnes Repplier and Cornelia Frothingham took dinner every other Sunday at the Brinley home on Spruce Street. These were not perhaps the brilliant, decidedly clever people the author ordinarily preferred, but, strangely, for that very reason she seemed particularly to enjoy their company. Apparently she found in the Brinley family a comfortable, sane, and gentle household that satisfied her by its very normality. Summer after summer Miss Repplier visited Mr. Brinley and his wife and children in Litchfield, or Dorset, or Magnolia. And here again there was what appeared to be contradiction. Decidedly an urban person all her life, the essayist took to the country existence that her weeks spent with the Brinley family offered with as much real pleasure as on other occasions teeming city life alone could give her.

Cornelia Frothingham came from New England stock, a fact she never forgot. She considered herself always as alien to Philadelphia where, more by force of circumstance than by choice, she made her home. Indeed, in order to insure the perfect clarity of her position, she assumed something of the role of recluse, living for the most part in admirable seclusion and independence. Yet the retiring Cornelia Frothingham and the somewhat ubiquitous Agnes Repplier, as it turned out, made excellent traveling companions. Their divergent personalities never clashed, but proved rather each to enhance and complement the other.

The trip with Cornelia Frothingham began leisurely: a

month in Paris, twelve days at Tours, a month of Amboise
"with the Chateau at our backs and the Loire at our feet,"
and a month at Vevey on the shores of Lake Leman.* Mary
Repplier was in London attending a host of parties that followed in the wake of King Edward's coronation. Displaying just the proper distortion of truth, the essayist wrote to
Harrison Morris: "I am glad with my whole heart [Mary]
is having such a good time, and gladder still I am not doing
that kind of thing. Pastoral pleasures for me!" A bit later
on she again wrote her friend, enclosing in her letter a
photograph of *La petite île á Clarens*. "This is the house
Miss Frothingham and I covet to madness," she declared.
"We want to live here together"—though she could scarcely
have meant that at all. It is somewhat difficult to picture
Agnes Repplier cooped up on a house-size island plumped
in the middle of a lake, miles from any city of distinction.

Later there came a further note:

Miss Frothingham . . . is striving to develop in me what she
calls a civic conscience. I believe its finest fruit is to be the de-
claring of my beggarly purchases at the Custom House when
I go home; but in the meantime I am expected to revere the
Pilgrim Fathers, to read Emerson and the newspapers, to dilate
with patriotic emotions, and not to throw match stumps out
of the windows. Think of me with that halo of virtue round
my head!

Ordinarily Miss Repplier did little or no writing while
on her trips. Travel constituted the keenest recreation for
her, and she was usually far too busy sight-seeing to take
time out for work. But occasionally, when a particularly
good idea struck her and when she was in the proper mood,
she would retire to some quiet spot and set to work.

* This in spite of Agnes Repplier's avowed distaste for Switzerland.

From Siena she wrote to Harrison Morris:

Would you like a paper on *Tourists*,—their peculiarities, their misdeeds and the animosity they bear one another, for Lippincott? I have just begun it, and it occurred to me that maybe you would like to have it. Heaven knows I don't lack experience on the subject. I rather think it will run to 2500 words. I have not been able to get any work type-written since I left Paris, and won't be until I reach Rome; but I can make you a decent copy, though it is an awful nuisance. One scrambles along under many disadvantages in this beloved land.

By the middle of November, Miss Frothingham and she had reached Florence. "Winter has come," she wrote Morris, "and the hills above Florence are white with snow. However, we are just returned from a two days' trip to Pistoja and Lucca—Greenland is sultry by comparison."

And from Florence she mailed him the promised essay:

I send you forthwith the paper on Tourists, and hope it won't greatly disappoint you. It would go better in an early Autumn than in a Summer number, for then readers freshly returned from touring would know whereof I speak.

Miss F. wrote me a delightful account of Mr. H. C. at the Bucknell football game and of the figure he made racing up and down with Dr. White . . . And why should you or anyone suppose that I was going to make a figure of *myself* by climbing—on my knees—the "Spanish Steps," which are every whit as unregenerate as is Dr. White? You don't know much about penitential observances!

ꙅ ꙅ ꙅ

Late in 1904, Agnes Repplier published her sixth collection, *Compromises*, fourteen papers in all, ranging from "Marriage in Fiction" to "The Spinster," and from "The Gayety of Life" to "Allegra," a moving account of Byron's pathetically appealing little daughter. *Compromises* offered as well the paper on "The Tourist" that the essayist had published not long before in *Lippincott's*.

As might be suspected, *Compromises* is replete with well-turned and telling comments. In "The Luxury of Conversation" the essayist says:

> But conversation . . . does not depend upon one or two able talkers. It is not, and never has been, a question of stars, but of a good stock company. . . .
> Perhaps the saddest proof of intellectual inertia, of our failure to meet one another with ease and understanding, is the tendency to replace conversation by story-telling. It is no uncommon thing to hear a man praised as a good talker, when he is really a good *raconteur*.

"The Spinster," interesting particularly in view of the maiden state of its author, goes beyond books and literary lore in its contentions and significance. Too many people assume, the author points out

> that there *are* no interests outside of marriage; no emotions, ambitions, nor obligations unconnected with the rearing of children. We are invited to believe that the great world, filled to its brim with pleasures and pains, duties, diversions, and responsibilities, cannot keep a woman going—even to thirty-five—without the incentive of maternity. Accustomed as we are to the expansive utterances of conjugal felicity, this seems a trifle overbearing. . . .
> It is not an easy thing to be happy. It takes all the brains, and all the soul, and all the goodness we possess. We may fail of our happiness, strive we ever so bravely; but we are less likely to fail if we measure with judgment our chances and our capabilities. To glorify spinsterhood is as ridiculous as to decry it. Intelligent women marry or remain single, because in married or in single life they see their way more clearly to content.

ರ ರ ರ

Over the months from December 1904 to November 1905, Miss Repplier offered the *Atlantic* a series of papers based on her experience at Eden Hall, the convent of her early school days. Harrison Morris congratulated her on the first, and she wrote him:

I am so very glad that you and Mrs. Morris liked Marianus. I really want to write some more convent sketches; but three people . . . have told me that it was a strange thing for a good Catholic to do. As if any one who was not a Catholic could ever know what the convent spirit was!

And because she discovered "Marianus" to be well received, at least by all readers save her three carping critics, Agnes Repplier continued the series, seven papers in all.

In December 1905 the collection was published under the title *In Our Convent Days*. "A charming human document," the critic for the *Catholic World* called the book, and continued:

It is impossible for us to renew our youth, but still it is in the power of genius to make the days of childhood live again. Miss Repplier . . . has recalled the past years and presented them with such living power that, in all the charm, the frankness, the mischievousness, and romance of childhood, they live again. . . . Miss Repplier, with praiseworthy humility, says: "Our successors to-day know more than we knew." We can but say, that if there are many pupils now in our convent schools who will attain to Miss Repplier's knowledge and power, the outlook for Catholic literature is promising indeed.

And it was of this book, one of her most popular through forty years of popularity, that Agnes Repplier was able to write with pride and pleasure:

The one book which I have written which has a Catholic background—a book designed for my own people, and which I thought would be acceptable only to those who, having shared my experiences, would also share my pleasure in recalling them —has been read with perfect good humor by a secular public.

ଚ ଚ ଚ

It was in the spring of 1906 that Mrs. Schuyler Neilson Warren of New York invited Agnes Repplier to lecture before the Philothea Society, a small group of Catholic women in that city. Mrs. Warren had been convent educated and her school too had been under the direction of the Order of the Sacred Heart. For years she had been reading Miss Repplier's essays, first in the *Catholic World* and then in the *Atlantic* and other magazines, but it was not until the publication of *In Our Convent Days* that she had been really attracted to the author. Mrs. Warren's childhood experience had been much like those of which the essayist had written. She was one for whom the book had been specifically designed. And she had not been outraged by any breach of etiquette or decorum on the part of the writer. On the contrary she had felt that the essayist had indeed captured whole and beautiful the spirit and flavor of convent life.

Agnes Repplier's lecture, "The Mission of Humor," delighted her audience that afternoon in New York. It was largely because of this lecture and as largely through the efforts of Mrs. Warren that she was introduced to the literary life of New York. She was known, certainly, by her writing long before she appeared professionally before any audience there, but she had needed an introduction. And Mrs. Warren had provided that necessary introduction.

What was perhaps even more important to Miss Repplier, out of this lecture to the Philothea Society, there grew up a firm and lasting friendship between the writer and her New York sponsor, a friendship that flourished in spite of differences of opinion on many important issues. Mrs. Warren was an ardent feminist, and Agnes Repplier cared not a whit for women's rights. Mrs. Warren fought for a cause with a display of energy that the other found impossible to muster. And, later, after Miss Repplier had discovered an issue for which she could and did expend every ounce of her energy, she and Mrs. Warren found themselves for the most part on opposite sides of the fence. But, though they might have their differences, their friendship was based upon an unassailable foundation, the Catholic-convent background they both shared.

Following the 1906 lecture, the essayist was invited to Mrs. Warren's summer home in Lenox, Massachusetts, where she delivered another talk before her hostess' friends. And it was there upon a later occasion that she met Edith Wharton. Mrs. Warren introduced the two to each other. "It is a very great pleasure to meet Mrs. Wharton," Agnes Repplier said in acknowledgment, for she felt her the author of finished and important work. "The pleasure is entirely mine," Mrs. Wharton graciously responded. "There isn't a writer in the country who hasn't been trying to achieve the perfection of style of the distinguished Miss Repplier."

ꙮ ꙮ ꙮ

A Happy Half-Century, and Other Essays appeared in 1908. The title essay begins:

There are few of us who do not occasionally wish we had been born in other days, in days for which we have some secret affinity, and which shine for us with a mellow light in the deceitful pages of history . . . For myself, I confess that the last twenty-five years of the eighteenth century and the first twenty-five years of the nineteenth make up my chosen period, and that my motive for so choosing is contemptible. It was not a time distinguished—in England at least—for wit or wisdom, for public virtues or for private charm; but it *was* a time when literary reputations were so cheaply gained that nobody needed to despair of one . . . Think of being able to find a market for an interminable essay entitled "Against Inconsistency in Our Expectations"!

Miss Burney, Mrs. Montague, Hannah Moore: this was the day of the famous "Bluestockings," the day of the ardent English literary *salon*. And this was the day selected by Agnes Repplier, who was labeled by one of her literary friends "our best Bluestocking."

"The Accursed Annual" describes a kind of gift book peculiar to the early years of the nineteenth century, a book so unreadable, the essayist contends, that the only thing that could be done with it was to give it away. "Our Great-Grandmother" tells of the innocent if useless occupations of young ladies of a bygone day: painting china, making "herbals" out of paper, weaving filigree baskets that would not hold anything, constructing Ionic temples out of Bristol board, an almost endless list.

Amusing and entertaining as these papers are, presenting as they do an extraordinary array of odd pursuits out of Agnes Repplier's "happy half-century," two other essays in the collection stand above all the rest by virtue of their cleverness and curious lore. "The Novelist" offers a delightful account of early nineteenth century novels, and sentimental and delicate in the extreme they were. Having pointed to the languishing heroines of these stories, the author turns to the men in them:

It was Miss Jane Porter who successfully transferred to a conquering hero that exquisite sensibility of soul which had erstwhile belonged to the conquering heroine,—to the Emmelines and Adelinas of fiction. Dipping her pen "in the tears of Poland," she conveyed the glittering drops to the eyes of "Thaddeus of Warsaw," whence they gush in rills,—like those of the Prisoner of Chillon's brother. Thaddeus is of such exalted virtue that strangers in London address him as "excellent young gentleman," and his friends speak of him as "incomparable young man". . . . Never do hero and heroine approach each other with such spasms of modesty as Thaddeus and Miss Beaufort. Their hearts expand with emotion, but their mutual sense of propriety keeps them remote from all vulgar understandings. In vain "Mary's rosy lips seemed to breathe balm while she spoke." In vain "her beautiful eyes shone with benevolence." The exile, standing proudly aloof, watches with bitter composure the attentions of more frivolous suitors. "His arms were folded, his hat pulled over his forehead; and his long dark eyelashes shading his downcast eyes imparted a dejection to his whole air, which wrapped her weeping heart round and round with regretful pangs." What with his lashes, and his hidden griefs, the majesty of his mournful moods, and the pleasing pensiveness of his lighter ones, Thaddeus so far eclipses his English rivals that they may be pardoned for wishing he had kept his charms in Poland . . . "Thaddeus of Warsaw" may be called the "Last of the Heroes," and take rank with the "Last of the Mohicans," the "Last of the Barons," the "Last of the Cavaliers," and all the finalities of fiction. With him died that noble race who expressed our great-grandmothers' artless ideals of perfection.

In "When Lalla Rookh Was Young" Miss Repplier makes gentle fun of the days when the Orient fired the life and literature of England and Europe generally. Moore's *Lalla Rookh* had taken everyone by storm. The Orient blossomed on every side. To illustrate one manifestation out of many, the essayist offers from "an arid wilderness of

Moorish love songs, and Persian love songs, and Circassian
love songs, and Hindu love songs" an "Arabian love song,
peerless amid its peers:

> 'Thy hair is as black as the starless sky,
>   And clasps thy neck as it loved its home;
> Yet it moves at the sound of thy faintest sigh,
>   Like the snake that lies on the white sea-foam.
>
> 'I love thee, Ibla. Thou art bright
>   As the white snow on the hills afar;
> Thy face is sweet as the moon by night,
>   And thine eye like the clear and rolling star.
>
> 'But the snow is poor and withers soon,
>   While thou art firm and rich in hope;
> And never (like thine) from the face of the moon
>   Flamed the dark eye of the antelope.' "

"The truth and accuracy of this last observation," the
writer comments dryly, "should commend the poem to all
lovers of nature."

The essay continues:

In the winter of 1821, the Berlin court presented "Lalla Rookh"
with such splendour, such wealth of detail, and such titled
actors, that Moore's heart was melted and his head was turned
(as any other heart would have been melted, and any other
head would have been turned) by the reports thereof. A Grand
Duchess of Russia took the part of Lalla Rookh; the Duke of
Cumberland was Aurungzebe; and a beautiful young sister of
Prince Radzivil enchanted all beholders as the Peri. "Nothing
else was talked about in Berlin" (it must have been a limited
conversation); the King of Prussia had a set of engravings
made of the noble actors in their costumes; and the Crown
Prince sent word to Moore that he slept always with a copy
of "Lalla Rookh" under his pillow, which was foolish, but
flattering.

But *A Happy Half-Century* stood for more than merely a collection of essays the charm of which surpasses even their impressive learning and out-of-the-way information. The year that marked its publication, 1908, approximated the end also of Agnes Repplier's half-century. Agnes Repplier was well aware that there was a certain undeniable discrepancy in dates between the one which saw the close of her half-century and that which witnessed the appearance of the collection of essays in its honor. But an acute awareness of the passing years made confession of the horrid fact all the more distasteful, and her admission she cleverly concealed in the Preface to her volume:

The half-century, whose more familiar aspects this little book is designed to illustrate, has spread its boundary lines. Nothing is so hard to deal with as a period. Nothing is so unmanageable as a date. People will be born a few years too early; they will live a few years too long. Events happen out of time. The closely linked decades refuse to be separated, and my half-century, that I thought so compact, widened imperceptibly while I wrote.

So much for confession and admission for any who might care to read between the lines. The essayist continued:

I have filled my canvas with trivial things, with intimate details, with what now seems the insignificant aspects of life. But the insignificant aspects of life concern us mightily while we live; and it is by their help that we understand the insignificant people who are sometimes reckoned of importance. A hundred years ago many men and women were reckoned of importance, at whose claims their successors today smile scornfully. Yet they and their work were woven into the tissue of things, into the warp and woof of social conditions, into the literary history of England. An hour is not too precious to waste upon them, however feeble their pretensions. Perhaps some idle reader in the future will do as much for us.

 එ එ එ

Agnes Repplier's first half-century was marked in another way than by the publication of a collection of date-encircled essays. It was just about this very time that, after twenty years of friendship, constant interchange of notes and letters, and seeking and receiving advice and encouragement, she and Harrison Morris decided he need no longer be "Mr. Morris" to her. In modest compromise, her letters to him bore for a time the greeting: "Dear Harrison Morris." But the final step was in view. And before very long "Harrison" it became.

In celebration of the event his friend paid him enviable compliment. "Neither you nor I are models of discretion in speech," she wrote. "But the older I grow, and the longer I know you, the more gladly I turn to your candour and loyalty, and straight ways, and semi-brutal directness."

A happy conclusion for a happy half-century.

CHAPTER X

The Coming of the War

1910–1914

ꙮ ꙮ

From March 1910 until the following November, Agnes Repplier and her friend Cornelia Frothingham were again in Europe. The two travelers landed at Antwerp in Belgium and spent a length of time in that city and at Bruges. Later they went to Brittany, on the Côte du Nord, and tried motoring through the pleasant countryside. But the cars went far too fast for them to see what they wanted to see even if the dust raised in the process had allowed a reasonable degree of visibility. It had been an experiment, and it had failed.

Not long after her return to Philadelphia Miss Repplier was one day greatly surprised and pleased to receive a telegram from President John Cavanaugh of Notre Dame University. It read: "For distinguished achievement in letters and a noble exemplification of Catholic womanhood, the University of Notre Dame bestows upon you the Laetare Medal, the highest honor within its gifts."

Here was distinction indeed! It was curious that first recognition of such a nature had come from her native city, usually not given to express good pleasure, and that the great Catholic university had waited some nine years to add its honors. But perhaps there were among her Roman Catholic readers certain ones who felt that Agnes Repplier was too independent to be a "good" Catholic, although Father Burke, a former editor of the *Catholic World*, declared her to be "as narrow as a toothpick."

Whatever may have stood behind the delay, that which prompted the presentation was clear enough. And it was gratifying, to say the least, to receive so high an honor.

ɔ ɔ ɔ

Of all the cities in the United States that Agnes Repplier visited, and her lecturing took her to a great many, few measured up for her to New York. She did not believe that "all Philadelphians when they die go to New York." Indeed she was rather scornful of the idea. But it was undeniable that the larger city had an infinity of interest for her. Whatever her taste of the moment, New York was in a position to satisfy it, be it social, literary, or artistic.

Mrs. Schuyler Warren headed the list of Miss Repplier's friends there, and she was a frequent visitor at the Warren home on Lexington Avenue. Rarely indeed did she pass through the city on her way to New England or Europe that she did not stop off for a short stay. Even the difference of opinion between them on the matter of woman suffrage could not mitigate Mrs. Warren's undeniably generous hospitality.

Then there was the theater. From her childhood when her father had on occasion taken her to see Booth at the old Walnut Street Theatre, she had loved the stage, And New York offered an abundance of plays. Agnes Repplier felt that, next to visiting a strange city for the first time, preferably one in Europe, there was no pleasure quite like that of waiting for the curtain to go up.

As for her literary connections, they remained largely Bostonian even though most authors had drifted to New York where the "big money" was to be found. According to Agnes Repplier, inasmuch as the publishers were in New York, "where the publishers are, there also are the crows."

But in general it was nothing more tangible than the extraordinary "go" of New York that attracted her, the uplift of spirit she felt when she had reached the city. Even the very air seemed open, especially in comparison with the shut-in atmosphere of Philadelphia.

On occasion New York made for real excitement, as, for example, the time Agnes Repplier was drawn into a controversy with Jane Addams over the question of the child actor. Augustus Thomas, the playwright and producer, and Francis Wilson, of comic opera fame, banded themselves with her against the great Miss Addams there in open debate over the matter. Agnes Repplier was convinced that the stage for children was a good and safe pursuit. Child actors do not go "to the bad," she felt, because "they know all about it."

But over and beyond her convictions, Miss Repplier heartily disliked Jane Addams, and that was reason enough for taking up cudgels against her. The essayist declared she never cared for "good" people, only tolerant ones, and Miss Addams was, as everyone knew, as "good as gold." She was rather a power in the land, the author asserted, laying down the law with incontrovertible authority and seeing to it that everybody followed it. Although Agnes Repplier knew Jane Addams only slightly, she felt that the prominent social worker despised her, and she was rather pleased at being so singled out for attention.

ᵓ ᵓ ᵓ

Horace Howard Furness, one of Miss Repplier's most amiable literary friends, died on August 13, 1912. The essayist felt in his passing an irreparable loss, for he had been companion and critic, friend and fellow writer. And above all this he had loved cats with a love equaled only by her own.

In an *Atlantic* paper of the following November, Agnes Repplier wrote of Dr. Furness:

His rare powers of conversation, his marvelous memory, his information . . . his unfailing humor, his beautiful vocabulary, rich yet precise, his swift light sentences, conveying important conclusions, all made him the most enjoyable of companions. . . .

A man of exquisite charity, speaking evil of none; a man of indestructible courtesy, whose home was open to his friends, whose scant leisure was placed at their disposal, whose kindness enveloped them like sunshine; yet none the less a man whose reserves—unsuspected by many—were proof against all; a past master of the art of hiding his soul, "addicted to silent pleasures, accessible to silent pains."

Six weeks before his death, being then in perfect health, he wrote to me: "My grave yawns at my feet. I look down into it, and very snug and comfortable it seems." In the gallant acceptance of life and death lies all that gives worth to man.

ᵓ ᵓ ᵓ

Nineteen-twelve saw the publication of *Americans and Others,* a collection of fourteen essays, five of which were printed for the first time. The volume is particularly interesting for several reasons, not the least of which is that it contrasts so strikingly with the one that was to follow.

In *Americans and Others*, Agnes Repplier exhibited her usual wit and felicitous ingenuity of phrase. Here appeared for the first time "The Mission of Humor," a transcript of her popular lecture. Dealing in the main with the American brand of humor, it branches into other forms—British, Latin, Teutonic—and concludes with a memorable note on the man "destitute of humor" who is "often to be respected, sometimes to be feared, and always—if possible—to be avoided."

Miss Repplier enjoyed lecturing on "The Mission of Humor" because it gave her opportunity to tell entertaining stories. And there are a number of excellent ones in the essay, one of the most amusing being that about an American usher at one of Matthew Arnold's lectures who opened the door for a late-comer with the whispered warning: "Will you please make as little noise as you can, sir? The audience is asleep."

"The Temptations of Eve," "The Customary Correspondent," "The Condescension of Borrowers," "The Grocer's Cat," and, best of all perhaps, though distinctly Philadelphian in its point, "The Greatest of These Is Charity:" these are in Agnes Repplier's true vein, half-serious, half-mocking, clever, entertaining. But "The Nervous Strain" marks a new note of seriousness in the essayist's writings. "The Estranging Sea," with its somewhat barbed handling of the British attitude toward anything beyond the Atlantic, and "The Chill of Enthusiasm," a sophisticated condemnation of those who allow themselves to become enthusiasts, carry with them a seemingly palpable contradiction of what in a few years' time was to be Agnes Repplier's own attitude. With the coming of the war, the writer was to forget all about her criticism of ways British and quite overlook her condemnation of emotional ardor.

Ꭷ Ꭷ Ꭷ

Nineteen-twelve ended with a plaintive appeal to Harrison Morris: "You know everything and everybody," Agnes Repplier wrote him: "Please tell me what is the American Social Science Association, of which I have been asked to become a member. It has dues and gives medals. Shall I accept?" To which she added a postscript: "I see by looking again at the card the name of the thing is the National Institute of Social Sciences. What are social sciences?"

Ꭷ Ꭷ Ꭷ

On June 5, 1913, Agnes Repplier wrote to Mrs. Warren:

I take my flight northward on the 16th carrying my convalescing niece Mrs. Witmer with me.* The convalescing Cornelia left a week ago with her nurse. And may Heaven see us all safe through the next three months!

Never has any work of mine attracted half as much attention as the paper on the Cost of Sentiment [*Atlantic Monthly*, May 1913]. I am still deluged with letters concerning it. One from a big corporation lawyer, one from the president of the Philadelphia and Reading Railroad, saying that at a meeting of prominent men in New York, it had been referred to and praised by all. Think of that, my lamb! I am trying hard to make the light minded young editor of the "Atlantic" [Ellery Sedgwick] recognize my true value. He only laughs (we are

* Emma Repplier Witmer, daughter of George Repplier, Agnes Repplier's half brother. The wife of the psychologist Lightner Witmer, Mrs. Witmer owns a summer home at Chester, Nova Scotia.

good friends) and says he has heard the article most cordially abused.

"The Cost of Modern Sentiment" is a scathing denunciation of the social and philanthropic feelings of the day. "The issues with which our modern sentiment chiefly concerns itself are the conditions of labor, the progress of women, the social evil, and—for the past two years—the overwhelming question of peace and war." The essayist found this sentiment often "a revolt from authority, which, to the sentimentalist, seems forever despotic; and this revolt," she adds, "or rather this easy disregard of authority, is fatal to the noblest efforts of humanitarianism."

Perhaps with such a reformer as her friend Mrs. Warren in mind, Agnes Repplier continued:

The women of wealth and position who from time to time fling themselves with ardour into the cause of striking shirt-waist-makers and garment-makers are always well intentioned, but not always well advised. In so far as they uphold the strikers in what are often just and reasonable demands, they do good work; and the substantial aid they give is sweetened by the spirit in which it is given—the sense of fellowfeeling with their kind. But there is no doubt that one of the lessons taught at such times to our foreign-born population is that the laws of our country may be disregarded with impunity.

Jane Addams, Chesterton, Annie Besant all come in for their share of castigation in this essay which, because of its note of distinctly contemporary social consciousness is far removed from what Agnes Repplier's readers had come to expect from her. Little wonder railroad presidents and corporation lawyers should take it up and hail its author as a new Daniel come to judgment. Little wonder, too, that some of the followers of the *Atlantic* should "cordially abuse" it.

And little wonder that Mrs. Warren, that summer of 1913, should suddenly shift the subject of her correspondence with her essayist friend. The staunch New York social reformer, in the face of her friend's diametrically opposed opinions, sensibly ignored her own social convictions and instead wrote in praise of the works of Francis Thompson. Possibly innocently enough she quoted Mrs. Meynell and others in support of her point of view.

But Agnes Repplier was in a rebellious mood. She wrote a letter of reproach to Mrs. Warren. Later she regretted her haste, and said as much to her New York friend, though she could not back down on her outspoken beliefs:

What an unsatisfactory friend I am, Alice darling! I hate to make you boil and let off steam. I want you to be happy in my friendship. And yet I blunder sadly. Now listen! I like Francis Thompson's work quite as much as you do. The volume you sent me is full of beautiful things: "Shelley," "Paganism," and the very curious and tense paper on "Health and Holiness." I brought the book here [Chester, Nova Scotia] with me, and Cornelia Frothingham and I read it together . . .

But Alice *dear*, you cannot frighten me away from my point of view by shaking Mr. Wyndham or Mrs. Meynell at me. I have not studied English prose for thirty years without knowing whereof I speak. I have not loved and honored chastity of style, and the stern labour of the file, without learning to discriminate between what is perfect and what is imperfect, between what is good and what is best. On this point I trust myself. In the matter of verse, I am as ignorant as my neighbor. It is not my stamping ground.

For the moment "The Cost of Modern Sentiment" and all the favorable and unfavorable comment that followed in its wake were forgotten. For both Mrs. Warren and Agnes Repplier, a discussion of the value of Francis Thompson—even with some disagreement—was safer ground.

From French Village, Nova Scotia, where Miss Repplier had gone for a few weeks, she wrote to Mrs. Warren who had lately lamented her own being in Spain:

It is droll we should both be in places we do not like, and writing disconsolate letters to each other. . . . I thought when I was in Spain, that everybody had quite perfect manners—not better than the Romans who are also perfect, but certainly as good, so composed, serious and kind. Even when the young men in Seville flirted shamelessly with the children [Sarah and Agnes Boone], they were never offensive. They knew how to go about it . . .

A week later there came a note from Chester; in it the essayist complained to Mrs. Warren:

I have had no letter from you in ten days, and it is a grievous gap. But the workings of the Nova Scotian mail are beyond all reckoning. One letter of importance took thirteen days to travel from Philadelphia to French Village. One that I registered never reached Boston at all. It perished of its registry on the way. Even St. Anthony fails to carry the letters so fondly confided to him through such a perilous district. . . .
I'm back in Chester, and more in love than ever with my niece's tranquil and beautiful abode. Five weeks and over in a country hotel have taught me the worth of my blessings. In another week I take the beastly journey south. It is cold and stormy on this strip of sea, and at night the little house rocks under the gale. Having never blown over in the past, we trust blindly for the future. . . .

From Magnolia, the old argument over Francis Thompson plus the additional attraction of John Millington Synge, who seems to have worked his way into the discussion, was given its final dismissal: "So you think Mrs. Meynell a better judge of English prose than I am?" asks Agnes Repplier of her friend. "Well, we won't quarrel over *that;* nor over

Mr. Synge's plays, which can hardly support the weight
of disagreement; nor even, I hope," the essayist could not
forebear to add, "over the suffrage, which is a pretty serious problem, and made none the less problematic by the
coming of the Pankhurst to our shores. In fact she is painfully embarrassing the 'cause.' Her allies don't dare to turn
her down, and don't think her any help, and are praying to
be delivered from their friends."

The matter thus settled, Agnes Repplier continued in a
less caustic vein:

Having spent the summer in archaic simplicity, I am winding
it up with a very gay visit to the Brinleys, who have a house
full of people, and many more coming in to lunch or dine.
Also I am trying to see all my friends in Gloucester, and to
spend nights with some of them; and these things are made no
easier by the fact that it has rained four days with unswerving diligence and fervour; and bids fair, as far as I can see, to
keep on the rest of the month. Before that time I shall be back
in town and at work.

Miss Repplier wrote Mrs. Warren about a week after
the letter from Magnolia:

It was simply beastly to pass through New York on my way
home, and know how far away you were. I could never have
believed it possible to miss anyone as much as I miss you when
I get off my car and see in fancy your dear familiar figure
standing by the gate. I wish you would come home instead
of moving blithely from foreign town to town.

I wound up my summer with a little heavenly visit to Caroline Sinkler* at Eastern Point, Gloucester. She and Cecilia
Beaux† have beautiful little houses close to one another. Her
house was full of guests . . . I did have such a good time,
Alice, so gay and so *clever!* Not one dull moment anywhere . . .

ꙮ ꙮ ꙮ

* Of Philadelphia, a friend of the essayist's.
† The well-known artist, also a friend of the essayist's.

On January 4, 1914, Dr. S. Weir Mitchell died. But the death of this second of Agnes Repplier's Philadelphia literary friends was not the cause of sorrow such as Horace Furness' passing had brought. Mitchell had been a friend in every sense but never the companion the Shakespearean scholar had been.

What may as well have lessened the sense of loss in the death of the doctor by its centering the focus with increasing intensity on other matters was the fact that this was the year 1914, not 1912. And an infinity of difference lay between the two.

Not many years earlier Agnes Repplier's friend Cornelia Frothingham had tried to generate a sense of proper patriotism in the essayist. At the time at least her effort brought little result. Miss Repplier had tossed the crusade aside with a few clever remarks. A patriotic tourist was more a matter for laughter than a source of inspiration. She could be proud of her country, but pride did not necessarily mean a constant display of emotional effusion. There was something evangelistic about a person given to an obvious show of love of country, something evangelistic that smacked of the common and vulgar.

But years before Cornelia Frothingham, Agnes Repplier had felt it an exceedingly difficult business to give herself over wholeheartedly to some cause—any cause. That was why Mrs. Howe had loomed as so admirable—even if formidable—a person. Agnes Repplier's sense of humor prevented her from taking herself with the seriousness necessary for devotion to a cause. It was impossible not to see oneself at times at least as just a trifle ridiculous.

In no sense of the word could Miss Repplier have been called a feminist. She was not interested in women's rights.

That had been largely her quarrel with Mrs. Warren. Such as the world is, she felt, men are responsible for it. Good or bad, it has been their doing. But more than that, it will be of their doing, she believed. If men are so generous to us, she would tell Mrs. Warren, as ever to give us a voice in the running of this world, it is only because they do not fear us very much. They know that they will hold the strings. "And personally," she would add, "I prefer to have someone look after me than have to look after myself."

It was through White that Agnes Repplier met the former President of the United States, Theodore Roosevelt. She found him "blundering perhaps but as honest as the sun." He could have won a bird off a bough, she commented. And, of course, he was a great admirer of the French diplomat and critic Jusserand. That alone, as far as she was concerned, was recommendation enough.

Theodore Roosevelt may not have approved entirely of the essayist. Once he said to her, "You're no good as a partisan for you never go the whole way." At the beginning at least she preferred to sit for the most part as comfortably as she could on the fence.

But Roosevelt knew that in Agnes Repplier he had found a person whom the public would read. She had a following, a following made up of people of taste and intellectual maturity.

The situation was in no degree Machiavellian. Miss Repplier certainly knew what she was about. And she had never been one to do that which she did not want to do. From her earliest school days, she had acted mainly on her own impulse, not as the result of any compulsion brought to bear by some outsider. But perhaps in the present instance she was somewhat flattered by the thought that she and her writing could be of assistance to this charming if blustering former President.

That White not only added his consent but was most anxious that she comply with Roosevelt's suggestions made Agnes Repplier doubly willing. It was in the doctor's hands that she had trusted her life. Surely he would be as wise now as he had been then. Her political life, if such indeed it could be called, would be safe with him.

But over and beyond Theodore Roosevelt and White, there was Agnes Irwin. In her biography of Miss Irwin, Agnes Repplier wrote:

In November, 1914, Madame Vandervelde, the wife of Belgium's ablest statesman, came to the United States to ask help for her ruined countrymen. She was warmly received (at least on the Atlantic Seaboard), and her appeal met with a generous response. The restraint she imposed upon herself, the absence of all denunciation, which she felt would be out of place in a country theoretically neutral, was not lost upon her hearers. They may have found it difficult to cherish within their own breasts a negative and skeptical neutrality, but they were none the less grateful for her forbearance. Indeed, a plain statement of facts needed no comment. Miss Irwin's wholehearted interest in her work is evidenced by a letter written to a former pupil of whose sympathy she felt sure:

"You are going to write an open letter for the Vandervelde meeting, are you not? If you would do it! But I know you will, and it is going to be a great help. I find that many persons who are willing and eager to aid know nothing about Madame Vandervelde, or her husband, or what she is trying to do. A few words from you would be very enlightening. But why am I writing this to you who know so exactly what to say and how to say it? Only because I care so much about the unhappy Belgians; I also care so much about your help in the matter.

It is one of the bright spots in this darkened sky that you are so staunch an advocate for what must always seem to me the right side of things. Seem to me! I believe it *is!*"

A month after writing this agitated and distressful letter Miss Irwin died. In the interval she said to this same friend (and it sounded as though she had some premonition of her death): "You will always do what you can for the cause, won't you? I know it seems to you so little as to be hardly worth doing. But it is at least the raising of a voice, and someone listens."

Agnes Repplier was the "former pupil" to whom Miss Irwin had addressed herself on both occasions.

"War is a rough trade," Miss Repplier had commented in *Books and Men*, more than twenty-five years before, "and if we choose to call names, it is as easy any time to say 'butcher' as 'hero.' " Butcher, hero: it all depended on the point of view and on in which camp one found oneself. If in after years Miss Repplier was to come to believe that "really and truly Helen wasn't worth it," in the year 1914 the question was not of ultimate value but of immediate price. Roosevelt and the heroes had far more appeal for the essayist just then than did Wilson and, if scarcely the "butchers," something less than the heroes.

ᔕ ᔕ ᔕ

In an *Atlantic* paper entitled "The Repeal of Reticence," Agnes Repplier hit hard at a certain type of reformer. Her antagonism for the "sex educator" was so strong that it quite pushed her concern over the coming war from her consideration:

There is nothing new about the Seven Deadly Sins. They are as old as humanity. There is nothing mysterious about them.

They are easier to understand than the Cardinal Virtues . . . Knowledge is the cry. Crude, undigested knowledge, without limit and without reserve. Give it to the girls, give it to the boys, give it to the children. No other force is taken into account by the visionaries who—in defiance, or in ignorance, of history—believe that evil understood is evil conquered. . . . *

For the most part, the essay is singularly devoid of that mark of distinction usually associated with the author's writing: literary lore. Brieux and his *Les Avaries*, presented in this country as "Damaged Goods," is granted its "stern warning to the pleasure-loving world," and Stevenson is mentioned briefly. But these are exceptions here. This is a paper dealing with a contemporary problem. It does not grow out of the browsings of fifty well-read years. It is sharp and brittle and very much to the point. But there is a certain undeniable harshness about it as well. It is as if its author were here rehearsing her talents so that when the game of poison darts that was to be played for keeps over the question of war should begin, she might not be caught inexperienced.

"I send you the March [1914] 'Atlantic' with my last paper in it," Agnes Repplier wrote Mrs. Warren. "*Not* for young people to read." The paper was "The Repeal of Reticence." The essayist no doubt sincerely felt that Mrs. Warren would be interested. But more than that, Miss Repplier took a delight in teasing her New York friend in the matter of reform. Sex education may not have been among Mrs. Warren's usual interests, but "wayward girls" were not too far removed.

Agnes Repplier informed Mrs. Warren:

* A seeming contradiction of Agnes Repplier's point of view in the Jane Addams-stage child controversy.

I wrote you last from Atlantic City, where I was scrambling through something akin to convalescence. If I did not get well, I at least gained enough strength to go to New York, lecture, go to New England, lecture, and wind up in Boston. . . . Boston is even more mad about prostitutes than Philadelphia and New York. She talks about little else, tells blood-curdling stories, which bear every evidence of ripe invention, and the Dedham Club at which I lectured had actually had a real live "white slave" (at least she claimed to be one, but she may have been only bragging) to address them last month. Now how can a respectable old lady like myself compete with such an attraction! I felt the tameness of virtue. . . .

Mrs. Warren was amused by Agnes Repplier's fanciful exaggerations—and by another letter to her from the essay- ist that concluded: "What do you think of the 'Plays and Players' Club'* asking me to act in a translation of Brieux's comedies. I said I could not act. They said that did not mat- ter. On my soul, I expect to be asked some day to dance on a tight rope for the benefit of the militants."

Little danger of Mrs. Warren's so urging her friend to perform. Besides, the two, while never losing sight of each other, nor allowing indeed their mutual love and respect to diminish to any degree, were to go quite divergent ways over the question of Wilson and the war. And that question would permit of precious little delay. A very few months, and the Eastern Hemisphere—or much of it at least—would be irrevocably embroiled.

* A Philadelphia amateur theatrical group.

CHAPTER XI

The War and After

1914–1919

ಲ ಲ

The spring and summer of 1914 found Agnes Repplier in Europe, this time accompanied by a Philadelphia friend of long standing, Christine Platt. The travelers were warned to be careful where they went, but although they had no real difficulty—and certainly were not afraid of what might happen to them—before long they decided to come home. Jaunting now in Europe, even though it might be accomplished with little inconvenience, was scarcely the proper pursuit, they felt. Besides, as Miss Repplier said, William White was calling her, urging her return so that she might come to the assistance of those who were of the opinion that war in Europe is war in the Western Hemisphere as well.

Once home, the writer set to work with fine fury. She and White collaborated on a pamphlet titled *Germany and Democracy, the Real Issue, the Views of Two Average Americans, a Reply to Doctor Dernburg.* A year later *Germany and Democracy* was republished in England and was translated into French, German, and Dutch.

For weeks the two worked over the composing of the pamphlet. White wrote very rapidly whereas Agnes Repplier took her usual infinite pains, working slowly and carefully. The essayist found her collaborator a very exacting person—in matters of content at least. It seemed he objected to everything she put down. But she had the satisfaction of knowing that she wrote better than he even though her repeatedly reminding him of the fact made absolutely no impression on him.

As it turned out, about two thirds of *Germany and Democracy* belonged to White and the remaining one third to Agnes Repplier. Her friends found it an easy business to pick out her parts. They were clearly literary whereas his contributions were not. But the cause being what it was, Miss Repplier had no objections to being harnessed with her medical friend. Some time later she wrote to Mrs. Warren of her association with White: "We are working very hard, he and I, and his inroads on my time would be frightful if I did not love it so."

Germany and Democracy, as its full title states, is a reply to a Dr. Dernburg, who, in the *Saturday Evening Post,* had recently presented the views of Germany on the war. Agnes Repplier and White took up Dernburg's arguments point by point, attacking the German apologist's veracity at every turn. The collaborators were particularly incensed over the plight of Belgium:

Germany's campaign in Belgium . . . is an affront to honor, a deathblow to integrity, a denial of just rights. It is a triumph and exposition of brute force, of a life morally worthy of no man. It is a rejection of civilization, and of all that civilization implies. It is an abrupt return to savage and elemental conditions.

They were not averse to hard-hitting sarcasm along the way:

In good truth, *all* German apologists, writing to enlist the sympathy of Americans, should be made to understand the value of an understatement. If they would claim a little less, we could believe a great deal more. If they did not whitewash so vigorously, we should not suspect so much dirt.

Miss Repplier's hand is clearly seen in certain passages. "The Prussian soldier, as painted by Herr Albert (in a paper in the *Atlantic Monthly*) is what old-fashioned people used to call 'too good for earth.' Shelley's apostrophe to Emilia Viviani, 'Seraph of Heaven! too gentle to be human,' is the only description which can be found to fit him."

Germany and Democracy was not Agnes Repplier's only writing bent on wakening the United States to the cause of war, but it was one that most surely had grown out of Miss Irwin's urgent pleas.

ɔ ɔ ɔ

Early in 1915, the essayist wrote to Mrs. Warren: "The death of Miss Sophy Irwin,* four weeks after the death of Miss Agnes, has plunged this city in gloom. I was so unhappy about Miss Agnes that there was no grief left for Miss Sophy; but it means the closing of a charming and brilliant house, the turning of a page in our social history. . . . "

Agnes Repplier's association with Agnes Irwin had lasted over more than forty years. Even though the start had not been particularly propitious, the dismissal from the school

* Sister to Agnes Irwin.

was to be graciously forgotten in view of the recalcitrant pupil's later accomplishment. Miss Irwin could not joke about what had been so froward an affront to her disciplinary methods. But at least she harbored no resentment.

Boston, lecturing, Europe, and at present the war: in all these Miss Irwin had guided her former pupil. Little wonder then that Agnes Repplier was to feel with the death of her mentor and guide that a very real source of certainty had gone out of her life. Her parents, Horace Howard Furness, Mitchell, and now Miss Irwin and Miss Sophy. The old world was fast fading, and though the new was exciting enough, it could never expect to match the old for charm and real worth.

Miss Irwin had lived long enough to see the Battle of the Marne, the decisive nature of which was not then wholly understood. She died before the sinking of the *Lusitania* had decreased the scanty stock of human hope and happiness. . . . Her life had never been easy, but it had been reasonably happy, reasonably triumphant, teeming with interest, and nobly led. Always she had accepted it as both gift and burden, imposing many responsibilities and bringing much delight. Always she had "reigned within herself," and her soul was free.

Thus Agnes Repplier wrote some years later in her biography of Agnes Irwin.

ꙮ ꙮ ꙮ

Mrs. Warren was in Europe the summer of 1915. From Salem, Massachusetts, Agnes Repplier wrote her:

Don't think that you will gain peace of mind by returning to the United States! Agnes Klots [nee Boone] is coming over in the autumn, filled with the same hope. But here we are torn with contentions, troubled beyond measure by the toying of

the Administration with grave issues, and infinitely distressed
by the German successes. You may find some distraction in
the suffrage; the suffragists are as interested in the Rev. Anna's
yellow motor car as if there were no war in Europe; but you
have been too long with the contending nations to take up
small matters cheerfully. . . .

And as Mrs. Warren was in Europe longing to return
to the sanity of the United States, Agnes Repplier was at
home, provoked beyond measure because she could not go
abroad. "Next month [Dr. White] goes to France to arrange the Philadelphia Ward of the American Ambulance
Hospital," she wrote Mrs. Warren. "I wish he would take
me with him; but he says it wouldn't be proper, which is
nonsense—à mon âge."

ꙑ ꙑ ꙑ

In 1916 the essayist published *Counter-Currents*, a collection of nine papers, all of which had first appeared in the
Atlantic over the preceding three years. Five of the essays
deal with the war, and in only one of the nine is it not referred to either directly or indirectly. Agnes Repplier had
found her "cause."

"It is strange to glance back upon a day when we had so
little to trouble us that we could vex our souls over feudalism and fiction; when—in the absence of serious problems—
we could raise pronunciation or spelling into a national
issue," Agnes Repplier wrote with something like assumed
nostalgia in her paper on "Americanism." She regretted
the war; every right-thinking person did. But here was an
opportunity to use a flail with far more determination than
she had ever used it before. Here was an opportunity to be
properly caustic.

In January, 1915, the month Agnes Repplier first published "Christianity and War," the United States appeared to her to be "a nation smugly content with its own safety, living its round of pleasures, giving freely of its superfluity, and growing rich with the vast increase of its industries and trade." "We are safe for a little while," she wrote a few months later in "Women and War." "Let us stand cringing by, and see injustice done." We were the "worms warranted not to turn."

And Christianity was made to yield its seeming justification. If "it is a common saying that the New Testament affords no vindication of war, which is natural enough, not being penned as a manual for nations," still to Agnes Repplier "to speak loosely of war as unchristian is to ignore not only the Christian right, but the Christian duty, which rests with every nation and with every man to protect that of which nation and man are the lawful protectors."

As for the feminists and their perennial question of suffrage, Miss Repplier took delight in telling them that "the only agreeable thing to be recorded in connection with Europe's sudden and disastrous war is the fact that people have stopped talking about women, and begun to talk about men." She gave women three precepts by which to live their war-directed lives: intelligence, "reasonable modesty," and self-sacrifice. As for the first, "they should have some accurate knowledge of what has happened, some clear understanding of the events they so glibly discuss." As for the second, the essayist believed a woman is terribly hampered by a conviction of her own goodness, and that she is no more sensitive than many men to the horrors of war. The third scarcely needed explanation.

THE WAR AND AFTER

In the most esteemed of his advisory poems, Mr. Longfellow recommends his readers to be "up and doing," and at the same time learn "to labour and to wait." Having, all of us, imbibed these sentiments in their harmonious setting when we were at school, we have, all of us, endeavored for many months to put such conflicting precepts into practice.

Thus the essay on "Waiting" begins, as direct an attack on the policy of the Wilson administration as Agnes Repplier was to offer.

Here and elsewhere Wilson received his share of invective. Miss Repplier wrote in "Women and War":

In the genial reign of Henry the Eighth, a docile Parliament passed, at the desire of the King, an "Act to Abolish Diversity of Opinion." President Wilson, less despotic, has recommended something of the same order as a mental process, a soul-smothering, harmony-preserving anodyne. It is called neutrality, and if it has failed to save us from shameful insults and repeated wrongs, it has kept us fairly quiet under provocation.

And certainly it was of Wilson that Miss Repplier was thinking when she wrote : "Only an American can understand the cumulative anger as affront is added to affront, and the slow lapse of time brings us neither redress nor redemption." She had refused Roosevelt when he had asked her to write directly against the administration, true. But this, apparently, was to her completely nonpartisan, a matter of larger issues than mere disagreement with a policy. Quite alone or aided and abetted by Roosevelt, White, and the ghost of Agnes Irwin—it made little difference in the final result—Agnes Repplier had worked herself up into a fury of indignation.

Bryan was perhaps the most belabored of all the essayist's antagonism-arousers, both publicly and privately. In a let-

ter to Mrs. Warren, she wrote of an Authors' League dinner in New York. "It was very amusing, and I met a lot of
people; but the committee made the fatal mistake of invit-
ing Mr. Bryan, and he consumed so much time pouring out
platitudes that I had to leave without hearing the best of the
speakers." "A pastmaster of infelicitous argument," she
called him. And she declared that, until she had seen the
man, she doubted the good Lord would make anyone so
ugly.

Although among the forefront of interventionists before
the United States was drawn into the conflict, once the war
was over, the older, more natural isolationism was to settle
down on Agnes Repplier as well as on many of her friends.
Wilson and the League were to be quite as great anathema
to her as Wilson and neutrality. In "Women and War"
(May 1915), she had written: "There is everything to be
hoped for in the sane and just settlement of national dis-
putes by an international tribunal . . . " By 1919, she
seems to have quite abandoned the idea.

As for *Counter-Currents*, Miss Repplier fell only once
in its pages into the same kind of bathos she so abhorred in
the pacifists. "The Lusitania children, lying in pitiful rows
to await identification in Queenstown, little meek and sodden corpses buffeted out of comeliness by the waves . . . "
Meek and sodden corpses: surely this is as obvious an appeal
to the emotions as any she railed against. Then as now, what
was honest sentiment and what was not was much a matter
of opinion.

But the war-provoked essays in *Counter-Currents* are of
less permanent value than the others in the volume, and
there is enough here in the essayist's more usual vein to pro-

vide delight along with penetrating observation as in her
work before the war began. "The Repeal of Reticence"
for one, attacking the unnecessary exploiting of sex problems in literature and in public addresses, deals brilliantly
with a problem even more pressing today than thirty years
ago. And in "Popular Education" Agnes Repplier wields
the flail in a fashion to make "educators" squirm and the
"educated" cry, "Encore!"

"This is so emphatically the children's age," the essay
begins, "that a good many of us are beginning to thank
God we were not born in it." Miss Repplier then tells of the
First International Eugenics Congress held in London in
1912 at which an Italian delegate stated that twenty-seven
is "the best age for parentage." "But," the writer asks, "how
bend all the complicated conditions of life to meet an arbitrary date; and how remain twenty-seven long enough to
insure satisfactory results? The vast majority of babies,"
she concludes, "will have to put up with being born when
their time comes, and make the best of it."

The education of my childhood was embryonic. The education of to-day is exhaustive. The fact the schoolchild of to-day
does not seem to know any more than we knew in the dark
ages, is a side issue with which I have no concern. But as I look
back, I can now see plainly that the few things little girls
learned were admirably adapted for one purpose—to make us
parts of a whole, which whole was the family. I do not mean
that there was any expression to this effect. "Training for ma-
ternity" was not a phrase in vogue; and the short views of life,
more common then than now, would have robbed it of its
savour. "Training for citizenship" had, so far as we were concerned, no meaning whatsoever. A little girl was a little girl,
not the future mother of the race, or the future saviour of the
Republic. One thing at a time.

"If Saint Augustine, who was punished when he was a little lad because he loved to play, could see how childish pastimes are dignified in the pedagogy of the twentieth century," the author comments, "he would no longer say that 'playing is the business of childhood.' He would know that it is the supremely important business, the crushing responsibility of the pedagogue. Nothing is too profound, nothing too subtle to be evolved from a game or a toy."

"Popular Education," if not so literary as the majority of Agnes Repplier's prewar papers, is every bit as clever. It deals with a current theme, as does "The Repeal of Reticence," quite as up to date as the war essays. But because education is a perennial problem—which war, it is to be devoutly hoped, is not—the essay rings almost as true thirty years after its publication as it did when first it appeared.

ↄ ↄ ↄ

Whatever else it may have done, the European war provided the Contemporary Club of Philadelphia with an infinity of topics for discussion. November 9, 1914, brought "Aspects of the European War at Close Range," and the following January "What Can America Do to Bring About Peace," a meeting at which Agnes Repplier herself was a speaker.

The next Contemporary Club season was to start with a discussion of "A Year of War—What It Has Taught Us" with Norman Angell and Dr. Kuno Francke heading the list of speakers. Harrison Morris was president of the club that year, and he wrote to Agnes Repplier asking her if she would take part in the debate with Angell and Francke. It would be great fun, he insisted, a real opportunity for her to express her beliefs.

The essayist fumed over her friend's letter. She wrote in burning reply:

I can't do it! Not for love or money! The war is not to me a matter for cheerful debate. It is an ever-present horror. There is no "great fun" to be extracted from it.

I wouldn't listen to a flabby ass like Norman Angell for a hundred dollars, and I wouldn't appear on the platform with Kuno Francke for a thousand. Do you suppose Dr. White would *argue* with Francke? He'd knock him down, which I can't do, and that would be all the fun you'd get out of him.

You see, Harrison, Germany is not only the enemy of Europe, she is our enemy as well. She has injured us deeply, and offered no redress. Why should we invite her representatives to gabble in our ears?

Harrison Morris was understandably upset over the matter. He was afraid that Agnes Repplier might have misunderstood him entirely, that perhaps she even wondered as to his sense of patriotism. After all, he was president of the club, and it was his responsibility that Angell and Francke were to be speakers. He sent his old friend a hasty note of explanation.

But there was no need for him to fear. Miss Repplier had "slept on" her letter of the day before and was already experiencing some qualms over its harshness. She offered apology in far calmer tones:

Of course I understood that your "great fun" referred to the smashing of German arguments, and I never doubted where your sympathies lay. You are sensible to be able to meet Germans, and to listen to them. I can't. Since the Lusitania was sunk, their presence on a platform insults me. The Contemporary Club is a good athletic field; but this is not a sporting proposition. . . . Forgive my "flaming" letter.

ᔕ ᔕ ᔕ

Easter Sunday, 1916, Agnes Repplier wrote to Harrison Morris refusing his invitation to dinner. Her friend White was dying, and she could not even think of a dinner party in view of such a tragic extremity.

It was curious that the doctor had come into her life to save it for her, and now he was slipping out though she felt she still needed him. For the past four years out of fifteen or so of their friendship, he had become the force behind most of her writing and thinking. He had introduced her to Roosevelt, and he had helped her with her papers in behalf of intervention and the Allies.

But White had been more than mere political adviser to her. He had been the happy companion of many an evening of pleasure when he and his wife and a few others would join in nothing more out of the way than two or three hours of good conversation—"the most soothing of occupations," as Agnes Repplier had once called talking.

This was a loss comparable, really, only to that when Miss Irwin had died. The deaths of her parents were closer sorrows, but the deaths of her wise and helpful friends went even deeper. And White's perhaps more subtly than Agnes Irwin's. Though she admired men as a class and preferred greatly their company to that of women, White had stood somehow apart from the others. She would miss him in many ways.

ᔕ ᔕ ᔕ

Louis Repplier was past fifty-seven years old. And for better than half of those years he had been Agnes Repplier's charge. His schooling, necessarily slight because of his constant poor health, had fitted him for little in the way of work.

After the loss of the Repplier fortune, Louis Repplier had gone to work in his father's commission office with duties hardly more responsible than those of an office boy. He ran errands and kept simple books for the business. He did what he could, but his ability was limited.

Since the death of their father, Louis Repplier had maintained the merest pretense of a job at the Philadelphia General Hospital. It kept him occupied, but it did not go very far toward supporting him. That fell to Agnes Repplier, who, it must be said, never begrudged him the expense involved. Louis had been bequeathed to her, as she would say, by her mother. He was her special obligation, her special care. She never thought of him as a burden.

But sometimes her brother was an embarrassment to her. Once she was accused of not taking care of him. Louis, people said, looked like a beggar. She wrote to Harrison Morris in considerable concern. Never, she declared, had she been so prosperous as she was now. She received five to ten cents a word for her writing, and had more work than she could possibly handle. Certainly she was in a position to help her brother. "To dress him cleanly and decently would be a bagatelle," she wrote her good friend. "But he is unhappily unhinged in this regard. I can do nothing with him."

ꙮ ꙮ ꙮ

For almost six years the majority of Agnes Repplier's writings had been motivated in one way or another by the war. Either she had been pointing out the—to her—plain duty of the United States, intervention, or she had been passing asides in other matters that put her beliefs just as plainly. "Waiting," "The Privilege of Being Murdered," "War and the Child," "The American Essay in War Time," to pick a few at random of the more obvious, stem directly from the war. All but the last were written and published before the United States entered. Bitter, caustic, even cruel, these papers were Agnes Repplier's contribution, her payment for friendship with Theodore Roosevelt, her ticket of admission in the anti-Wilsonian band wagon. Though for all this, they were honest expressions of an honest if somewhat stridently determined opinion.

But others of her essays, only vaguely referring to the war or hinting at it in the most indirect of ways, revealed all the good humor and brilliance of expression of the happy papers before Germany turned open belligerent and Agnes Repplier became crusader in a cause. In "The Virtuous Victorian," for example, there is as deft a criticism of both Victorian literature and twentieth century art as one could possibly wish for: "A pre-Raphaelite Corsair languished as visibly as a pre-Raphaelite seraph. He could be bowled over by a worsted ball; but he was at least more vigorous and more ruddy than a cubist. One doubted his seared conscience and his thousand crimes; but not his ability to walk unassisted downstairs."

Becky Sharp's "successors," writes Agnes Repplier, already weary of the psychologically probing clinical novel, "sin exhaustively, and with a lamentable lack of *esprit*."

As for feminists, the essayist insists that "women . . . are only the equals of men," quoting in support of her contention a Cornish adage to the effect that "Lads are as good as wenches when they are washed."

Some of Miss Repplier's readers may have been disappointed when, at the bidding of her conscience and her friends White and Roosevelt, she had taken up cudgels in behalf of war. Some doubted that she would ever turn again to her former literary pursuits free from world-embracing convictions. Some went so far as to suspect that she ever could return to the old and delightful ways. But "The Virtuous Victorian," "Money," and even "Cruelty and Humor" might have dispelled their misgivings. The old learning and curiosities were still there if, as they felt, largely misdirected and as a consequence somewhat obscured.

ე ე ე

One evening in the year 1919, Agnes Repplier stood in the doorway of her home on Pine Street awaiting the arrival of her cab.* It was a quiet street, pervaded, as she might have put it, by the odor of decayed gentility. The war was over, and with its end had passed the great and burning cause. Somehow the very life seemed to have gone out of things. In its way, Pine Street, eminently respectable, almost unbearably restrained, rather symbolized the depressing calm after the excitement of the storm. In a moment the cab drew up and Agnes Repplier gave the driver an address. She was going to a dinner in honor of Joseph and Elizabeth Pennell.

As Miss Repplier had known it would, the occasion offered little more than a parade ground for Pennell's several dicta. To make matters worse than usual, he had chosen to sing the praises of Germany even though everyone else present was completely pro-British, or at least pro-Allies.

* The Clinton Street apartment came a few years later (1921).

Pennell was warming to his subject. His assertions were coming thick and fast and with more and more exasperating assurance the more violently opposed he found himself to be. At last, as climax to his claims, he declared in ringing tones: "Mark my words! You'll all live to see the day when the German Army and the British Army march arm in arm down Chestnut Street!"

An impressive silence followed this astounding declaration. Then, leaning forward ever so slightly in her place, Agnes Repplier spoke up in a voice that was deadly calm. "Oh, dear Mr. Pennell," she said slowly and distinctly, "do have them come down Pine Street. Nothing ever happens on Pine Street."

CHAPTER XII

Aftermath

1919–1928

Beyond doubt, one of Agnes Repplier's most amusing friends was A. Edward Newton, the Johnsonian collector and bibliomaniac. There was something almost quixotic about him, something very clever, and something quite naïve as well. Endowed from the beginning with all the tastes of a scholar, by the time he launched himself on literary society Newton was widely read and professionally learned in the matter of booklore. He had begun humbly enough both as to income and library; but with the amassing of his fortune, he purchased judiciously so that before long his was one of the famous collections in the country.

Agnes Repplier claimed to have "forged" Newton and the great Samuel Johnson. She had been a Johnsonian almost since childhood, and was well prepared to recommend the eminent eighteenth century scholar to his newest devotee. If there were some who felt that Newton became the Johnsonian he did mainly because he had the money to buy the books, there were others who felt as strongly that his love was genuine and sincere.

Having read Miss Repplier's essays and having recog-

nized in them the work not only of an able writer but of one
delightfully familiar with most of the literary great of the
past, Newton wrote asking if he might call upon her. The
essayist was pleased and amused by his visit, and the two
became fast friends. Frequently she would travel out to
"Oak Knoll" in Dalesford, not far from Philadelphia, for
tea or a browsing in the famous library, which Newton
generously put at her disposal. Although at times it seemed
hard that he should have so many books and she so few, still
she was appreciative of the opportunity of making use of
her friend's good fortune.

☙ ☙ ☙

Nineteen-nineteen saw the publication of *J. William
White*, Agnes Repplier's biography of her friend and coun-
selor. The book was designed more as a tribute to the doctor than as a profit-gaining enterprise, for its appeal and
consequent sale was limited. But its author found deep satisfaction in doing the work and in seeing it reach a moderately large audience. She felt that by this book she had repaid at least in part her great debt to the man.

The following year Agnes Repplier brought out another
volume of essays, *Points of Friction*. Unlike *Counter-Currents*, this collection was evenly divided between papers of
purpose designed for the immediate present, as "Living in
History" and "The Strayed Prohibitionist," and papers of
entertainment drawn from past and present.

In "The Beloved Sinner," to choose one of the latter
group, the author demonstrates all her sharp wit and felicity of expression. It is, indeed, as clever an essay as any in
the volume, perhaps almost as any she had written. It
begins:

All the world does not love a lover. It is a cultivated taste, alien to the natural man, and unknown to childhood. But all the world does love a sinner, either because he is convertible to a saint, or because a taste for lawbreakers is an inheritance from our first parents, who broke the one and only law imposed upon them.

" 'The criminal is a sick man, the prison is his hospital, and the judge who sentenced him is his physician,' " the essayist quotes an authority as having said. Her answer later in the paper is as deft in its expression as it is—or was—accurate in its claim:

An interesting circumstance . . . is the reluctance of professional burglars to ply their craft on very cold and stormy nights. It would seem as though bad weather might be trusted to stand their friend; but the burglar, a luxury-loving person, dislikes being drenched or frozen as much as does his honest neighbor. Happily for his comfort and for his health, a high-speed motor now enables him to work on sunny days at noon. It is pleasant to reflect that the experts who robbed three Philadelphia jewellers at an hour when the shops were full of customers, and the streets were full of pedestrians, ran no risk from exposure. They may have been sick men from the psychologist's point of view, but they were as safe from bronchitis as they were from the Philadelphia police.

Agnes Repplier uses her flail to considerable advantage in this attack on the sentimentality with which criminals are handled by modern society. If her point of view is not exactly "an eye for an eye," at least she is of the opinion that the violator of the law merits some punishment suitable to the nature of his crime.

"The Strayed Prohibitionist," though it has now lost its *raison d'être*, is too amusing to be overlooked. It begins:

The image of the prohibition-bred American youth . . . straying through the wine-drenched and ale-drenched pages of English literature captivates the fancy. The classics, to be sure, are equally bibulous; but with the classics the American youth has no concern. The advance guard of educators are busy clearing away the debris of Greek and Latin which has hitherto clogged his path. . . . As for the Bible, where corn and oil and wine, the three fruits of a bountiful harvest, are represented as of equal virtue, it will probably be needful to supply such texts with explanatory and apologetic footnotes.

"The banishing of the classics, the careful editing of the Scriptures, and the comprehensive ignorance of foreign languages and letters which distinguishes the young American, leaves only the field of British and domestic literature to enlighten or bewilder him," the writer continues. "Longfellow," she comments later, "wrote a 'Drinking Song' to water, which achieved humor without aspiring to it, and Dr. Holmes wrote a teetotaller's adaptation of a drinking song, which aspired to humor without achieving it."

These are but a sampling of the jibes with which "The Strayed Prohibitionist" is liberally dotted. But best of all perhaps is the account of how the secret of the making of "heather ale" was lost:

The story goes that, after the bloody victory of the Scots under Kenneth MacAlpine, in 860, only two Picts who knew the secret survived the general slaughter. Some say they were father and son, some say they were master and man. When they were offered their lives in exchange for the recipe, the older captive said he dared not reveal it while the younger lived, lest he be slain in revenge. So the Scots tossed the lad into the sea, and waited expectantly. Then the last of the Picts cried, "I only know!" and leaped into the ocean and was drowned. It is a brave tale. One wonders if a man would die to save the secret of making milktoast.

Although in *Points of Friction* Agnes Repplier is frequently concerned over some problem of the day, and even though her beliefs and opinions may still be "counter-

currents" in some instances, there is a considerable difference between this volume of essays and the one that preceded it. In the former collection, she was ahead of the
majority, so to speak, pulling the lagging public after her.
Here in this volume, though she may be at variance with
the general reader, her position is somewhat in the rear
guard. Here the tendency is to pull back rather than to
forge ahead. In *Points of Friction* Agnes Repplier has begun to assume, or, better, reassume, the role of conservative.

"Living in History," in addition to its comment on the
war so recently concluded, is a plea for the older, grander
kind of history. "The Beloved Sinner," as has been pointed
out, is a damaging criticism of the ways of modern crimi-
nology. "The Virtuous Victorian" offers a defense of Victorian reticence. And, most obvious of all, "Consolations
of the Conservative" ably presents the conservative point
of view. In it Miss Repplier justifies what might seem to be
her sudden shift in motivation. "Resistance," it is pointed
out, "which is the function of conservatism, is essential to
orderly advance. It is a force in the social and political, as
well as in the natural order." "This day shall be transient
as the days which have preceded it," the essay concludes.
Five years earlier and less, though the "day" no doubt was
just as "transient," the author's attitude toward it and its
potentialities demanded far more force and energy than
now. Five years earlier and less there were few if any consolations for the conservative.

ᵔ ᵔ ᵔ

Although Agnes Repplier was working as hard as ever
through the years 1921, 1922, and 1923, she revealed in her
letters to Harrison Morris a depression of spirit not charac-

teristic of their writer. Plainly she was feeling a letdown
following the close of the war. There was a dullness to life
now that made the usual round of work, duties, even pleasures, more burdensome than ever before.

She wrote Morris late in 1922: "I am lecturing north, and
south, and east, and west . . . and am worn into a heap of
tired bones." Laryngitis, she later informed her friend,
would prevent her attending the January meeting of the
Contemporary Club. And a few months later she refused
an offer from the Penn Publishing Company for a book on
the social and literary aspects of the Victorian period because she was "old and in ill health."

There were occasional lifts in the monotonous round,
as when Harrison Morris invited her to a lecture to be given
by Hamlin Garland at the Art Alliance and to dinner later.
Miss Repplier wrote in reply: "Of course I'll go with pleasure to hear Mr. Garland. . . . I did not know that art was
his bailiwick."

"The dinner," she added, "seems a bit vague. It is a far
cry from 4:30 to dining time. Are you the host or is it a
penny-in-the-slot dinner, or is it the kind of dinner at which
guests are expected to speak out? The last possibility
gives me pause. Otherwise, if I knew the hour, I'd like to
attend."

But the general effect was one of indifference plus a certain slackening off. When Mrs. Warren's son from New
York made a special trip to seek Agnes Repplier's support
for the League of Nations, he found her most uninterested.
She who a few years ago in the heat of battle had been all
eager intervention, was now deaf to pleas of international
settlement. Wilson, she felt, was an idealist but not a very

wise man. And she had learned her lesson so well at the hands of Theodore Roosevelt, White, and others, that she was incapable of changing her mind about him. The League was a meddling, muddled affair as she saw it. And since to her mind it obviously would do no good, why should she concern herself about it? Mr. Warren left for New York and home disappointed not only that his mother's friend should refuse her support in so vital a work as the establishing of the League of Nations, but also disturbed as well over what seemed to him a decided withdrawal from reality. It was as if Agnes Repplier had burned herself out over the war, he felt. She seemed to him completely dispirited, indifferent, coldly cynical about regenerating the world.

And the feeling her friends detected in Agnes Repplier's attitude toward the League carried over to each phase of her life in general. In her thank-you note to Harrison Morris for his gift and good wishes at Christmas, 1923, she wrote: "Personally, I have lost my taste for New Years. They are uncommonly like the Old Years, and I'd like something different and better."

At sixty-seven, Agnes Repplier was beginning to admit she was old—an admission she would rarely make twenty years later.

ꙮ ꙮ ꙮ

Early in 1924 Agnes Repplier published her thirteenth volume of essays. *Under Dispute* is made up of eleven papers ranging from "The Happiness of Writing an Autobiography" to "Are Americans a Timid People," and from "The Preacher at Large" to "The Idolatrous Dog."

"The Divineness of Discontent" offers an interesting exposition of the degrees, variations, and sources of discontent. There is that species, the author points out, "which is more fervently optimistic than all the cheerfulness the world can boast . . . the discontent of the passionate and unpractical reformer." And, later: "There is a discontent which is profoundly stimulating, and there is a discontent which is more wearisome than complacency. Both spring from a consciousness that the time is out of joint, and both have a modern background of nerves."

The paper has its share of clever comment as when Emerson's "invincible optimism" is mentioned, and the essayist remarks: "It was easier to be a transcendental philosopher, and much easier to cherish a noble and sweet content, before the laying of the Atlantic cable." And the paper evidences as well its author's ability to make a deft expression: "It may be possible to construct a state in which men will be content with their own lot, if they be reasonable, and with their neighbor's lot, if they be generous."

In "The Masterful Puritan" Agnes Repplier turns her criticism on the Puritan pioneers of New England. She recognized that "in our day it is generously conceded that the Puritans made admirable ancestors," but she is far from being in accord with the concession. Although she is fully aware that "a vast deal of sympathy has been lavished upon the Puritan settlers because of the rigours of their religion, the austerity of their lives, their lack of intellectual stimulus, the comprehensive absence of anything like amusement," she herself finds it difficult to be sympathetic.

On two issues the essayist belabors the Puritan most heartily: religious intolerance and slavery. And, as always, her comments are pointed with a sharpness of expression that would be difficult to improve upon. In partial illustration of the terrors that only a Puritan soul might experience, Miss Repplier relates a story of "a woman of Boston, driven to desperation by the uncertainty of salvation," who "settled the point for herself by drowning her baby in a well, thus ensuring damnation, and freeing her mind of doubts." As for slavery, she tells of John Bacon of Barnstable, who in his will bequeathed a slave woman, Dinah, to his wife: "If, at the death of my wife, Dinah be still living, I desire my executors to sell her, and to use and improve the money for which she is sold in the purchase of Bibles, and distribute them equally among my said wife's and my grandchildren." To which the author adds the comment: "There are fashions in goodness and badness as in all things else; but the selling of a worn-out woman for Bibles goes a step beyond Mrs. Stowe's most vivid imaginings."

Eight years before the publication of *Under Dispute*, Agnes Repplier had written: "It is strange to glance back upon a day when we had so little to trouble us that we could vex our souls over feudalism and fiction . . . " And yet in this present volume she does little more. "The Masterful Puritan" is not concerned with "a national issue," but rather a sectional one. Neither is "The Divineness of Discontent." And in "They Had Their Day," a study of Victorian heroines, and "Strayed Sympathies," a severe criticism of contemporary methods of biography, the writer is plainly dealing with fiction and near-fiction. *Under Dispute* offers as conservative an Agnes Repplier as had *Points of Friction*. That there is no deep, underlying "cause" behind the essays in this new volume mitigates not a whit their pungency. In "The Happiness of Writing an Autobiography," to give further illustration, she writes: "Mr. Theodore Dreiser's 'A Book About Myself' sounds like nothing but a loud human purr." But it remains that here there is no cause, the result not only of the author's apparently having forgotten about such, but of the fact that essentially there is no need for a cause in her type of essay.

�’ �’ ’

The following May, Agnes Repplier sailed with a friend for three months in France, Belgium, and England. "It will be the last time before I die," she wrote to Harrison Morris.

And a few months later there came another letter to him from Bruges:

We are lingering in Bruges, a city I have always loved and of which I never have enough. Strange to say, I was told here of the one good deed I ever heard accredited to the accursed Germans. When they occupied the town, they had all the dogs killed. To appreciate this, one must live in Bruges, which has more dogs than any city in Christendom. All night long they bark, bay, howl, and occasionally squeal like a pig. I never thought I'd live to praise a German act!

This trip was not to be the essayist's last, for two years later she received word of her appointment to a commission for the Ibero-American International Exposition to be held in Seville in 1929. Although she could never decide how it was that she, of all persons, had been chosen to the position, the appointment had been made by President Coolidge.

"I wish I could feel I would ever be of any earthly use as a commissioner in Spain or elsewhere," she wrote Morris in reply to his letter of congratulation following her appointment. But when the time came, although she may still have doubted her usefulness to the commission, Agnes Repplier never regretted the unexpected trip. As it turned out, the Spanish Exposition was a considerable high light in the years between the World War and her eventual retirement from an active literary life.

ᢒ ᢒ ᢒ

Agnes Repplier's first honorary degree had come from the University of Pennsylvania in 1902. Nine years later Notre Dame had offered her the Laetare Medal. And now in rapid succession two more academic citations were to be extended to her. On June 17, 1925, the essayist received the degree of Doctor of Laws from Yale University, and two years later, on June 2, 1927, a third degree, this from Columbia University.

The second woman to be recognized by Yale with an honorary degree, Miss Repplier was understandably proud of the distinction. With characteristic succinctness she wrote to Harrison Morris: "I was puffed up with pride," then added modestly, "But have returned to my normal condition."

Two more major honors were to be added to Agnes Repplier's list in the following years: one from Princeton University and one from the National Institute of Arts and Letters. And all of them were a constant source of wonder to the essayist who, as she would say, had "carved her niche out of Philadelphia."

ᢒ ᢒ ᢒ

For all his somewhat blatant absurdities, Newton was a
good friend. And to Miss Repplier, his eccentricities and
little vanities only made his pleasantness and generosity the
more agreeable. Let Harrison Morris vent his scorn on the
"upstart" literary figure. Ellery Sedgwick, for one, thought
him immensely clever. And Agnes Repplier was inclined
here to side against her old friend and with the editor of
the *Atlantic.*

When she had received and read her copy of Newton's
newest volume, *This Book-Collecting Game,* she was grat-
ified to see herself in its pages. Newton is pointing out the
foolishness of American collectors who pass over the best
of native writers to grab at foreign firsts—generally
English.

Take Agnes Repplier, for example. For the price of half a
theatre ticket one can buy a volume of her essays, compounded
of wit, wisdom, humor, irony, and exquisite learning, the like
of which one would look for in vain in England to-day. The
reader will not wish to laugh loud, certainly not, but a persistent chuckle should not displease him, and Miss Repplier's
best volume, *A Happy Half-Century,* will certainly produce
it.

"I was present once," Newton continues, "when she was
introduced by a man, at a Blue-Stocking Club, as America's
most distinguished female essayist. I felt that her introducer
was in for his bad quarter of an hour, and I was not
mistaken . . . "

Agnes Repplier never begged any gentler treatment for
being a woman. Certainly she had never stood on her sex;
that attitude she had learned from Miss Irwin who never
cared whether a person was, as she would say, "male, fe-

male, or neuter" as long as that person was of interest and worth in Miss Irwin's eyes. And on this particular occasion of which Newton had written, the introducer had been so very patronizing, Miss Repplier had been unable to resist the temptation to set him straight in the matter. From her reading she had seen that throughout the years there had always been a great distinction between writers and female writers, and she was determined to avoid classification under the second head. Sex, she insisted, had had absolutely nothing to do either with her writing on the one hand or—at least she devoutly hoped—her reputation on the other.

But, having paid his compliment, having told his little story, Newton required his fee. "Candor compels me," he concluded his account of Agnes Repplier in *This Book-Collecting Game*, "to say that the lady has one grave fault: 'first editions' leave her cold, very cold. Some people are like that."

And on that score Agnes Repplier had nothing to offer. She enjoyed Newton's little joke, but she ventured neither apology nor excuse. She was perfectly willing to leave it with "some people are like that" for the time being.

ꙮ ꙮ ꙮ

Late in December 1928, Miss Repplier wrote to Harrison Morris about a paper of hers in the *Yale Review* "written with my heart's blood, which," she added, "shows the severance the gods have ruled between you and me."

The paper was "Town and Suburb" in which the emphatically urban Agnes Repplier came out strongly against suburbanites—traitors to the city—motor cars, and kindred disrupting entities. "The present quarrel . . . is between the town and suburb," she wrote, "that midway habitation which fringes every American city, and which is imposing or squalid according to the incomes of suburbanites." And, she insisted, "it is the all-prevailing motor which stands responsible for the vast increase of suburban life in the United States . . . "

The essayist, like many writers of the eighteenth century whom she so much admired, had always been a city person. Even the evils, that she was perfectly willing to admit, could not make her change her position. The country, certainly the suburb, had its manifold evils as well. Santayana knew what he was about when—and Agnes Repplier quotes him—he wrote: "I prize civilization, being bred in towns, and liking to hear and see what new things people are up to."

Unfortunately, not all of Miss Repplier's friends shared her beliefs. And not all were, as a consequence, city dwellers. Horace Furness had lived far enough away, and Newton was little nearer. It would have been unseemly to have pointed the finger of scorn at Furness: he had been too fine and noble a friend. But Newton? "If Dickens still has readers as well as buyers . . . " And she might have added "suburban buyers," though perhaps she hesitated at being quite so blunt.

Furness, Newton, even Harrison Morris was not beyond reproach in the matter of town and suburb living. True, his home was in the city; but it was so far toward being suburban that it might as well have been beyond the urban limits. It took Agnes Repplier hours to make the trip from her home, comfortably tucked away in the very heart of the city, out to his palatial place, just this side of the "fringe."

Once she had written him: "It is no use loving people who live in the country. I intend to transfer all my affection to town dwellers, who are an affectionate race, preferring their friends to grass and vegetables." And again: "Don't you think that some day you will give up living in the heart of nature, and draw a bit closer to the people who love you? I loathe those estranging acres."

But Harrison Morris remained as blithely unaware of Agnes Repplier's cajolings as did Newton. Only in the case of Morris, with the passing of the years the city grew out to him; the "estranging acres" were built upon; and the charge of suburbanite could no longer be made.

CHAPTER XIII

The Eighth Decade

1929 and After

ꙮ ꙮ

The winter of 1929 was a busy one for Agnes Repplier. That was the year she published the first of a series of biographies, and it was the year of the Ibero-American International Exposition in Seville.

Some time before, a New York publishing firm had asked her to write a biography of Père Marquette, and although she had refused another New York concern their request for a book also, the biography held special appeal for her. Besides, the other request had been for a memoir, and Miss Repplier was unwilling to make use of her friends by writing of them.

The biography of Père Marquette, the French Jesuit missionary and explorer who had accompanied Joliet down the Wisconsin and Mississippi rivers and up the Illinois in 1673, proved an arduous task. Most of the "spade work" had to be done by the writer herself, although in this she was aided by Father McShain, a Jesuit priest, to whom in gratitude she dedicated the finished work.

The reviews of *Père Marquette* praised the essayist, who in this volume had tried her hand a second time at "full length" biography. One critic called it "history written by an artist," and continued, "Miss Repplier steers a happy course between the ponderous footnote school of biography and the clever but shallow group of modern iconoclasts." Another, in an article headed "Miss Repplier Triumphs," wrote: "The Catholic book-shelf, which holds Dryden's Saint Francis Xavier, Francis Thompson's Saint Ignatius of Loyola, and Chesterton's study of Saint Francis of Assisi, can now receive Agnes Repplier's *Père Marquette*." And a third, in what was perhaps the most gratifying notice of all, declared:

Everything that discriminating mankind most cherishes in its best reading is to be found in this extraordinary book—a great story, greatly told: great human characters, moving and suffering; great deeds for great ends; great perils bravely withstood; great difficulties vanquished. . . . If from the endless old records artists like Agnes Repplier can bring stories of fact as great and inevitable as this, what is fiction but a primitive vanity and the making of it a lost motion?

As he had done on so many previous occasions, Harrison Morris asked for a copy of the biography to round out the "Repplier Collection" in his private library. The essayist answered his request: "I should like to send you 'Père Marquette' (it is my only work which has not gone to you in the long years of our friendship); but it is essentially a 'rum, Romanism and rebellion' book, and, as such, can have no place upon your godly shelves.

"I am sailing February tenth," she added, "on the Marques de Comellas, Royal Spanish Mail Line, for Seville, a city of rum and Romanism, and perhaps of rebellion, too. I am glad to go, but very sad at leaving, and I have a lost and lonely feeling in my heart."

Miss Repplier was in her middle seventies, and the thought of a trip abroad, particularly one bearing such responsibilities as this one, was somewhat unnerving. It had never occurred to her in the past that one day she would ever feel like refusing a journey to Europe. Forty years earlier such had seemed a reasonably ridiculous possibility. But she was tired, and more than anything else, she wanted to be let alone.

ꙫ ꙫ ꙫ

Thomas E. Campbell, former governor of Arizona, had been appointed by President Coolidge as commissioner general. A former Wyoming judge, a San Francisco publisher, and two women in addition to Agnes Repplier comprised the committee for the Ibero-American Exposition.

Miss Repplier's main duties at first were to arrange a library of standard American works that had been contributed by various bookstores in the United States. As it turned out, they filled three cases, and the arranging of them covered three days. After that, the author's time was taken up largely with receiving distinguished visitors, attending bull fights, and witnessing the unveiling of Mrs. Harry Payne Whitney's memorial statue to the discoverer of America. The distinguished visitors Agnes Repplier found both interesting and amusing. The bull fights, which she attended in the company of a Spanish lady whose idea of entertainment consisted mainly of copious amounts of indigestible food, appeared to her as indecent if grand shows. And Mrs. Whitney's statue turned out to be "a trifle bewildering, looking more like an old woman than the great adventurer." But, Miss Repplier was some years later to comment with a marked lack of conviction, "we were told that it was meant to be glimpsed by mariners far out at sea, and that to them it was noble and imposing." To her on land and close by, it was decidedly not.

The King of Spain was the most interesting of the visitors and Queen Marie of Rumania the most amusing—though she was scarcely aware of that. The essayist recorded later:

She sent word that she was travelling privately, and wished no attention to be paid her. The commissioner general, who did not know the lady, and whose duties had grown very onerous, was delighted to take her at her word. He provided some handsome flowers . . . a tastefully draped Roumanian flag . . . summoned his weary but faithful followers, and awaited the royal visitor. She arrived with a longer line of motors than we had yet seen, made a stately entrance into our building, and evaded looking at the exhibits. The commissioner, however, succeeded in getting her shut up in the cinema theatre, and we sank into our seats, hoping for a half-hour's respite. We did not get it. In twenty minutes the queen had seen as much as she could bear, and made a break for the door, followed joyously by her ladies. As she emerged into the dazzling sunlight, she was received in respectful silence by a large circle of our employees, and a much larger circle outside—the crowd which gathers in Spain on the smallest possible provocation. The royal photographer was waiting to chronicle every move. In our front row stood the commissioner general's chauffeur, wearing his new khaki uniform. He was a young Cuban of much skill, but so ill-mannered that petitions for his dismissal were of daily occurrence. The queen caught sight of the khaki, drew a swift but erroneous conclusion, walked nimbly across the open space, and shook hands cordially with the smiling young man while the photographer recorded her urbanity. Then she and her ladies stepped into their motors and disappeared from our sight.

The Feria, the Romero, and most of all, Holy Week in

Seville were all well worth the trouble and anxiety the exposition caused as far as Agnes Repplier was concerned.
From her early days in the convent, Spain had been dear
to her heart. Time and again during her stay in Seville she
recalled the smart that had stung her when, during the
course of one of the games she and her little friends had
played at Eden Hall, she had been required to forfeit Castile in place of Tuscany. "Loveliest of cities" she called
Seville, and she had defied King Alfonso to make her
change her mind in favor of Madrid.

Seventy-five or no, Miss Repplier found the exposition
an unqualified success. More months than she had ever
spent in Spain before had come to her because she had
been thought capable of arranging three cases of books—
and months with salary, she was pleased to remark to her
friends, in an effort to impress them with the commercial
value of a bookish reputation.

ͻ ͻ ͻ

In the course of the next four years, Agnes Repplier
published as many books, a not inconsiderable output for
anyone, let alone one of her years. *Times and Tendencies*,
a collection of twelve essays, combines papers after the
fashion of her older, more characteristic work as well as
the war-provoked, social-conscious writing that had first
intruded itself largely as a result of Miss Irwin's deathbed
pleas to her.

"Peace and the Pacifist," an essay belonging to the latter group, is almost as harsh as many of the papers written
immediately before and during the war.

Now that the world is at peace (excepting only China, and India, and Afghanistan, and possibly a South American Republic or two that cannot be betted on with security, and some strips of country policed by American marines whose activities are not officially recognized as fighting)—now, I repeat, that the rest of the world is at peace, and ardently desires to remain so, it is time that pacifists reduced their sentimentalities to order.

Thus the essay begins. Pacifism has no place in the world, the essayist contends, because "nothing can make men and women who lived as adults through the World War consent to witness another." Of that she is very sure. And she is equally as certain that all pacifists are misguided as she is that the League of Nations, the World Court, and the Kellogg Pact are unnecessary.

"Peace and the Pacifist" is redeemed, however, by its author's cleverness which cannot be suppressed no matter how irked she may be. (Indeed on occasion it would seem that the more annoyed Agnes Repplier is, the sharper is her expression of annoyance.) She writes:

If patriotism becomes an emotion too expansively benevolent to make men willing to live and die for something concrete like a king or a country we shall have nothing left to fall back upon but sexual love, which is a strong individual urge, but lacks breadth and scope of purpose. It burned Troy; but it did not build Rome, or secure the Magna Charta, or frame the Constitution of the United States.

"Cure-Alls" presents an examination of panaceas ranging all the way from pills, through "colour psychology" and Dr. Eliot's famous five-foot shelf, to the Eighteenth Amendment. "The American Credo" offers the contention—and none too gently—that in America "the creed is education, the temple is the school house, the conviction

is the healing power of knowledge," and that "our passionate desire, not so much to acquire education as to bestow
it, is the most animated of American traits." These and
several other essays in the collection bear little more re-
semblance than the deftness of expression and the delight
of incisive wit to Agnes Repplier's earlier work. And in
these essays the wit frequently is barbed almost beyond
the limits of "fair play."

But in "The Pleasures of Possession" the essayist is her
usual self. This is a charming essay dealing with the joy
one has in owning anything, a joy that "lies in showing
these things to friends who are experiencing no immediate
urge to look at them." In it are related many delightful accounts of collectors and their collections, but none more
delightful than this:

I was asked once to see a collection of silhouettes, and found
that there were seven thousand of them. It was a marvelous
collection. Many were very beautiful, many were very valuable, some had historical significance. But there *were* seven
thousand. Now seven good silhouettes hung on a wall properly
toned for their reception are a gracious sight; seventeen are
not too many for enjoyment; but seven thousand under one
roof challenged endurance. Their owner was courteous, kind,
patient, and hospitable; but he did cut off our retreat when
from time to time we made a break for liberty. Years of his
life, and apparently all of his income, had been spent in searching for these shadow pictures in every corner of Europe and
America. The search, begun as a pastime, had become the
absorbing principle of his life. It had doubtless given him
hours of anxiety and hours of ecstasy. Yet here was the
magnificent result, the vastest collection of silhouettes in the
world; and three visitors, dazed and fagged, trying to escape
from its vastness. My word! Cornelia's Roman friend who
was asked to look at two school boys had an easy time of it.

The reviews of *Times and Tendencies* were not all in commendatory agreement as had been the majority of the reviews of Agnes Repplier's other collections of essays. One critic apparently did find this most recent volume of much the same value as the rest. "Those who . . . continue to think a little and who can endure a wholesome astringency of phrase and thought," she felt, "will be proud of this book. They will even enjoy it enormously." But this notice was rather the exception. "The shade of difference between this and most of [Agnes Repplier's] earlier books is in the subjects," a second critic wrote. And that he did not altogether appreciate the difference is indicated by his explanation of it. "It is due perhaps to the changes . . . in the demands of the magazines that were formerly called literary. The typical magazine essay now is a sort of extended editorial. Its topic is current. It is all about today and tomorrow, about here and now." A third critic agreed more with the second than with the first, though he would lay the fault at the writer's door rather than place the blame upon the editors and their changed demands. He commented:

Miss Repplier's precision is dulled and her clarity dimmed in this book by a note of personal weariness and vexation. The genial satire reaches toward cynicism . . . The writing is that of one who, though thoroughly urbane, is getting very tired of the foolishness of the world and perhaps a trifle impatient with her own urbanity.

Whether the difference between *Times and Tendencies* and, for example, *A Happy Half-Century* was the result of a changed market and changed demands, as the one critic had suggested, or of a personal weariness, as the other had believed, may be a matter of question—though Agnes Repplier was now seventy-six and might reasonably be expected to feel somewhat weary, it might be pointed out. Certain it was that for those who could remember—as well as think, to use the third critic's comment—this latest volume could not approach many an earlier collection when it came to the matter of sheer reading pleasure. One regretted both the "times" and its consequent "tendencies."

Mère Marie of the Ursulines, another biography in the fashion of *Père Marquette*, was published in the same year as *Times and Tendencies*, and was made a selection of both the Literary Guild of America and the Catholic Book Club. It tells the story—"A Study in Adventure" is its subtitle—of Mère Marie de l'Incarnation who helped in the founding of the Ursuline convent at Quebec in 1641. As was the case with *Père Marquette*, *Mère Marie of the Ursulines* contains almost as many literary allusions and quotations from the lore of the centuries as any single volume of Agnes Repplier's essays. But the mark of the essayist, though it be here plainly stamped on the work of the biographer, never impedes the story, adding rather only to the enjoyment of the reader.

In 1932, Agnes Repplier published a book entitled *To Think of Tea!* which endeavored to do for that drink something similar to what *The Fireside Sphinx* had done for cats. This is not a complete history of tea by any manner of means, but it is a consideration of certain historical aspects of the drinking of tea. There is a chapter on "The Coming of Tea to England," one on "The Blue-Stocking Tea-Drinkers of England," one on "Some Recent Tea-

Drinkers of England," and finally, one on "The Drinking of Tea Today."

To Think of Tea! is Miss Repplier at her best. Here is no caviling at contemporary social mispractices, no objecting to earnest if misguided feminists, no railing against stupid reforms. The war, now almost fifteen years in the past, has been quite forgotten, and books and booklore, and the praises of a day that meant far more to Agnes Repplier than the present, be it wartime or no, hold full and happy sway.

Mr. Newton enjoyed *To Think of Tea!* with almost extravagant abandon. He wrote to all his friends, issuing invitations to a Sunday luncheon, with a curious combination of crassness and generosity. The invitation to luncheon was accompanied by a note that read:

My friend Agnes Repplier's new book TO THINK OF TEA! is a sheer delight. It is compact with learning and wisdom— which is not the same thing—and it is ironical and witty.

I am pleased to note that as the lady grows older—she is no longer in her thirties—she, like Dr. Johnson, is "prepared to call a man a good man on easier terms than heretofore."

The format of the book is admirable. It is published by Houghton Mifflin Co. of Boston and costs $2.75.

I regret that times being what they are I cannot afford to send you a copy. But I'll tell you what I will do. If you buy a copy and don't like it I will take it off your hands for $1.50 and give it to some appreciative friend at Christmas. Thus it will cost you only $1.25 to read one of the most delightful volumes of essays that has appeared in years.

And so Agnes Repplier traveled west to Oak Knoll one Sunday in November to receive the congratulations of Mr. Newton's friends who had braved the cold as well as put up the necessary two dollars and seventy-five cents for the privilege of attendance at tea in honor of the essayist. And duly she was photographed on one side of a tea table, caught in the act of pouring, with Newton seated in his inevitable checkered suit on the other, clutching rather obviously a copy of *To Think of Tea!*

The year following *To Think of Tea!* brought forth the third in the series of biographies of Roman Catholic figures from the past. *Junípero Serra, Pioneer Colonist of California* tells the story of the adventurous priest who founded eight missions in what is now the state of California. In the Foreword to the biography, Agnes Repplier wrote:

From Serra's own diary, from the diaries and letters of Franciscan friars, from the correspondence of viceroys and *visitadores*, from the casual comments of contemporaries, and from the pages of earlier biographers, this pioneer priest emerges a finished portrait which I have endeavored to put upon paper. If I can awaken but a tithe of the admiration and affection I have felt for my subject, I shall be well content.

That the reviewers at least did feel something of the author's "admiration and affection" is evidenced by the notices *Junípero Serra* received. One calls it "a labor of love;" another "a noble [biography] in a great tradition." And a third remarks that this latest book "demonstrates once again that felicitous mastery of English expression made famous by [Agnes Repplier's] essays."

ᛒ ᛒ ᛒ

Nineteen-thirty-five was made memorable to Miss Repplier by the fact that it was the year in which she received two citations (the last, as it happened) to add to her list of honors. In June of that year Princeton University

Charles G. Osgood

Mrs. Newton

A. Edward Newton

Miss Repplier

awarded her the degree of Doctor of Letters, Agnes Repplier's fourth such academic honor. Pennsylvania, Notre Dame, Yale, Columbia, and now Princeton: the universities had been generous in their recognition of the writer's more than fifty years of steady writing.

Some nine years before, the National Institute of Arts and Letters, in which Harrison Morris had been active as Treasurer for many years, had granted membership to four distinguished women of letters: Edith Wharton, Margaret Deland, Mary E. Wilkins Freeman, and Agnes Repplier. That had seemed honor enough, but there was to be more for the essayist.

One day she received notification that the Institute had presented her with its Gold Medal in recognition of her long years of excellence in the field of writing. Her Boston publishers ran a large advertisement in the *Transcript:* "Felicitations to the American Institute of Arts and Letters for their award of the Gold Medal in Essays and Belle Lettres to Agnes Repplier," to which was appended a complete list of the books by the recipient that they had published. The author was sincerely affected by the honor that had been done her. "And," as she would say, "the medal is so big and gold and handsome."

ಶ ಶ ಶ

Louis Repplier was seventy-five years of age. Latterly he had taken it upon himself now and again to journey out of the center of the city to visit his nephew and his family in one of Philadelphia's suburbs. Dr. Sidney Repplier was the oldest child of Lancaster Repplier, and Uncle Louis was particularly fond of his children. His great delight was

in calling upon them, armed with a jar of hard candies
which his grandnephew and grandnieces found much to
their liking even though their pleasure in receiving the
sweets was somewhat mitigated by the ordeal of having
to bury their faces in Uncle Louis' whiskers in order to
reward his kindness with a kiss.

It was in returning from one of these excursions that
Louis Repplier was struck by an automobile and so seriously injured that it seemed doubtful he would ever walk
again. His sisters had him taken to a nursing home in Ger-
mantown where, every few days, one or the other of them
would visit him. The constant journeys were a considerable
drain on Agnes Repplier's health and strength (she was
seventy-nine at the time of the accident), but for five years
she traveled back and forth, in good weather and bad, seeing to her brother's wants with all the care and love she
felt was her responsibility.

In his eightieth year Louis Repplier died and was buried
in the Repplier brothers' vault at St. John's on South Thirteenth street, the final resting place of all the Repplier
family for generations. The little church, settled within its
somewhat cramped churchyard across the street from the
vast Wanamaker store, the hub of the city to all good Philadelphians, offered at last its peaceful sanctuary to "the helpless one."

When the simple ceremony was over, and Agnes Repplier and the few mourners were about to leave the church,
the essayist turned to her sister and was heard to remark
with characteristic directness: "Well, it's a blessed
relief that Louis is at his rest—and so convenient to
Wanamaker's!"

ɔ ɔ ɔ

In 1934, Agnes Repplier published a slim but effective biography of Agnes Irwin. Like her book about Dr. White, it was more a gesture of gratitude, a tribute to friendship, than a financial venture, and it gave its author real pleasure in the writing. From its pages Miss Irwin emerged as a strong personality, the champion of worthy causes, a force in American education. And its style was that of Agnes Repplier at her most pleasing. She could well be satisfied with the book; Miss Irwin would have been proud of her former pupil.

Two more volumes remained before Agnes Repplier's career as writer would be largely finished. *In Pursuit of Laughter*, published in 1936, follows *The Fireside Sphinx* and *To Think of Tea!* rather than her more usual collections of essays. In a sense it traces the history of humor from the Middle Ages to the twentieth century. But it is "no dry and sober history of humor. It is the flight of a subtle and penetrating mind lightly pursuing laughter down the centuries." The Middle Ages, Elizabethan England, the Restoration, the Eighteenth Century, each yields its store of good tales, its contributions to gaiety, its wit and learning that no one knew better how to present to modern readers than Agnes Repplier.

Ellery Sedgwick, in the *Atlantic Monthly*, sang the praises of author and book:

For full two generations Miss Agnes Repplier has not ceased to be a bright and finished ornament of American Letters. Who matches her in craftsmanship? Who excels her in discipline, in the honest withholding of praise, or in its just bestowal? She is the inheritor of a more ancient excellence than ours, and among Americans she has become a sort of contemporary ancestor, a summation of the best that has gone before. She it is who traces the "Pursuit of Laughter," and her quest is recorded in a book of delights to be read and digested with smiles but not with laughter, for laughter is dead and this book is its epitaph.

Agnes Repplier's last volume of essays and her final book, *Eight Decades,* was published the year following *In Pursuit of Laughter.* It is made up of sixteen essays gleaned from the preceding thirty and more years, the best, she felt, of her work. And in addition there is the title paper, "Eight Decades," "a slice of autobiography," as the publishers called it.

Eight Decades proved once more Agnes Repplier's "very real gifts of style, wit, wisdom and urbane tolerance." More than that, the writing which these papers exhibits is of an all but uniform excellence, even though the first essay in the collection is separated in time from the last by more than three of the author's eight decades. Most telling of all perhaps, the book does not date, for, as one reviewer put it, Agnes Repplier "has something to say which holds the reader of the nineteen-thirties as her earlier work held the reader of the eighties and nineties." "The Masterful Puritan," "Allegra," "Town and Suburb," "When Lalla Rookh Was Young:" in them all Agnes Repplier writes with as sure a touch as the best of her calling. And her "learning leaves us gasping." Well may we ask with Mary Ellen Chase: "Has she read all her life and forgotten nothing?"

ᵓ ᵓ ᵓ

Agnes Repplier's work was almost over. Nineteen-thirty-eight saw the publication of eight essays, but the following year none at all. Then in January 1940, the essayist appeared for the last time in the *Atlantic Monthly* with a paper on "The Brothers Housman." Its author was shortly to celebrate her eighty-fifth birthday. It was time, she felt, to call a halt. As she would say, in her time she had endured the dribblings of too many octogenarian authors. She had no use for the last feeble utterances of people. She would inflict none on what it pleased her to label a "long-suffering public."

Two years later, in 1942, when an anthology of the "best" of some ninety or more "greatest living American authors" was proposed, Agnes Repplier was asked to contribute. Her niece, Mrs. Witmer, wrote the editor: " 'My aunt, Agnes Repplier, received your letter, but she has been ill for the last two years, very weak and frail and confined to her bed. She is not able to write . . . ' " But she did select an essay for the anthology, a paper of six years earlier on "Horace," for, she said, " 'There never would be a time when people would not want to read about Horace.' "

Essayist, biographer, wit, stylist among stylists, Agnes Repplier had earned the right to rest from her labors of more than sixty years.

CHAPTER XIV

Agnes Repplier: Literary Artist

I

Although it is possible that a casual reader coming upon a copy of *Books and Men* with its title page missing would not suspect the author of being an American, it is even more likely that he would not suspect the author of being a Roman Catholic. That the writer was a woman would no doubt be surmised. But the only conclusion that could be hazarded with any degree of certainty would be that the essayist was a person displaying an extraordinary range of reading interests, and, in addition, an unusual ability to put ideas into words.

Although there was a gradual infiltration of native material into Agnes Repplier's writings as she progressed from volume to volume, it was not until more than half of her books of essays had been published that she swung definitely and, for a time at least, almost completely to the consideration of American problems as distinct from the English facts, fancies, and foibles that had been her particular delight. But such mundane material, vital as it appeared to be for nearly twenty years, could not lure her indefinitely. So compelling was the earlier, more sympathetic contemplation of things English, that Agnes Repplier was drawn irresistibly to concluding her career in the very vein in which she had begun it.

"Look where we will, we find the author's future work reflected in the intellectual pastimes of his childhood," she had written in her first collection of essays. *To Think of Tea!* (1932) and *In Pursuit of Laughter* (1936) are far closer to *Books and Men,* published almost fifty years earlier, than they are to their immediate predecessor, *Times and Tendencies* (1931). Her rightful field was not the stupidities of contemporary America, for the "intellectual pastimes" of her childhood had concerned themselves almost exclusively with the English literary history of another day.

ᵔ ᵔ ᵔ

To exclude an extended account here of the biographies, one finds among the various volumes of essays certain ones that are as books distinctly feminine as well as certain individual essays in other collections that exhibit unmistakably the author's sex. Most obvious among the books that are themselves feminine as units is *In Our Convent Days,* and this because it is biography in a sense, if perhaps somewhat romanticized biography. The long biographical title essay in *Eight Decades,* the only part of this volume not a reprint from previous collections, belongs in the same category. These could not, by their very nature, avoid being the peculiar product of a feminine mind inasmuch as they are the picturings of the life of the author.

Two other books may be classed with *In Our Convent Days,* not because they are in any way autobiographical, but because their content is of a sort usually considered— in this country and in this day at least—feminine. *The Fireside Sphinx*, being as it is a history-of-sorts of the domestic cat down through the ages, offers material appealing primarily to women. The cat has, rightly or wrongly, and in spite of Agnes Repplier's constant references to the feline pets of masculine literary figures of the past which would seem to indicate that the contrary was so, come to be associated more with women than with men. Just as a dog is man's pet, so a cat is woman's. And *The Fireside Sphinx* is a woman's book.

The second of these two books distinctly feminine because of their material is *To Think of Tea!* The very fact that Agnes Repplier does not consider tea drinking in any way a feminine taste, nor the fact that once it was not here in this country so considered, cannot alter the case that for the most part tea drinking is in truth just that. Books on tea have been written by men* but largely from a commercial point of view, not a literary or an artistic one. And *To Think of Tea!* remains feminine or at best a curiosity to the average masculine reader.

For the most part, what applies to certain of her books applies as well to individual essays of Agnes Repplier's. Thus there are a number of papers that are undeniably feminine, not only because of treatment, but also because of material: "The Eternal Feminine," "The Spinster," "The Literary Lady," "The Temptations of Eve," to name only a few. And they prove to be interesting reading to the men in her audience because of their style, because of their literary and historical references, and in spite of their

---

* Witness, for example, William H. Ukers' work.

subject matter. That indeed is one of the wonders of Agnes Repplier: she could win a man to an avid reading of her by the way in which she expressed herself, even when that of which she wrote would have been scorned by that very man if offered to him by a less consummate artist.

There are in addition to this class of essays distinctly feminine by virtue of their material, certain other essays feminine more through treatment than because of content. Such are "Allegra," a sympathetic and fundamentally womanly essay on Byron's ill-starred daughter, and "When Lalla Rookh Was Young," a most amusing account of the extraordinary effects of Moore's poem upon his audience. Such also is "Three Famous Old Maids." "Women and War," and "Woman Enthroned," to choose two more at random, had they been written by a man, would have been far different from what they are as offered by Agnes Repplier.

But this is not all. If perversity be a characteristic peculiarly feminine—and one perhaps had better avoid dogmatic assertion here—then certain of Agnes Repplier's essays are feminine because of what might be labeled their perversity. Whatever else may on occasion have added its weight to the balance, it is clear that Miss Repplier more than once chose deliberately to tread a nobly aloof and independent path. If this were perversity, and if perversity be an attribute of the feminine make-up, then in these instances the essayist displayed herself in an obviously feminine fashion.

Agnes Repplier held no special brief for women. "The right to be judged as men are judged is perhaps the only form of equality which feminists fail to demand," she wrote with evident scorn in "Woman Enthroned." On the other hand, she was not one to allow men to cow her. " 'Never has a virgin, young or old, produced a work of art,' " she quotes Edmond de Goncourt as having said, and comments witheringly: "One makes allowances for the Latin point of view. And it is possible that M. de Goncourt never read 'Emma.' " But in the final analysis, Agnes Repplier took no pains to disguise her sex, for she was neither ashamed nor regretful that she had been born a woman. "The girl who lounged opposite us in the carriage, and who would be a very pretty girl in any other conceivable hat . . . " is both typical of its author and of her kind.

ɔ ɔ ɔ

It was not often that Agnes Repplier devoted an entire essay to the delineation of some phase, interest, or manifestation of the Roman Catholic Church, the church in which she herself had been brought up. There are some essays, such as "The Pilgrim's Staff," an account of pilgrims, pilgrimages, and famous European shrines, as well as several papers designed for the special audience of the *Catholic World*, which are Roman Catholic to the core. And there are certain other essays in which one strongly suspects that the author's interest was to some extent at least stimulated by her religious background. "The Cavalier," a picture of Graham of Claverhouse, and "The Pietist," an account in part of how the "happy half-century" treated Roman Catholics, papers not given over entirely to Catholicism, are sufficiently inclined sympathetically in that direction to indicate unmistakably her own affiliation. In fact, it would not be too much to contend that Miss Repplier's unqualified dislike for most things Puritan stemmed, and understandably so, from her religious training.

In Our Convent Days Agnes Repplier labeled her one book "designed for my own people." But *In Our Convent Days* remained unique. Her biographies of Mère Marie, Père Marquette, and Junípero Serra were not designed for her "own people." Each, although an undeniably prominent figure in the Roman Catholic Church, was sufficiently significant to the non-Catholic world to have appeal merely as a historical personage. As biographer she imposed no limitation upon them.

Agnes Repplier's faith reveals itself largely in subtle ways in her writing. Now and again it crops out in some such obvious declaration as: "There is a charming and gracious dogma of Roman Catholicism which would have us believe that all good deeds and holy prayers make up a spiritual treasury, a public fund, from which are drawn consolation for the church suffering, and strength for the church militant." But most often it is evidenced no more than in a general liberal conservatism of outlook plus a fine sense of proportion, the result of her having had to supplement the Catholic viewpoint she had learned at home and in her convent training with the Protestant viewpoint she found in the world around her.

ᴆ ᴆ ᴆ

The general impression a casual reader of Agnes Repplier's essays might gain of her attitude toward Americans would be one of amused toleration or, from those written during the period of the First World War, of something approaching contempt. "Sixty-two years ago Mr. James Russell Lowell published in the *Atlantic Monthly* an urbanely caustic essay, 'On a Certain Condescension in Foreigners,' " she wrote in one paper. "Yet the condescension which Mr. Lowell deprecated, and which was based upon superiority of culture, seems like respectful flattery compared to the condescension which Americans now daily display, and which is based upon superiority of wealth."

As for the amused toleration, we find ready illustration in "Actor and Audience":

A veteran actor has asked, rather superciliously, if anyone has ever heard an intelligent comment upon a play made by a member of the departing audience. Intelligence is a large order; but if we are content to be amused at such moments, we may have our fill of entertainment. When the curtain fell upon John Barrymore's *Hamlet*, and I was making my way out of the theatre, wondering what principle had dictated the ruthless and arbitrary cutting of the text, a lady in front of me said to her companion: "What I liked best was that we had the play just as Shakespeare wrote it. There wasn't a line left out." "Oh, but there was," said the second lady. "I waited all evening to hear the queen say, 'Out, damned spot.' and she never said it."

If our casual reader confined himself to the first half-dozen volumes of essays Miss Repplier published, he might come to the conclusion that the essayist thought nothing one way or the other of Americans, so slight are her references to them in these books. The English and the French (with occasional excursions among the Italians and the Germans) would, by the very weight of preponderance, appear to crowd her native countrymen almost entirely off the scene.

Yet her amused toleration, her open contempt, her seem-

ing indifference, all this was apparently much a matter of
the moment, the interest immediately at hand, for in "A
Question of Politeness" Agnes Repplier wrote with evident sincerity: "The American is not without gentleness of
speech and spirit. He is not always in a hurry. He is not
always elbowing his way, or quivering with ill-bred im-
patience. Turn to him for help in a crowd, and feel the
bright sureness of his response . . . "

America itself was not unknown to Agnes Repplier. Her
lecturing took her far and wide, and she had made one
long pilgrimage to California and Alaska. Her biography of
Mère Marie carried her in study to Canada, that of Père
Marquette to the valley of the Mississippi, that of Junípero
Serra to the Southwest. Her travels in and reading of
America, as well as her constant keen observation, would
forestall any criticism of her as unaware of the American
scene.

But for all her loyalty to her native land, Agnes Repplier loved Europe with almost an equal devotion. She was
never surfeited with travel abroad. "The pretty adage,
'Tout homme a deux pays: le sien et puis la France,' is truer
of us than of any other people in the world," she wrote
in "The Estranging Sea." If her own life and interests did
not always bear out such a contention (for surely England
held sway over France, even in spite of her inherited Gallic
inclinations), the comment is worth noting. It indicates an
attitude of mind and spirit that is typically Repplierean.
Her own country, yes; but ever since her first, long-
dreamed-of trip had been realized, travel abroad as often
as possible.

Agnes Repplier cared little for scenery as such. Her

heart lay in the cities of the world. In them she met people, and from people she learned the ways of their country. Her essays are filled with the unusual, the out-of-the-way, so that they become almost anthologies of lost, forgotten, or unfamiliar customs and manners.

To this endless curiosity to know about people, literary people out of the happy past, satisfied to a considerable extent by travel in the cities their hearty ghosts still haunted, the essayist brought as well an extraordinary love and appreciation of history. "I used to think that ignorance of history meant only a lack of cultivation and a loss of pleasure," she wrote in "Living in History." "Now I am sure that such ignorance impairs our judgment by impairing our understanding, by depriving us of standards, of the power to contrast, and the right to estimate. We can know nothing of any nation unless we know its history; and we can know nothing of the history of any nation unless we know something of the history of all nations."

The ordinary essayist of Agnes Repplier's period, coming out of Philadelphia and feted primarily in Boston, might well deserve the charge of provincialism or, at best, sectionalism. But her writings know no limits in geography at least, whatever other limitations may have been set upon them by virtue of the personality of the author.

ɔ ɔ ɔ

Early in her career as essayist, Agnes Repplier had openly declared herself opposed to unbridled reformers and their reforms. In "What Children Read," an essay belonging in her first collection, she had admitted quite frankly that she disliked "reform" books for children, the sort produced by Flora Shaw and Susan Warner. In the same volume she wrote of "the intolerable sting of that modern gadfly, the professional agitator and socialistic champion of the poor." A dozen years later Miss Repplier was still of the same mind. "Reformers have unswervingly and un-pityingly decreased the world's content that they might better the world's condition," she complained in "The Gayety of Life." And as time passed, she remained adamant in her attitude.

In all this rebuffing of the endless tide of reform, Agnes Repplier's frame of mind can be seen to have resulted from the workings of two characteristics instinct with her. The author, both through inheritance and through her formal education and lifelong reading and study, was a patrician. True, she was not a social aristocrat, not by birth; she belonged in a far more worthy class, for hers was an intellectual aristocracy. And coupled with this, derived to a certain extent from it, was her ability to see through to bedrock fundamentals. Hence sentimental reform of the somewhat spectacular sort that called for demonstrations, strikes and the like, could never hold appeal for her if for no other reason than that she was constitutionally incapable of entering into such demonstrations. Even after she had turned to the writing of ardent interventionist papers during the First World War, her ring, so to speak, remained her study or the eminently genteel, tight, socially and intellectually correct Contemporary Club. And because, as she saw it, the reforms demanded by the clamorers of her day ("Give the business of running the world to the women, and there will be no more wars," for example) were so patently surface, their value left her unmoved, for she saw no value in them.

There was no hardness, save superficially, and certainly

no indifference in Agnes Repplier's relation to humanitarian reform. She was endowed with a sense of proportion that could not countenance the excesses, the extraordinary limits, as she saw them, that popular reformers would demand. And her sense of humor was too keenly developed to allow her to overlook the fact, as she regarded it, that much of the proposed reform and many of the proposing reformers were plainly ridiculous. For the most part, Miss Repplier preferred to let the world work out its problems in the age-old way, that is, by letting the problems work themselves out. Her inbred conservatism rebelled at short cuts that sacrificed common sense and good taste in an effort to achieve reward not deserved except by honest effort.

ꙅ ꙅ ꙅ

Agnes Repplier was not without her unreasonable prejudices. It could scarcely be expected that she would be; after all, she was quite human. More than that, she was a woman. And even more, she was distinctly a gentlewoman. During the First World War she was eminently unfair, narrow-minded even, where the Irish were concerned. Perhaps her dislike for the Irish can be explained in part by the fact that it had been ingrained by her mother, and she had come, further, to resent the fact that in the United States the Irish had seemingly preëmpted the Roman Catholic Church, though neither may condone her attitude.

The essayist was even more ungraciously prejudiced toward the Germans. " 'The Germans are a rude, unmannered race, but active and expert where their personal advantages are concerned,' wrote the observant Froissart many years ago. He could say neither more nor less were he traveling over the Continent to-day," she commented in a paper written some ten years before the outbreak of the First World War. In all her volumes of essays one sympathetic reference to a German stands out as striking because it is unique.

For all her evident love of the English, Miss Repplier bore no illusions where their faults were concerned. She knew them too well. But it was both easy and natural for her to rush to their aid in whatever way she could when war threatened that country. It was doubly easy, as it happened, because Germany, a country whose people had never aroused her sympathy or esteem, stood as the enemy.

The writer's tried and trusted friend Agnes Irwin urged her; Dr. White sought her collaboration; and Theodore Roosevelt added his cajolings. The air was full of pro-British sympathy. America was plainly shirking its duty. She would not shirk hers.

And so there was offered to the public a long list of essays motivated, not by literary history, the field Miss Repplier knew and loved so well, but by a new and suddenly purposeful creed. The essayist became an ardent crusader, a reformer as it were, and this in spite of her equally ardent dislike for crusaders and reformers. It is true that the issues were, at least to her, more vital than those that attracted the ordinary crusader. But what difference there may have been between the two was one of degree, not of kind.

The majority of essays Agnes Repplier wrote during the nearly three years between the beginning of hostilities in Europe and the entry of the United States into the war deal with the cause of intervention in one way or another. And the general tone of these papers is one of bitterness. They are characterized by caustic, wry humor, by biting sarcasm, by invective verging on the openly libelous.

The aftereffect of these war papers was felt, in the essays of Agnes Repplier, for more than a dozen years following the cessation of that which had called them forth. Having experienced the excitement of a crusade, and evidently having enjoyed the feeling, the writer uncovered others to replace the one that no longer existed. Thus she loosed her scorn upon suffragettes, upon penal reform, upon the prohibitionist, upon almost any topic that would allow her to continue in the biting, caustic vein that had become a part of her during the siege against the pacifist and the isolationist. Commenting on the aftermath of the war in "Peace and the Pacifist," she confessed: "There are many of us who have failed to regain the lightness of heart which seemed a normal condition before this horror came." As far as her writings were concerned, it was as if she had become so wound up immediately prior to and during the war that time was needed for her in which to unwind. And it was not until 1932 and the publication of *To Think of Tea!* that, in her essays at least, she had reached the degree of equanimity that had been hers before the "horror came."

It is not so curious as it might on first consideration seem that Agnes Repplier lost all interest in intervention in world affairs after the war was over. Agnes Irwin was dead; Dr. White and Theodore Roosevelt were gone. Such chilling facts had their effect. But at the core of the change lay the essayist's true affections. She was not a crusader; she was not a politician. She was not comfortable with those who advocated causes. And she could no more forswear the power of the intellectual pastimes of her childhood, which, as she had said, an author's work reflected, than she could forswear the power of love itself. It was inevitable that she should return to the older, far happier pursuits.

It is a woman's prerogative, we are told, to change her mind. If in *Counter-Currents*, *Under Dispute*, and *Times and Tendencies*, Agnes Repplier had seemingly contradicted in content and in tone much of what had gone before and much that was to come after, she may merely have been exercising her prerogative. For first and last, she was a very woman among women.

II

Although Agnes Repplier was the author of some eight extended pieces of biographical writing, three of these alone stand as being of primary importance. The other five, undeniably excellent as writing per se, remain somewhat less than the others as biography by virtue either of their size, their intent, or their general appeal. Without question *Mère Marie of the Ursulines*, *Père Marquette*, and *Junípero Serra* are the three volumes that give Agnes Repplier rank among the foremost of American biographers.

Of all the biographies Miss Repplier wrote, the one which most marks her as a Philadelphian is that dealing with her native city. An outsider could well have written as historically accurate a biography, but it took an insider to achieve the subtleties of significance that distinguish *Philadelphia, the Place and the People* (1898). However, although it was written at the behest of Macmillan for that company's "Travel Series," and, presumably, would have sale beyond the city limits, it remains a book of greatest interest to its own people whose history it recalls and records.

Because they are autobiographical in nature, *In Our Convent Days* (1905) and the title essay in *Eight Decades* (1937) stand apart from the body of Agnes Repplier's biographical writings. That the former is a somewhat romanticized account of incidents out of the author's early stay at Eden Hall and the latter a tantalizingly brief summary of her life up to her eightieth year both adds to and takes away from what at first might appear to be their real worth as autobiographies. *In Our Convent Days*, although fully detailed, is a bit too smooth for total accuracy, and "Eight Decades," uncompromisingly honest, is too cursory to allow of much detail.

Agnes Irwin: A Biography (1934), a slight volume if judged by bulk alone, was something of a labor of love, even though it had been sponsored by the Agnes and Sophy Dallas Irwin Memorial Fund. Agnes Repplier had the warmest affection for her early mentor, an affection that had grown through the years, for although Miss Irwin was considerably Miss Repplier's senior, theirs had been a close friendship after the initial failure. But *Agnes Irwin* is not among Miss Repplier's more important works, though as an appreciative gesture it is pleasant, and as a source of information concerning the author's days at the Irwin School, as well as after, it is valuable.

A far larger work in every respect than the book about Miss Irwin is *J. William White, M.D.: A Biography* (1919). And this is so not only because the friendship between the author and her subject was more complete than that between the teacher and her former pupil (Miss Irwin being somewhat too formidable a person for such friendships), but also because Dr. White was a considerably more colorful individual than the first Dean of Radcliffe College. *J. William White* is a rewarding book. It must have offered its author considerable pleasure in the writing. But its limitation is the limitation of its subject: prominent as he no doubt was in medical circles, Dr. White is not a "large" subject when compared with the figures with whom Miss Repplier deals in her three most important biographical works.

In *Père Marquette: Priest, Pioneer and Adventurer* (1929), Agnes Repplier wrote the first of a series of three biographies dealing with early figures in the history of the Roman Catholic Church in America. In all three she lays aside of necessity all considerations purely contemporary, all those immediate likes and dislikes that, for example, quite naturally marked her biographies of Agnes Irwin and Dr. White. In all three she returns to the style of her former writings before the war and problems of the day beset her.

Père Marquette tells the history of that pioneer-priest's coming to New France, of his work in and around Quebec, and of his discovery, along with Joliet, of the Mississippi River, which, as the author comments, "for a stream of its magnitude . . . was singularly elusive." Of its nineteen chapters, five have little to do with the central character, contributing instead both proloque and epilogue, though not so designated, to the main drama. But although these chapters may on the surface appear to have been included to give book proportions to an otherwise brief story, one does not resent them. They are so marked by the author's artful selection of detail and by her excellence in expression that they become in themselves outstanding as essays. Thus "The Lure of the Mississippi" or " 'The Indians of the Prayer,' " to choose two of the five, are, unless one insists that Agnes Repplier is at her best only when she is writing of literary history, as effective essays as any she ever wrote. Furthermore, because the picture is thus supplemented with authoritative related material, *Père Marquette* becomes a book that has worth not only as biography, but as history.

"M. André Maurois, who has told us—and shown us—how to write biographies, says that in every life there is a hidden rhythm," Agnes Repplier notes in this story of Père Marquette. "The biographer's business," she continues, "is to discover this mysterious music, and to note its correspondence with outward circumstances, its response to any influence, seen or felt, which strikes an impelling note." And this Agnes Repplier succeeds in doing in *Père Marquette.* Thus she makes of him, not just a priest of the Catholic Church sent out to proselytize the native Indians, but a pioneer, because he was motivated in large part by a reaching out into the unknown, and a discoverer, because that, even more than converting the Indians to Catholicism, was his destiny.

The central theme in the "mysterious music" of Père Marquette's life was the drumbeat of the "Red Gods;" the chant remained a secondary motive, strong, impelling, but not prime in his life. Had Père Marquette been merely a priest, even a missionary, he could have carried on a respectably productive life much nearer his native Laon. But he was not. He was an adventurer—to use that word in its purest sense—of the Catholic Church.

And his biographer does not hesitate to make him out such an adventurer:

Although the conversion of heathen tribes is understood to be the aim and end of a missionary's existence, it is impossible to read Père Marquette's narrative (Joliet's was unhappily lost in the swollen waters of the St. Lawrence) without a pleasant realization that the sentiment uppermost in the hearts of these two young men was a keen anticipation of the remarkably venturesome voyage, its risks and rewards. They were about to penetrate into the unknown. They were bound on a magnificent errand. They had been selected from dozens of other young men to perform a signal service for France. They were abandoning comparative comfort (food and shelter) for real hardships, and comparative safety for certain danger. What wonder that Père Marquette closes an account of their meager equipment with these exhilarating words: "We were ready to do and suffer everything for so glorious an undertaking."

As one would expect—even as one would hope—there are certain touches in *Père Marquette* that place it in the ranks of Agnes Repplier's most characteristic work. And none is more characteristic than what she has to say concerning something particularly dear to her heart. Although scattered here and there throughout the whole body of her writings there are occasional allusions to the beneficent effect of tobacco, it is here in this story of the priest of New France that the author writes her fullest apostrophe to "My Lady Nicotine:"

Our debt to the Indians for the discovery and use of tobacco, of that inestimable solace in a hard—and sedative in a noisy—

world, is so great that no heart is wide enough to hold it, and no words are warm enough to give it proper expression. Therefore it is a pleasure to know that to many of these Indians the pipe was an august and holy thing, the emblem of all they held hallowed and dear.

Agnes Repplier found in Père Marquette a figure eminently satisfying to her. And in her simple telling of his death, to choose but one illustration out of many, the sympathy she felt for her subject and the art that was by now instinct with her combined to produce a singularly moving picture:

On the 18th of May the canoe passed the mouth of a small and rapid stream with sloping banks. On the left shore was a gentle eminence crowned by oaks. Père Marquette asked his companions to land. His hour had come, and the little hill would make a fitting site for his grave. Quickly they beached the canoe, and with the practiced dexterity of woodsmen built a shed of saplings, branches, and bark. To this poor shelter they carried the dying man, and laid him on a mat by the side of a freshly lighted fire. When he had rallied a little he gave them a few simple directions for his burial, thanked them for the care and devotion they had shown him ("the charities which they had exercised in his behalf"), and confessed them both—his last priestly function. Then he bade them sleep, saying he would call them, or ring his little mass bell, when he grew worse. Three hours later they heard the summons and hastened to his side. He whispered to one of them to take the crucifix from his neck, and hold it before his eyes. Faintly he breathed familiar words of prayer: *"Sustinuit anima mea in verbo ejus." "Mater Dei, memento mei."* When he had ceased, and the watchers thought the spirit had fled, one of them cried in a loud voice, "Jesus, Mary." At the sound of those beloved names Père Marquette's eyes opened wide. Distinctly he repeated them: "Jesus, Mary," and died.

In *Mère Marie of the Ursulines* (1931) Agnes Repplier wrote the second in the series of three historical biographies of early Catholic figures in America. The stories of Mère Marie and Père Marquette overlap in point of time, but the two books present quite different pictures. Not only is this the story of a woman, but its scene is laid almost entirely in the town of Quebec instead of the wilderness around, for this is a story in part of colonization rather than of exploration.

Mère Marie tells the history of Marie Guyard, who at thirty-two, being then a widow with a half-grown son, entered the Ursuline convent at her native Tours, and, some eight years later, sailed for Quebec where she founded the convent for which she is remembered. It is a simple narrative of hardship, relentless effort, modest accomplishment, undistinguished by any climax in action as was the story of Père Marquette. In one respect only does Mère Marie go beyond her fellow pioneer: in 1922 she was declared venerable, the first step toward canonization.

As was *Père Marquette*, this biography is built up with supplementary material illuminating its main figure. Thus there is a chapter on Saint Ursula, one on Champlain, as well as whole sections of other chapters dealing with the Indians and the efforts of the missionary priests. And as was the case with the former work, here too this additional material serves the valuable purpose of reinforcing the scene, so that *Mère Marie* is quite as much a picture of an era as is *Père Marquette*. But because Mère Marie had been granted a longer life than the explorer-priest, and in consequence a fuller history, there is about this book a greater sense of unity, for the surrounding information is as a result less extensive.

The "mysterious music," the "hidden rhythm," of the life told in these pages, although related to that of *Père*

Marquette, inasmuch as the overtones are those of the Catholic chant, is of a different sort from that found in the earlier biography. Mère Marie had in her being the love of the unknown that marked Père Marquette, else she never would have been so eager to leave the Ursuline convent at Tours, but she was not motivated by this impulse to the extent that the priest had been. She was a teacher primarily, an organizer of a school that sought to bring the native Indians into the church by way of their children. "As Quebec developed," the biographer notes, "Mère Marie's letters reflect every phase of the development. She writes less and less about the things of the spirit, and more and more about what is going on around her." Although a mystic, she was a distinctly human person. "Her ecstatic piety never obliterated her practical qualities," the author states with finality.

"It is the lamentable habit of hagiographers to exclude from their narratives any circumstances which might possibly link them with life, to deny to the subjects of their pious memoirs any characteristic which savors too strongly of humanity. In their desire to be edifying they cease to be convincing," Agnes Repplier early declares in her story of Mère Marie. Hence with the purpose of giving life to her subject clearly defined at the outset, she draws the very essence of life into her work and provides a strong and unmistakable chain of links between the convent founder and the life around her. There is no forgetting here that Mère Marie was first and foremost a woman beset by the trials of her kind and of her day. "Mère Marie was by nature a daughter of Mary. All mystics are. She would fain have sat at the feet of Christ in blissful quiescence and contemplation. But the role of Martha had been assigned her, and she ennobled and sanctified it."

Mère Marie is not without its glints of characteristic Repplierean humor, though quiet for the most part as befits the occasion. One night in December of 1650 the Ursuline convent in Quebec burned to the ground, and the little Indian children stood shivering in their night clothes. "The nuns," we are told, "were not much better off, though some of them had snatched up their cloaks as they fled. Mme de la Peltrie [patroness of the convent] made her escape in her night dress—'quite an old worn night dress,' observed Mère Marie with regret." Concerning this information the biographer comments dryly: "She evidently considered that a new one would have been more appropriate to the situation."

Here and there the book is enlivened by a note of levity that would be truly remarkable in many Catholic authors, though through the years it had come to be looked upon as quite an accepted—almost an expected—mark of Agnes Repplier's attitude toward certain aspects of her church. The biographer is writing of the Vicar Apostolic and first Bishop of New France, a considerable person in the story of Mère Marie. "Laval," she remarks, "the fighting bishop, has been pronounced venerable by the Church he served. He is en route for sainthood, though outstripped in the race by the eight Canadian martyrs who were canonized in June, 1930," a neat figure indeed.

Mère Marie is in several respects a better book than *Père Marquette*. And this is so not only because the story is in itself a rounder, fuller one, a more clearly defined unit. This second historical biography takes precedence over the other because, although the author was in entire sympathy with the priest-explorer, she could bring an even deeper understanding to the delineation of the nun-teacher. All writers are in a sense teachers, and the critic even more so than most others. The biographer being a woman was better prepared to understand Mère Marie than Père Marquette. And being of a critical turn of mind, she was further marked by nature to evaluate Mère Marie's teaching mission. Although she could appreciate the wanderlust that took Père Marquette on his journeys into the mapless wilderness, for travel in foreign lands stimulated her immeasurably, she was a true explorer in the intellectual sense only. Her essential urbanity found far greater appeal in the Quebec of *Mère Marie*, primitive as it no doubt was, than in the most thrilling of discoveries drawn from the tangled forests of *Père Marquette*. If in Père Marquette Agnes Repplier had found a figure satisfying to her, in Mère Marie she found another even more satisfying, for Mère Marie was in many ways a woman after her own heart.

Junípero Serra, Pioneer Colonist of California (1933) is the third and last volume in Agnes Repplier's historical trilogy. In this biography the author travels across the country, far from the Canada of *Père Marquette* and *Mère Marie*, to the distant land claimed by Spain as the other had been claimed by France. But although there is a divergence in cultures here, and no bond exists between Junípero Serra and his fellow colonists such as existed between Père Marquette and Mère Marie, the Roman Catholic Church ties the three together in one common endeavor and gives a certain homogeneity to the group.

The story of *Junípero Serra* is that of the founding of nine missions in California, dating from the first in 1770 to the last in 1782. It is the history of an heroic priest who ignored his own physical handicaps, combatted the difficulties raised by rash military incompetents, and toiled unceasingly in the realization of a dream. It is the history of the beginnings of that which has come down to this day as an integral portion of the Spanish survival in California.

The technique, practiced in *Père Marquette* and *Mère Marie*, of supplementing the account of the main figure with additional material to produce a full story is carried here in this biography somewhat beyond reasonable limits and brings about an ultimate effect different from that of the other two books. Because Agnes Repplier does go rather far afield, as, for example, in the chapter "What Happened Afterwards" in which a long recounting of the efforts of Russia to take a hand in the development of California is given, the "history" of *Junípero Serra* appears to outweigh the "biography," with the result that the book is divided against itself. In the final analysis, this is not true biography but something lying between biography and history. That which had achieved such a neat balance in *Mère Marie* is lost here in *Junípero Serra*, and consequently the central personality is submerged almost to the point of being forgotten altogether.

Just as Père Marquette and Mère Marie were found to have been motivated, the one by the lure of the unknown and the other by the urge to teach, so Junípero Serra has his individual "hidden rhythm." The Majorcan friar moved to a "mysterious music" removed in its way from that which stirred either of the other two. Although he was a hundred years closer to the contemporary scene than Mère Marie or Père Marquette, Junípero Serra

was mediaeval. He had the qualities of those emotional, penitential, and migratory years, when endurance was the keynote of existence, and when the love of life was balanced by the honor paid to death. His harsh asceticism, the boards on which he slept, his meagre diet, the cruel mortifying of his flesh, all savored of the Middle Ages; and so, too, did his habit of putting his mind and soul into his work.

Père Marquette and Mère Marie had been forward-looking persons; Junípero Serra, of the present in his founding of the nine missions for the further glory of the Catholic Church, sought his inspiration in the past. His ear was attuned to the muffled, subdued music of a day long since gone.

Here in *Junípero Serra* Agnes Repplier offers a final note on her attitude toward hagiographers and their "pious memoirs:"

There was something very vital and direct in the relations between the Church Militant and the Church Triumphant which in the time of Fray Serra clasped hands across the gulf of death; something that has faded out of our more complicated lives. Cardinal Newman, aware of our loss, said that the fault lay with the hagiographers who eliminated every spark of humanity from these profoundly human servants of God. When a good churchman can write in an ecclesiastical magazine: "There is no disguising the fact that in general the sanctity of the saints affrights us, their selflessness fills us with self-reproach, their burning charity leaves us cold," we feel that Newman's reasoning was just. We cannot blame ourselves for this icy remoteness, and we assuredly cannot blame the saints.

If in the three biographies, *Père Marquette*, *Mère Marie*, *Junípero Serra*, there is any approach to "icy remoteness," it is in this last, though not because Agnes Repplier does not labor to make the friar human, but because of the distant, unapproachable, unassailable medieval asceticism of the man. Of the three closest to us in point of time, Junípero Serra is most removed from us in spirit and underlying in force.

Père Marquette, *Mère Marie*, and *Junípero Serra* demonstrate Agnes Repplier at her best in biography. Here in these three books the artist in her holds with the scholar the balance of power, and as a result the biographies are free from the extreme of bias that came to mar much of the author's late work. One might have expected that Miss Repplier, having given herself over in the essay to a kind of excess following the First World War, would take advantage of the one aspect of the lives she was to relate to indulge in further emphasis of expression. Such would have been understandable here inasmuch as religion frequently looms particularly large in old age, and Agnes Repplier was past seventy when she set out upon the writing of these books. But just as an emotional leveling had turned her back in the essay to old ways, so a reasonableness governed her in the historical biographies.

Although all three of these biographies are drawn from the Roman Catholic Church, and as such are religious books, they are entirely free from any considerations of theology. Indeed, every step along the way the author reveals herself as opposed to the common practices of hagiographers. As far as church is concerned, save for a controlled yet pronounced sympathy, it is almost as if the Catholic

part of the picture as such were taken for granted. Part of
Agnes Repplier's concern here seems to have been to show
that worthy biographies of church figures could be written
that would be free from the charge of sanctimoniousness.
Of the validity of such an opinion she has offered more
than sufficient proof. That *Mère Marie* is the most success-
ful of the three and *Junípero Serra* the least, is understandable in view of both the material at hand and the qualities
the author could bring to bear upon it.

III

"We read The Bostonians and The Rise of Silas Lapham
with a due appreciation of their minute perfections; but we
go to bed quite cheerfully at our usual hour, and are content to wait an interval of leisure to resume them," Agnes
Repplier wrote in her first volume, *Books and Men*. And
she asked: "Could Daisy Miller charm a gouty leg, or
Lemuel Barker keep us sleepless until morning?" She was
never to change in her attitude toward Howells, although
she did in regard to James. Thirty years after her comment
on *The Bostonians* and *Daisy Miller*, Miss Repplier was to
recognize James as a "great novelist."

It is not difficult to understand why Agnes Repplier was
at distinct variance with William Dean Howells, who by
1888, the date of the public expression of her lack of interest in him, had become well established both as editor and
novelist. Howells and realism were synonymous, and the
essayist at the time found the latter at least "arid and
dreary." The "democratic theory of art" advocated by
Howells, with its emphasis upon the middle class, left Agnes

Repplier unmoved. An ardent believer in the great individual, she could find little sympathy for the average human being.

That Agnes Repplier should profess a keen enjoyment over the novels of Dickens, for example, in whose tradition Howells belongs, and at the same time profess as great a dislike for the later novelist is not the contradiction it may at first appear to be. Dickens was English; and with little deviation throughout her entire career, she preferred English authors to American. Furthermore, the time of Dickens' novels was just sufficiently removed from her own to lend them, in spite of their realism, an aura of the romantic. The long ago and far away, particularly when the vista was English, provided an irresistible combination for Agnes Repplier.

As far as Howells and his brand of realism is concerned, Miss Repplier's opinion of both is not difficult of explanation. Henry James offers a somewhat more complicated problem. It is clear that the early work of the expatriate American meant little to the essayist. But as James progressed from realist to symbolist, that is, from *The Bostonians* and *Daisy Miller* to *The Wings of the Dove* and *The Golden Bowl*, it may well have been that his appeal grew for her. Gide's complaint that James "proceeds through subtleties," that "his strokes are too fine," certainly would not have been hers; nor could James's emphasis upon an intellectual approach to character delineation have disturbed her, though she preferred the novel of incident to the novel of character. His position toward America, even when finally he renounced his citizenship, did not alienate her. In the biography of Dr. White she carefully and sympathetically explains James's feelings in the matter. And James is made something of a hero because of his stand.

Henry James may have paved the way for the "stream of consciousness" novel of Virginia Woolf whom Agnes Repplier found "thin" and "self-conscious." But it was in the late novels of James that his characters became increasingly introspective; and it was in 1919, long after the appearance of *The Golden Bowl,* that Miss Repplier called him "great." It is quite possible that the essayist, unsympathetic toward the realists generally, took an early dislike to James for something of the same reason she took an even stronger dislike to Howells: each in his way was an advocate of realism, and realism at the time was anathema to her. Then as she herself, during the period of the First World War, arrived at a far more realistic way of looking at life, and as she came to know James personally through her friend Dr. White, she found in him a greater artist than she had at first suspected. That he had become less obviously the realist undoubtedly helped them to meet at some point midway between the extremes that for each had been a mark of an earlier interest.

It was inevitable that from the start Agnes Repplier should belong outside the literary realm then being charted by Howells and James. By nature and training a conservative, she resented the intrusion of the new. And when, particularly as with Howells, that new was to her mind also mundane, she took an even deeper refuge in the old. The very fact that, although for twenty years almost in the midst of her career she was to concern herself with matters both new and mundane, she eventually returned to the old proves beyond question which in the final analysis had the greater attraction for her.

ↄ ↄ ↄ

Agnes Repplier chose her "happy half-century," the last twenty-five years of the eighteenth century and the first twenty-five of the nineteenth, or thereabouts, she said, because "it was a time when literary reputations were so cheaply gained that nobody needed to despair of one." But far more significant to her than this, the happy half-century was the time of Johnson and Sheridan, of Wordsworth, Coleridge, Byron, Shelley, Keats, Lamb, Jane Austen, to say nothing of the Fanny Burneys, the Hannah Moores, and Maria Edgeworths. This was the period dearest to the essayist's heart, the period she knew and loved the best. This was the period to which she turned again and again for inspiration in her essays.

But Miss Repplier's knowledge of English literature was far from limited only to the happy half-century. Her reading had taken her back to the time of Shakespeare and the Elizabethan lyrists and, with the exception of the drama to which her essays are for the most part singularly void of reference, down to the very days of her eighth decade. Certain writers, it is true, received fuller treatment than others, as would be expected in an author who had been led more by personal taste than by the somewhat sterile attractions of purely objective study. But many more than those appearing at length in her papers belonged in the lists of the elect as far as she was concerned. And even though they may not have figured obviously in her work, they were close to her and she to them.

American literature was never the attraction to Agnes Repplier that English literature was. In "French Love-Songs" she commented: "We are tethered to our kind, and the wisest of all limitations is that which holds us well within the sphere of natural and harmonious development." Agnes Repplier's "kind" was, first and foremost, the English writer and, most of all, the English writer of her "happy half-century."

This is not to say that the essayist had no knowledge of literature outside the English-speaking part of the world, for she had. Greek and Roman writers, from the early days of her schooling when she discovered Horace, her favorite of them all, meant much to her. Her very first volume of essays, in "Some Aspects of Pessimism," exhibits a considerable understanding of classic literature. And one of her late papers deals in sympathetic appreciation with the Sabine satirist.

As would be expected of one brought up to a certain extent in a French tradition, Agnes Repplier had read considerably in the literature of that country. But a simple comparison of two essays, "French Love-Songs" and "English Love-Songs," shows unmistakably which was the closer to her.

Russian literature she knew primarily through the work of Tolstoi, for whom she had scant love. "Count Tolstoi," she wrote in "The Gayety of Life," "has, with the noblest intentions, made many a light step heavy, and many a gay heart sad." The realism of the Russian was as unappealing to her as that of Howells, and the moral uplift supposedly to be gained from a reading of the count was to her small compensation indeed for the lack of pleasure to be derived in the process.

Although one recognizes that Miss Repplier's major pre-occupation was with writers of the nineteenth century and earlier—inevitable in view of the period to which she belongs—one finds in her later work considerable reference to twentieth century authors. Thus in "The Strayed Prohibitionist" she had this to say of Galsworthy:

If the young prohibitionist be light-hearted enough to read Dickens, or imaginative enough to read Scott, or sardonic enough to read Thackeray, he will find everybody engaged in the great business of eating and drinking. It crowds love-making into a corner, being, indeed, a pleasure which survives all tender dalliance, and restores to the human mind sanity and content. I am convinced that if Mr. Galsworthy's characters ate and drank more, they would be less obsessed by sex, and I wish they would try dining as a restorative.

And in "Eight Decades" she wrote of Robert Nathan:

In those joyous months [that is, when in her first decade she had learned to read] which followed my conquest of print . . . I read the books I loved best over and over again. When I had finished [*The Young Crusaders*] I gave a long sigh, turned back to the beginning, and started anew upon its absorbing pages. Thank God I have been able to do the same thing in my old age, notably with Robert Nathan's "Road of Ages," which I re-read instantly while its delicate loveliness was fresh in my mind and heart.

From her very early reading days, the novel held particular appeal for Agnes Repplier, and throughout her career as essayist she frequently passed judgment upon it as an art form. In an essay on "The Novel of Incident" she commented with striking effect: "For my part, the good novel of character is the novel I can always pick up; but the good novel of incident is the novel I can never lay down." But, both because she essayed the form herself, and with marked success, and because her reading in the form was even more extensive than in the novel, the biography is given fuller consideration than any other single literary type. André Maurois's dicta on biography she quoted with approval in *Père Marquette*, and there too as well as in *Mère Marie* and *Junípero Serra*, she offered comment at length on hagiography, a division, so to speak, of the larger form. Elsewhere throughout her essays one finds many telling remarks that reveal clearly the writer's various criteria where biography is concerned. But it is in one of her journals that Agnes Repplier gives what might be considered the key to good biography as she saw it when she wrote, along with a number of damaging quotations concerning Strachey, "The amazing and unconcerned inaccuracies of the modern biographer." Realism—in the novel, for example—annoyed her because too often the realist emphasized the grubby and the completely dull either for the sake of a "photographic likeness" or, what to her was worse, for didactic purposes. But in biography she insisted upon exactness and would admit of neither flights of fancy parading as fact nor of the glittering generalization.

From all this, however, it would be a mistake to conclude that Miss Repplier was free from any limitations as a critic. She was not. And the principal source of her limitation was an undeniable love for phrase-making, the lure of the neat remark even on occasion at the cost of her equally undeniably good "reading sense." Nowhere is this fault more obvious than in her war-provoked essay "Waiting," in which she deliberately misread Longfellow's "Psalm of Life" for mere effect:

In the most esteemed of his advisory poems, Mr. Longfellow recommends his readers to be "up and doing," and at the same time learn "to labour and to wait." Having, all of us, imbibed these sentiments in their harmonious setting when we were at school, we have, all of us, endeavored for many months to put such conflicting precepts into practice. Mr. Longfellow, it will be remembered, gave precedence to his "up and doing line;" but this may have been due to the exigencies of verse.

The essayist was angry and bitter at the time over what appeared to her and many of her pro-British friends to be the cowardly delaying of the United States to enter the conflict. But here in this essay she was most certainly guilty of a lack of fairness for which she would as certainly have taken any other writer at any other time to severe task.

ᴐ ᴐ ᴐ

In her essay "Wit and Humor" Agnes Repplier defines these two oft-confused manners, both of which mark much of her writing, though of the two, the former is more prominent. It is to be expected that in the work of this writer, fundamentally the intellectual, wit should play a larger part than humor. On occasion, it is true, humor is her special interest. Thus in "Humor: English and American" and "The Mission of Humor" she deals with this form at some length. And, incidentally, it is interesting to note that in the latter essay, written some eighteen years after the former, the author is far less favorably inclined toward the American brand than she is toward the English. It is equally curious that in the earlier paper, coming at a time when nearly all things English seemed the brightest the world had to offer, the essayist favored the American to the English. Frequently when one thinks he has the writer neatly pigeonholed in one regard or another, some contradiction or near contradiction disrupts all patent plan.

Agnes Repplier's wit, demonstrated so ably and so often in her essays, defies cataloguing as successfully as do on occasion her varying points of view. Sometimes, as in "What Children Read," it is the result of a skillful use of incongruity alone. The writer is complaining in this paper of the ridiculous fare of the modern child-reader, lamenting that the old books of worth have been replaced by present-day twaddle:

> "How much of our poetry," it has been asked, "owes its start to Spenser, when the Fairy Queen was a household book, and lay in the parlor window-seat?" . . . We know that in the window-seat of Cowley's mother's room lay a copy of the Fairy Queen, which to her little son was a source of unfailing delight, and Pope has recorded the ecstasy with which, as a lad, he pored over this wonderful poem; but then neither Cowley nor Pope had the advantage of following Oliver Optic through the slums of New York, or living with some adventurous "boy hunters" in the jungles of Central Africa.

Or again, as in "The Beloved Sinner," the main thesis of which is that "All the world does not love a lover . . . But all the world does love a sinner," Miss Repplier's wit results from a blend of the incongruous with something else. Here, as elsewhere in her writings, the ridiculousness of a situation or idea is revealed, not only by a deft use of the incongruous, but also by the simple expedient of applying merciless logic to that which usually receives some other, generally sentimental, handling. In "The Beloved Sinner" the essayist directs her wit at the misguided public that would sympathize, not with the victim, but with the victimizer.

Frequently Miss Repplier makes use of a kind of exaggeration that is the result of logic applied in a different direction. In such instances, cold reason plus exaggeration is used to prick a bubble, a bubble that itself is evidence of exaggeration. In *The Fireside Sphinx* she tells of a wonderful cat that belonged to a Scotch friend of hers, a cat that was in the habit of eating the sparrows that came to feed upon the crumbs its owner tossed from the dining-room window. In order to circumvent the cat, the Scotchman stopped scattering the crumbs, whereupon the astute animal stole a roll from the breakfast table, thus providing its own bait for the unwary birds. This is the tall story; and this her comment: "It only remains to be told that [the cat] first baked the bread, and this veracious chronicle will be complete."

"If men of real wit have been more numerous in the world than men of real humor, it is because discernment and lenity, mirth and conciliation, are qualities which do not blend easily with the natural asperity of our race," Agnes Repplier wrote in "Wit and Humor." And she recognized the further fact that "edged tools are dangerous things to handle, and not infrequently do much hurt." In her essays written during and for some years after the period of the First World War, Miss Repplier resorted to wit of a far more biting sort than that which distinguishes the larger part of her writings. Aroused by American indifference, later somewhat embittered by American foolishness, she forgot her sense of humor in an almost relentless display of wit. The essays of this period so marked are in a sense uncomfortable essays, verging on the irritable and peevish. Sarcasm replaced satire, and the earlier good humor was cast aside. "Few things in the world are more wearying than a sarcastic attitude towards life," the essayist had written years before the conflict. And the truth of her assertion, because the assertion itself was unfortunately forgotten, was largely borne out as a result of the disrupting effect of the war upon her.

It is not every writer who appreciates the usefulness and true worth of the neatly turned phrase as does Agnes Repplier. Early in her career she confessed to valuing form over content. And if on occasion she allowed the former to wield too obvious a control over the latter for the sake of effect alone, when the full scope of her work is taken into account, the occasions are slight indeed. "There are many who affirm that the humorist's point of view is, on the whole, the fairest from which the world can be judged. It is equally remote from the misleading side-lights of the pessimist and from the wilful blindness of the optimist. It sees things with uncompromising clearness, but it judges of them with tolerance and good temper." Although, strictly speaking, one cannot class Miss Repplier as a humorist, she was endowed with the "humorist's point of view," and for the most part it did indeed allow her to see "things with uncompromising clearness" and to "judge of them with tolerance and good temper."

ꙩ ꙩ ꙩ

Some critics have passed judgment upon Agnes Repplier to the effect that her work shows little more than assimilation, that she merely gathered appropriate ideas and quotations together and made her essays out of her gleanings. She herself, amused by the idea, remarked lightly: "Why should I do the writing when there was someone else to do it for me?" But there is far more to the matter than just that. It is true that some assimilation does not create; but it is equally true that, on the other hand, some does. And Agnes Repplier's is certainly of the latter kind. Out of her gatherings of material, both ideas and quotations, she invariably made something new, something, furthermore, that was given additional interest and worth by the way in which she presented it.

Although in the essays of the war period and immediately following Miss Repplier turned aside from the main current of her inspiration—though the means of expression remained almost of constant excellence—essentially she was not interested in the kind of writing, be it poetry or prose, that, parading as art, existed for some ulterior purpose. For the essayist, art was first and foremost a source of pleasure. "Any book which serves to lower the sum of human gayety is a moral delinquent," she wrote in "A Plea for Humor." And again: "Art is never didactic, does not take kindly to facts, is helpless to grapple with theories, and is killed outright by a sermon." It is for this reason that Tolstoi meant no more to her than he did. "The hundred and one excellent reasons for becoming acquainted with Tolstoi or Ibsen," she wrote in "Literary Shibboleths," "resolve themselves into a single motive when we turn to Scott. It is 'for human delight' or nothing."

Agnes Repplier never offered any justification of or explanation for her abandoning the principle of pleasure for the didactically purposeful essays of the war period. Patently she felt no explanation was necessary. The war itself was sufficient justification. But some among her friends felt that she "burned herself out" in the white heat of her propagandist vehemence. They were of the opinion that she never fully recovered from the devastation her excess of vituperation worked upon her. Happily *To Think of Tea!* and *In Pursuit of Laughter* as well as the historical biographies stand as ample refutation of such a contention.

Ꙩ Ꙩ Ꙩ

In one of her journals Miss Repplier quotes T. S. Eliot as having said that "he does not believe that 'Marius the Epicurean' has influenced a single first-rate mind or a later generation," to which she added, "As he did mine." And in her paper on Pater's book she wrote that the lesson it teaches is "to help us to be as happy as we can, by increasing and refining our sensations, by identifying ourselves with every form of beauty, and by opening our hearts freely to all high emotions." The essayist was indeed a lover of beauty. No further proof is necessary than is to be found in what she wrote of the Elizabethan lyric, revealing as it does a sensitivity to beauty exquisitely expressed, though further proof there is to be found in plenty. In her essay "On the Benefits of Superstition" she declared that "beauty is one of the tonics now most earnestly recommended to our sick souls." And in "Curiosities of Criticism" she tied her critical credo in with beauty and wisdom. "Criticism," she wrote in that paper, "does not mean a random opinion on the last new novel, though even the most dismal of light literature comes fairly within its scope. It means a disinterested endeavor to learn and to teach whatever wisdom and beauty has been added by every age and every nation to the great inheritance of mankind." Wisdom and beauty blended

in the critical approach to life and literature is the essence
of the writings of Agnes Repplier save when the First
World War led her into a foreign and not altogether congenial field.

In her essay "Words" Miss Repplier wrote:

The felicitous choice of words, which with most writers is
the result of severe study and unswerving vigilance, seems with
a favored few—who should be envied and not imitated—to be
the genuine fruit of inspiration, as though caprice itself could
not lead them far astray. Shelley's letters and prose papers
teem with sentences in which the beautiful words are sufficient
satisfaction in themselves, and of more value than the conclusions they reveal. They have a haunting sweetness, a pure perfection, which makes the act of reading them a sustained and
dulcet pleasure. Sometimes this effect is produced by a few
simple terms reiterated into lingering music. "We are born,
and our birth is unremembered, and our infancy remembered
but in fragments; we live on, and in living we lose the ap-
prehension of life." Sometimes a clearer note is struck with the
sure and delicate touch which is the excellence of art. "For
the mind in creation is as a fading coal, which some invisible
influence, like an inconstant wind, awakens to transitory
brightness." The substitution of the word "glow" for "brightness" would, I think, make this sentence extremely beautiful.

This, then, the effect of words upon the essayist, this in
evidence of the attention she paid to the nuances of language. And this the brief summation of the whole matter:
"Every word misused revenges itself forever upon a writer's
reputation."

To Agnes Repplier, style in writing was preëminent.
"The stern labor of the file" was one of her favorite phrases,
and in a letter to her friend Mrs. Warren, wherein it is to be
found, she emphasized the fact that the study of words, of
styles, of means and manners of expression had been a life-

long work with her. It is for this very reason that, even though on occasion one may not agree with what the writer has to say, seldom indeed can one argue over the way in which it has been said. It is for this very reason that Miss Repplier was able to interest a host of readers in matters long considered dead, and in the byways of history and literature.

ꙮ ꙮ ꙮ

This, then, is almost the entire picture. It remains but to point again to her liberal-conservative attitude, to her extensive knowledge, to her attitude on intolerance. By training, both that which had been self-imposed and that the result of her schooling, and by nature a lover of fundamentals, Miss Repplier sought the very basis of things for her consideration of any question. Her Catholic education gave her an insight into matters frequently unknown or misunderstood by non-Catholic writers. And her wide reading in the world at large gave her a firm footing beyond the confines of her religion.

Possessing such a solid foundation on which to build, the essayist, save in some of those papers directly effected by the First World War, seldom demonstrates more than a completely justifiable intolerance. In "The Strayed Prohibitionist," for example, she is wrathful over what she felt was an infringement upon her personal rights. Law-made crime was not crime as she saw it. Independent all her life, she would not have others tell her what she should eat and drink, and she was of the strong opinion that those who felt that such indeed was not only their privilege but their right were guilty of an intolerance incompatible with proper freedom. The only intolerance with which she could sympathize was that directed against stupidity and sham. Guilty of neither fault herself, she saw no reason for allowing or condoning them in others.

But current topics, no matter how ardently discussed for the moment, were not Agnes Repplier's real interest. The written word alone she allowed to dominate her life. "When the standard of criticism is high, when the influence of classical and foreign literature is understood and appreciated, when slovenly and ill-digested work is promptly recognized as such, then, and then only, may we look for the full expansion of a country's genius. To be satisfied with less is an amiable weakness rather than an invigorating stimulant to perfection." This was the admirable creed to which Agnes Repplier showed admirable devotion through sixty years and more of constant labor. Weaknesses, amiable or otherwise, were not for her.

NOTES

Chapter I

Page 5: Biographical sketch: See Agnes Repplier's letter to Harrison Morris, p. 115.

Page 9: "Wagner is thundered . . . ": Letter to Mrs. Schuyler Neilson Warren. Sept. 21, 1913 (Philadelphia).

Page 11: "I learned my . . . ": *Points of View*, pp. 65–67.

Page 14: "When I was . . . ": *J. William White, M.D.*, p. 3.

Page 14: "Once more I . . . ": *Essays in Idleness*, pp. 48–49.

Page 14: "Having never been . . . ": *Ibid.*, p. 50.

Chapter II

Page 21: "At that Spartan . . . ": *In Our Convent Days*, pp. 2–3.

Page 21: "Those little imps . . . ": *Eight Decades*, p. 7.

Page 21: "No one had . . . ": *In Our Convent Days*, p. 107.

Page 22: "*Then*, over an . . . ": *Ibid*, pp. 165–66.

Page 28: "The scene was . . . ": *Ibid.*, pp. 70–71.

Page 31: "Francis was first . . . ": *Ibid.*, p. 114.

Page 36: "On one occasion . . . ": *Agnes Irwin*, p. 20.

Page 36: "A clever little . . . ": *Ibid.*, p. 18.

Chapter III

Page 50: "If form was . . . ": See letter to Harrison Morris, p. 116.

Page 52: "Of all the . . . ": Letter to Harrison Morris. March 17, 1937 (Philadelphia).

Page 55: "I am glad . . . ": Letter to Harrison Morris. March 19, 1895 (Rome).

Page 58: "About July 1884 . . . ": In *Celestial Homespun, The Life of Isaac Thomas Hecker* (New York, 1943), Katherine Burton gives an account of this meeting. The date is said to be 1877. However, Miss Repplier said the meeting came *after* she had published for some time in the *Catholic World,* and it would seem reasonable that the meeting took place immediately before the publication of the paper on Ruskin (1884), not seven years before as would be the case according to Miss Burton. It might be noted also that in *Celestial Homespun* Agnes Repplier's age is given as twenty in 1877. Actually she was twenty-two at that date.

Page 59: "The first criticism . . . ": *Catholic World,* XC (Nov. 1909), 172–74.

Page 62: "At the risk . . . ": *Ibid.,* pp. 172–73.

Chapter IV

Page 67: "Mary and I . . . ": Letter to Harrison Morris. Feb. 3, 1892 (Philadelphia).

Chapter V

Page 87: "It was said . . . ": *Eight Decades,* pp. 13–14.

Chapter VI

Page 100: "After French, Dutch . . . ": Letter to Harrison Morris. Aug. 16, 1890 (London).

Chapter VII

Page 120: "He bade me . . . ": *Eight Decades,* p. 21.
Page 125: "Miss Repplier's function . . . ": *Chap Book,* VII (Nov. 1, 1897), 478.
Page 125: "It has insight . . . ": *Critic, N. S.,* XXIX (Jan. 15, 1898), 42–43.

Chapter VIII

Page 129: "There is something . . . ": *Eight Decades,* pp. 294–95.
Page 139: "Once, long ago . . . ": *Ibid.,* pp. 304–5.

Chapter IX

Page 144: "We have invited . . . ": From the records of the Secretary of the University of Pennsylvania.
Page 149: "The one book . . . ": See p. 63.

Chapter X

Page 157: "For distinguished achievements . . . ": In the Warren letter collection. (March 25, 1911.)

Chapter XIII

Page 205: "history written by . . . ": *Catholic World*, CXXIX (April 1929), 116.
Page 205: "The Catholic book-shelf . . . ": *Commonweal*, IX (Feb. 13, 1929), 434.
Page 205: "Everything that discriminating . . . ": *New York Herald Tribune Books*, V (Jan. 13, 1929), 2.
Page 206: "a trifle bewildering . . . ": *Eight Decades*, p. 41.
Page 207: "She sent word . . . ": *Ibid.*, p. 40.
Page 211: "Those who . . . ": *Catholic World*, CXXXV (April 1932), 120.
Page 211: "The shade of . . . ": *Saturday Review of Literature*, VIII (Jan. 2, 1932), 431.
Page 211: "Miss Repplier's precision . . . ": *New York Herald Tribune Books*, VIII (Nov. 29, 1931), 12.
Page 214: "a labor of . . . ": *Nation*, CXXXVII (Nov. 29, 1933), 627.
Page 214: "a noble [biography] . . . ": *Commonweal*, XIX (Dec. 22, 1933), 222.
Page 214: "demonstrates once again . . . ": *Saturday Review of Literature*, X (Dec. 23, 1933), 369.
Page 217: "no dry and . . . ": From the publisher's notice.
Page 218: "has something to . . . ": *Commonweal*, XXVII (Dec. 31, 1937), 276.
Page 218: "learning leaves us . . . ": *Yale Review*, N.S., XXVI (March 1937), 602.
Page 219: "My aunt, Agnes . . . ": *This Is My Best*, Whit Burnett, ed. (New York, 1942), p. 657.

Chapter XIV

Page 224: "Never has a . . . ": *Poems of Friction,* p. 182.

Page 224: "The girl who . . . ": *Points of View,* p. 209.

Page 225: "There is a . . . ": *Compromises,* p. 22.

Page 226: "Sixty-two years ago . . . ": *Times and Tendencies,* pp. 73–74.

Page 246: "Thirty years after . . . ": *J. William White, M.D.,* p. 118.

Page 246: "arid and dreary": *Essays in Miniature,* p. 121.

Page 246: "The 'democratic theory . . . ": Arthur Hobson Quinn, *American Fiction* (New York, 1936), p. 273.

Page 247: "proceeds through subtleties . . . ": *The Question of Henry James,* F. W. Dupee, ed. (New York, 1945), p. 252.

Page 248: "thin and self-conscious . . . ": Agnes Repplier's Journal. In the Library of the University of Pennsylvania.

Page 256: "Few things in the world . . . ": *Essays in Idleness,* p. 181.

Page 256: "There are many . . . ": *Americans and Others,* p. 32.

Page 261: "When the standard . . . ": *Books and Men,* p. 154.

Bibliography

Published Books:

Agnes Irwin. New York, 1934.
Americans and Others. Boston, 1912.
A Book of Famous Verse. Boston, 1892. (Editor)
Books and Men. Boston, 1888.
Compromises. Boston, 1904.
Counter-Currents. Boston, 1916.
Eight Decades: Essays and Episodes. Boston, 1937.
Essays in Idleness. Boston, 1893.
Essays in Miniature. Boston, 1892.
The Fireside Sphinx. Boston, 1901.
Germany and Democracy, the Real Issue, the Views of Two Average Americans, a Reply to Doctor Dernburg. Philadelphia, 1914. (With J. W. White)
A Happy Half-Century, and Other Essays. Boston, 1908.
In Our Convent Days. Boston, 1905.
In Pursuit of Laughter. Boston, 1936.
In the Dozy Hours and Other Papers. Boston, 1894.
Junípero Serra, Pioneer Colonist of California. New York, 1933.
J. William White, M.D.; a Biography. Boston, 1919.
Mère Marie of the Ursulines; a Study in Adventure. New York, 1931.
Père Marquette; Priest, Pioneer and Adventurer. New York, 1929.
Philadelphia, the Place and the People. New York, 1898.
Points of Friction. Boston, 1920.
Points of View. Boston, 1889.

Times and Tendencies. Boston, 1931.
To Think of Tea! Boston, 1932.
Under Dispute. Boston, 1924.
Varia. Boston, 1897.

Manuscript Collections:

The Mrs. Schuyler Neilson Warren Letter Collection.
The Harrison Morris Letter Collection.
Two Journals kept by Agnes Repplier, now in the possession of the Library of the University of Pennsylvania.

Periodical Writings:

An extensive bibliography, compiled by the biographer, of the periodical writings of Agnes Repplier, as well as reviews and criticisms of her work, is on deposit with the Library of the University of Pennsylvania.

Index